FOUR DISSERTATIONS and ESSAYS ON SUICIDE
AND THE IMMORTALITY OF THE SOUL

KEY TEXTS
Classic Studies in the History of Ideas

FOUR DISSERTATIONS
and ESSAYS ON SUICIDE AND
THE IMMORTALITY OF THE SOUL

David Hume

With Introductions by
John Immerwahr
(*Four Dissertations*)

John Valdimir Price
(*Essays on Suicide and the Immortality of the Soul*)

Preface by
James Fieser

 ST. AUGUSTINE'S PRESS
South Bend, Indiana

Library of Congress Cataloging in Publication Data
Hume, David, 1711–1776.
      Four dissertations ; and, Essays on suicide and the immortality
   of the soul / David Hume.
         p. cm.
      First work originally published: Bristol, UK : Thoemmes Presss,
   1992. 2nd work originally published: Bristol, UK : Thoemmes
   Press, 1995.
      ISBN 1-890318-57-4 (alk. paper)
      1. Natural theology – Early works to 1800. 2. Emotions – Early
   works to 1800. 3. Tragedy – Early works to 1800. 4. Aesthetics
   – Early works to 1800. 5. Suicide - Moral and ethical aspects –
   Early works to 1800. 6. Immortality Early works to 1800.
   I. Title: Four dissertations ; and, Essays on suicide and the
   immortality of the soul. II. Hume, David, 1711–1776. Essays
   on suicide and the immortality of the soul. III. Title: Essays on
   suicide and the immortality of the soul. IV. Title.
   B1493.F64 2000
   192 dc21   00-037275

Publisher's Note

These reprints are taken from original copies of each book. In many cases the condition of those originals is not perfect, the paper, often handmade, having suffered over time and the copy from such things as inconsistent printing pressures resulting in faint text, show-through from one side of a leaf to the other, the filling in of some characters, and the break up of type. The publisher has gone to great lengths to insure the quality of these reprints but points out that certain characteristics of the original copies will, of necessity, be apparent in reprints thereof.

Please note that because these two works are facsimile editions, page numbers repeat.

Contents

PREFACE

During the 18th century, the name of David Hume (1711–1776) was almost synonymous with philosophical and religious controversy. His first work – the monumental *Treatise of Human Nature* (1739–1740) – raised problems with a range of philosophical issues, most notably our ideas of cause-effect relations. Many religious leaders were infuriated at Hume's skepticism and felt that his view of causality in particular undermined the causal argument for God's existence. Several clergymen retaliated by blocking Hume's chances of getting a university teaching appointment. About a decade later Hume published his *Enquiry concerning Human Understanding* (1748), which contained an essay titled "Of Miracles." Hume argues here that it is never reasonable to believe in secondhand reports of miracles. The essay generated a flurry of harsh attacks, and even today Hume's argument is at the heart of philosophical discussions about miracles.

By the mid-1750s, Hume's reputation was firmly established as a brilliant but skeptical philosopher, and he entered his last sustained period of philosophical writing. Hume only sporadically touched on religious issues in his early philosophical publications, but now he focused on the topic with a vengeance. It was during these years that he composed his *Dialogues concerning Natural Religion*, which attacks the main philosophical arguments for God's existence.

Because of its controversial nature, the *Dialogues* remained unpublished until after his death. During this time he also wrote a series of essays on religious subjects, which in many ways were as scandalous as his *Dialogues*. Hume's initial plan was to publish these and some other essays together in a volume titled *Five Dissertations*. The proposed contents included these items: (1) The Natural History of Religion, (2) Of the Passions, (3) Of Tragedy, (4) Of Suicide, and (5) Of the Immortality of the Soul. The second and third items – though very original — were comparatively innocent. Hume undoubtedly expected that the other three would be controversial, and the essays indeed had the desired effect. "The Natural History of Religion" reduces common religious belief to psychological factors, such as fear and the tendency to anthropomorphize. He also argued that polytheism is in many ways morally superior to monotheism. "Of Suicide" argues that suicide does not violate moral duties to God, oneself, or others. "Of the Immortality of the Soul" defends the view that the human soul dies with the human body.

As common for 18th-century publishing conventions, pre-release copies of *Five Dissertations* circulated among influential readers and, apparently under threat of prosecution, Hume and his printer Andrew Millar agreed to alter the first essay and completely remove the last two. Book reviewer William Rose recounted the story some decades later:

The Writer of this article [i.e., Rose] knows that the essays here mentioned [i.e., "Of Suicide" and "Of the Immortality of the Soul"] were written by Mr. Hume. That almost thirty years ago they made part of a volume, which was publicly advertised to be sold by Mr. Millar; that, before the day fixed for publication, several copies were delivered to some of the Author's friends, who were impatient to see whatever came from his pen; that a noble Lord, still living, threatened to prosecute Mr. Millar, if he published the essays now before us; that the Author, like a bold veteran in the cause of infidelity, was not in the least intimidated by this menace, but that the poor bookseller was terribly frightened, to such a degree, indeed, that he called in all the copies he had delivered, cancelled the two essays, and, with some difficulty, prevailed upon Mr. Hume to substitute some other pieces in the room of those objected to by the noble Lord; that, by some means or other, however, a few copies got abroad, and have been clandestinely circulated, at a large price, as already mentioned. [*Monthly Review* 70 (June 1784), pp. 427–28]

In place of two removed essays, Hume inserted a new essay, "Of the Standard of Taste." The work was then retitled and published in 1757 as *Four Dissertations*.

The changes to the "Natural History of Religion" involved two passages that were especially critical of monotheism. The first implies that the God of the Old Testament was first only a regional God, but was later elevated to the status of the creator of the world: \

Original: "Thus the deity, whom the vulgar Jews conceived only as the God of *Abraham*, *Isaac*, and *Jacob*, became their *Jehovah* and Creator of the world."

Revision in the first three editions: "Thus, notwithstanding the sublime ideas suggested
by <Moses> and the inspired writers,
many vulgar <Jews> seem still to have
conceived the supreme Being as a mere
topical deity or national protector."

Revision in the six succeeding editions: "Thus, the
God of A/BRAHAM\, I/SAAC\, and
J/ACOB\, became the supreme deity of
J/EHOVAH\ of the J/EWS\."

The second passage indirectly criticizes Old Testament
depictions of God as overly anthropomorphic – especially as appears in Muslim tradition:

Original: "Were there a religion (and we may suspect Mahometanism of this inconsis-
tence) which sometimes painted the
Deity in the most sublime colours, as
the creator of heaven and earth; sometimes degraded him so far to a level
with human creatures as to represent
him wrestling with a man, walking in
the cool of the evening, showing his
back parts, and descending from heav-
en to inform himself of what passes on
earth . . ."

Revision in all editions: "Were there a religion (and
we may suspect Mahometanism of this
inconsistence) which sometimes painted the Deity in the most sublime
colours, as the creator of heaven and
earth; sometimes degraded him nearly

to a level with human creatures in his powers and faculties."

Although the "Natural History of Religion" was published, Hume never authorized any publication of the removed essays on suicide and immortality. Nevertheless, as Rose indicates in the above letter, in 1770 and 1777 the essays clandestinely made their way into print – apparently in limited copies. In 1783, though, essays were more widely published. Along with Hume's two essays, the anonymous editor of the 1783 edition included his own critical notes to Hume's two pieces, and excerpts from Rousseau's *La Nouvelle Heloise* on the subject of suicide.

The present text is a facsimile reprint of both *Four Dissertations* (1757) and *Essays on Suicide and the Immortality of the Soul* (1783). Thus, the long separated essays are finally united as Hume intended.

James Fieser
University of Tennessee, Martin

FOUR DISSERTATIONS

INTRODUCTION

Hume's *Four Dissertations* (published in 1757) is an unusual work in a number of ways.[1] It was the last philosophical book Hume published during his lifetime. Indeed, its concluding essay, 'Of The Standard of Taste', is the last piece of extended philosophical analysis that Hume ever wrote.[2] *Four Dissertations* was also Hume's most troublesome book. Its publication brought Hume to the brink of a criminal prosecution, and the volume went through a frustrating series of revisions and changes.

The Context

The mid-1750s were a difficult time in Hume's life. On the one hand, he was beginning to see some of his works achieve the kind of attention he craved for them. But much of the growing attention to Hume as a writer was driven by controversy about his religious works, such as 'Of Miracles' and 'Of Providence and Any Future State'. (One 1749 pamphlet, for example,

---

[1] I am grateful to the staff of the Swarthmore College Friends Historical Library for permission to work with their copy of *Four Dissertations*, and for their advice on the details of printing and binding.

[2] The only essays written after 'Of the Standard of Taste' were 'Of the Jealousy of Trade', 'Of the Coalition of Parties', and 'Of the Origin of Government'. None of these really qualify as a philosophical essay in the contemporary sense. For a useful chronology of Hume's publications, see the notes to the Foreword in David Hume, *Essays, Moral, Political, and Literary,* edited by Eugene F. Miller (Indianapolis: Liberty Classics, 1987), pp. ii–xiv.

described Hume as 'the Most Impudent Man Living'.)[3]
While controversy (then as now) motivated book sales,
it also created real dangers of religious persecution.

Precisely in the months that Hume was bringing the
Dissertations to press, the Scottish Presbyterian Church
met in a General Assembly to debate the excommuni-
cations of both David Hume and his friend Lord
Kames. It was not entirely clear what the effect of
excommunication would be, and the motion was in fact
defeated. But Hume was concerned enough to insure
his contact with 'discrete families, who have promised
to admit me after I shall be excommunicated'.[4]

A Troubled Publication

These ecclesiastical debates help explain the complex
publication history of *Four Dissertations*.[5] Hume's
original intention is described in a letter to his publisher
Andrew Millar in 1755:

> There are four short Dissertations, which I have kept
> some Years by me, in order to polish them as much as
> possible. One of them is that which Allan Ramsey
> mentiond to you (The Natural History of Religion).
> Another of the Passions; a third of Tragedy; a fourth
> some Considerations previous to Geometry &
> Natural Philosophy.[6]

---

[3] Quoted in Ernest Campbell Mossner, *The Life of David Hume* (Austin:
University of Texas Press, 1954), p. 289.

[4] Letter 112, June 1755 in *The Letters of David Hume*, edited by J. Y. T.
Greig (Oxford: Clarendon Press, 1932), I:224.

[5] A full account of the unusual history of this publication is included in
Ernest Campbell Mossner's 'Hume's Four Dissertations: an essay in
biography and bibliography', in *Modern Philology*, 47 (1950),
pp. 37–57.

[6] Letter 111, May 1755, *Letters*, I:223.

Such a book would have been attractive to Hume for several reasons. First, he could have expected 'The Natural History' to further increase the attention to his works that had already been fuelled by other religious writings such as 'Of Miracles' and 'Of Providence and a Future State'. This publication would also mark the completion of Hume's goal of recasting his first work, the *Treatise of Human Nature,* for more popular consumption. While Hume himself came to accept the public's negative judgement of the *Treatise* he always remained convinced that its lack of success 'proceeded more from the manner than the matter'.[7] He thus tried to revive the thinking of the *Treatise* by recasting both the first and the third volumes as shorter and better-written works. This rewriting effort resulted in the *Enquiry Concerning Human Understanding* (1748) and the *Enquiry Concerning the Principles of Morals* (1751). The second essay in *Four Dissertations* ('Of the Passions') is an abbreviated version of Book II of the *Treatise*; with its publication all three books of the *Treatise* would have been reincarnated in more accessible forms.

Sometime in the next few months, Hume dropped the essay on Geometry because he became convinced that 'there was some Defect in the Argument or in its perspicuity'. Hume next attempted to publish the remaining three essays as a set. Millar objected that the three essays were not in themselves long enough to make up a volume, so Hume added two other essays

---

[7] 'My Own Life', in David Hume, *Essays, Moral, Political, and Literary,* edited by Eugene F. Miller (Indianapolis: Liberty Classics, 1987), p. xxv.

('Of Suicide' and 'Of the Immortality of the Soul') which he 'had never intended to have published'.[8]

The trouble began when pre-publication copies of what was now *Five Dissertations* were distributed. A copy of the work fell into the hands of William Warburton, one of Hume's more vitriolic critics. Hume (or Millar) became convinced that Warburton would be able to use the suicide and immortality essays as evidence in a criminal prosecution. The fact that Hume was at that very moment facing excommunication from the church must surely have increased his concern about possible sanctions from secular government as well. At any rate, Hume withdrew the two essays, made some minor revisions in 'The Natural History' and wrote a completely new essay, 'Of the Standard of Taste', to bulk up the volume. Rather than reprinting the entire book, the publisher physically cut out the offending essays (leaving four page stubs between pages 200 and 201) and bound in 'Of the Standard of Taste' at the end of the book.

There were also problems with the 'Dedication' for the *Dissertations*. Hume began the volume with a lengthy dedication to his cousin, John Home, a young clergyman who had written a tragedy entitled *Douglas*. Home was a controversial figure in his own right, because of orthodox hostility to stage plays in general and especially because of the perceived impropriety of a minister writing a play. Hume hoped to bring favourable attention to *Douglas* by lavishly praising it in the dedication. After writing the dedication, however, Hume became concerned that a public link between himself and John Home might do damage to

---

[8]   Letter 465, January 1772, *Letters*, II:253.

them both. He therefore asked Millar to delay the publication while he rethought the matter. Eventually Hume decided to go ahead with the publication, but in the meantime Millar, contrary to Hume's instructions, had sold 800 copies without the dedication. Hume was deeply upset by this and said that he had 'not been so heartily vexd at any Accident of a long time'.[9]

The *Dissertations*, begun with high hopes, ended up as a series of frustrations and problems, having gone from four dissertations, to three, up to five, and then back to four, and having been published both with and without the dedication. Indeed, the troubles with *Four Dissertations*, mixed with his disappointment with the reception of the *History* were discouraging even to the usually optimistic Hume. Years later Hume said of this period of his life that 'had not the War been at that time breaking out between France and England, I had certainly retired to some provincial Town of the former Kingdom, have changed my Name, and never more have returned to my native Country'.[10] Perhaps because of these difficulties Hume dismantled the volume only a few months after its original publication.[11] Although his usual practice was to keep collections of essays together even after they were integrated into larger anthologies, the essays in *Four Dissertations* were scattered throughout a new one-volume edition of his *Essays and Treatises on Several Subjects*. The essay 'Of the Passions' was renamed as *A Dissertation on the Passions* and placed between the two *Enquiries*. The two shorter essays on taste and tragedy were bound

[9] Letter 128, February 1757, *Letters*, I:243.

[10] 'My Own Life.'

[11] Letter 131, April 1757, *Letters*, I:247.

with Hume's other essays, and 'The Natural History' was placed after the *Enquiries*. This way of organizing the materials was maintained in all subsequent editions and in the definitive posthumous edition of 1777.

Unifying Themes in Four Dissertations

One unfortunate effect of breaking up *Four Dissertations* was to obscure several unifying themes that run through the essays in their original configuration. Specifically, *Four Dissertations* can be seen to be a sustained application of the theory of the passions developed originally in Book II of Hume's *Treatise*. Furthermore, the *Dissertations* are an extended response to the sectarian firestorms of the 1750s. These themes are obscured when the essays are viewed outside of their original context. A review of the various parts of the volume reveals this unity.

1. *The Dedication*

Although Hume prided himself on not beginning his books with dedications ('I never dealt in such servile Addresses'),[12] he began the *Dissertations* with a long dedication 'To the Reverend Mr. Hume [Home], Author of Douglas, a Tragedy'.[13] Hume was extremely proud of this dedication, which is reprinted in this edition for the first time since 1757. In one letter Hume says 'I am sure I never executed any thing, which was either more

---

[12] Letter 127, January 1757, *Letters*, I:241.

[13] The spelling of John's name as 'Hume' rather than 'Home' is probably an insider's joke, since the proper spelling of the name was a point of friendly dispute between the two cousins, with David favouring the modern 'Hume' and John favouring the more traditional 'Home'. See Mossner, *Life*, p. 276 for an account of David Hume's attempt to settle the dispute once and for all by casting lots.

elegant in the Composition, or more generous in the Intention'.[14]

The dedication begins with a call for religious tolerance. Hume describes his own relationship to his more religious cousin as a model for how people of good will can be mutually enlightened by religious differences. Hume uses the dedication, in other words, as a not-so-subtle critique of the intolerance of the conservative Scottish church. Hume next moves to an unabashed tribute for Home's tragedy *Douglas*, especially for its ability to move the passions of the audience and for its superiority to other tragedies (including Shakespeare's). The dedication touches, in other words, on the central themes of the dissertations themselves: a critique of religious fanaticism ('The Natural History'); the power of the passions ('Of the Passions'); the nature of tragedy ('Of Tragedy'); and the warrant for claims of aesthetic superiority ('Of the Standard of Taste'). As we will see, these themes are developed in the essays that follow.

2. 'The Natural History of Religion'

'The Natural History' was clearly written by Hume as a companion piece to the posthumously published *Dialogues on Natural Religion*. As Hume tells us in the Introduction to 'The Natural History', the two primary questions about religion concern its 'foundation in reason' and 'its origin in human nature'. The former is the subject of the *Dialogues*, while the latter is the subject of 'The Natural History'.

Hume begins with an imaginative discussion of the origin of religion. He argues here for two main claims:

[14] Letter 128, February 1757, *Letters*, I:242.

first that polytheism was the original religion of humankind, and secondly that all popular religion originates not in any attempt at a rational understanding of the universe but in the most primitive and basic human passions: fear of the unknown.

> Convulsions in nature, disorders, prodigies, miracles, tho' the most opposite to the plan of a wise superintendent, impress mankind with the strongest sentiments of religion; the causes of events seeming then the most unknown and unaccountable (p. 44).

Hume argues that the same irrational forces that drive human beings to polytheism motivate belief in monotheism as well. Hume concludes the essay with a detailed comparison of these two varieties of religious experience. His thesis is that on most counts, popular monotheism is even less attractive than polytheism. While both forms of religion are based in irrational fears, polytheism, with its emphasis on courage and tolerance, is morally superior to monotheism.

Despite Hume's claim to be a neutral observer of the origins of religion, 'The Natural History' is, as has been frequently observed, a not-very-subtle attack on Christianity.[15] His strategy is to show that popular Christianity, which his readers presumably accept, is even less compelling and attractive than polytheism, which his readers reject.

The central psychological concept in 'The Natural History' is that religious experience is driven by the passions, especially the emotions of fear and hope. Essentially then, 'The Natural History' is an exercise in

---

[15] See, for example, Mark Webb, 'The Argument of *The Natural History*', *Hume Studies*, 17:2 (November 1991), pp. 141–60.

applied psychology. The theoretical basis for that exercise is supplied in the next essay, 'Of the Passions'.

3. *'Of the Passions'*

'Of the Passions' is surely Hume's most neglected and disparaged philosophical work. The scholarly literature has usually ignored it completely, mentioned it only briefly, or treated it negatively.[16] Kemp Smith, for example, wrote that 'by general consent it is the least satisfactory of all of [Hume's] writings'.[17] Indeed, prior to this republication of the *Four Dissertations,* the most recent print edition of this work was the Green and Grose edition of 1892 (all of Hume's other philosophical works have been republished numerous times since then).[18]

Rather than rewriting *Treatise* II, Hume produced 'Of the Passions' by selecting and editing certain paragraphs from the earlier work. In fact, of the 119 paragraphs in the dissertation, approximately two-thirds are taken virtually word for word (with minor editorial changes) from the *Treatise.* Many of the remaining paragraphs are summaries or transitions. Comparing 'Of the Passions' to *Treatise* II thus provides a key to understanding Hume's goals for the later revision.

---

[16] For a more detailed discussion of 'Of the Passions' and its reception by Hume scholars see John Immerwahr, 'Hume's *Dissertation on the Passions*', *Journal of the History of Philosophy*, 32:2 (April 1994), pp. 224–40.

[17] Norman Kemp Smith, *The Philosophy of David Hume* (London: Macmillan and Co., 1941), p. 535.

[18] David Hume, *The Philosophical Works*, T. H. Green and T. H. Grose (eds.), (London: 1882; reprint edition Darmstadt: Scientia Verlag Aalen, 1964), IV:139–66.

Two changes between 'Of the Passions' and *Treatise* II emerge as particularly striking. Both of these changes are clearly meant to support the arguments of the other essays in *Four Dissertations*.

a) *Direct Passions*
In the *Treatise* the major emphasis is on indirect passions, such as pride and humility, love and hatred. The direct passions (such as joy and grief, fear and hope) are discussed in only one chapter of Part III.

In 'Of the Passions' this balance is completely changed. The discussion of the direct passions is moved to the beginning of the essay, and is retained almost in its entirety from *Treatise* II. By contrast, the material on the indirect passions is moved back, and drastically shortened. Thus after a few introductory remarks, Hume begins 'Of the Passions' focusing on direct passions. The direct passions which he finds 'curious or remarkable', however, are 'hope and fear'.

What is especially remarkable about hope and fear, of course, is that Hume has just finished explaining (in 'The Natural History') that these particular emotions are the source of popular religion. Hume's decision to emphasize and move forward the material on the direct passions can clearly be seen as an attempt to make the material from *Treatise* II relevant to the practical problem of the origin of religion.

b) *The Predominant Passion*
The second major change between 'Of the Passions' and *Treatise* II is also designed to heighten the connections to another of the *Four Dissertations*, 'Of Tragedy'. In *Treatise* II, Hume explores the question of how contrary passions affect one another when they are experienced simultaneously. This doctrine, which is a

sideshow in the *Treatise* (Part II, sect 4), is retained intact in the radically shortened 'Of the Passions'. Hume's view is that in certain cases, the conflict of two contrary passions makes the stronger of the two passions even more intense. As Hume explains it, 'The predominant passion swallows up the inferior, and converts it into itself' (p. 173). This material is also repositioned in 'Of the Passions' so that it is the concluding section.

As we will see in a moment, the theory of the predominant passion is important because it is the philosophical underpinning for 'Of Tragedy'. By placing it at the end of 'Of the Passions' Hume makes this material also serve as a technical introduction to 'Of Tragedy'.

4. *'Of Tragedy'*

'Of Tragedy' is one of Hume's better-known essays, but when it is read in the context of *Four Dissertations* it takes on a new meaning both because of its relationship to John Home's tragedy, *Douglas*, and because of its dependence on the theory of the predominant passion. In effect, *Douglas* raises the problem which concerns 'Of Tragedy', and the answer to that problem is to be found in the psychological theory in 'Of the Passions'.

We know that Hume was deeply preoccupied with *Douglas*, which he described as the 'only tragedy' in the English language. Hume read and commented on early drafts of the play, appears to have acted in a stage reading and served as the ticket seller for the premiere in December 1756 (just a few weeks before the publication of the *Dissertations*).[19] It is fair to say that 'Of Tragedy' is a commentary on *Douglas* in the same way

---

[19] Mossner, *Life*, p. 358–9; Letter 130, March 1757, *Letters*, I:246.

that Aristotle's *Poetics* is a commentary on Sophocles' *Oedipus Tyrannos*.

In the 'Epilogue' to *Douglas*, John Home describes how tragedy 'gushes pleasure with the tide of woe'.[20] Hume begins his essay 'Of Tragedy' by calling our attention to the same phenomenon, by describing the 'unaccountable pleasure, which the spectators of a well-wrote tragedy receive from sorrow, terror, anxiety, and other passions, which are in themselves disagreeable and uneasy' (p. 185). What fascinated and puzzled Hume about *Douglas* was the mixture of aesthetic enjoyment with the 'unfeigned tears which flowed from every eye' in the audience (p. v). It is just this problem that concerns him in 'Of Tragedy'.

After dismissing as incomplete the answers to this paradox given by Dubos and Fontenelle, Hume advances his own answer by referring to the theory of the predominant passion which he has just explained in 'Of the Passions'. Hume's view is that in a tragedy, the audience undergoes two simultaneous and seemingly contradictory passions. On the one hand the audience experiences pleasure from the eloquence with which the subject is portrayed. At the same time, the audience is presented with scenes that would typically cause negative emotions. Because the scenes described are known to be fictional, the emotions that they cause are weaker than the pleasure caused by the eloquence. In this type of conflict, according to Hume, the negative emotions are converted into positive ones:

---

[20] 'Home's *Douglas*', edited with Introduction and Notes by Hubert J. Tunney, in *Bulletin of the University of Kansas, Humanistic Studies*, 3:3 (November 1924), p. 87.

The subordinate movement is converted into the predominant, and gives forces to it, tho' of a different, and even sometimes tho' of a contrary nature (p. 193).

Rather than cancelling each other out, the weaker emotion gives new force to the stronger emotion. Indeed, we would receive less pleasure from the same degree of elegance used to describe an emotionally less intense scene. The pathos of the events described heightens our pleasure in the eloquence of the description. Seen in this light, 'Of Tragedy' is thus an application of theoretical principles originally developed in *Treatise* II and highlighted in 'Of the Passions'.

5. 'Of the Standard of Taste'

Hume concludes the *Dissertations* with his famous essay, 'Of the Standard of Taste' which, he tells us, he wrote specifically for this volume after the essays on suicide and immortality were suppressed.[21] Again Hume focuses on a paradox about the passions. On the one hand, aesthetic judgements are based on passions which are seemingly indisputable, and yet, on the other hand, we feel that some aesthetic judgements can have greater warrant than others. Hume seeks the origin of 'a rule, by which the various sentiments of men may be reconciled; at least, a decision, afforded, confirming one sentiment, and condemning another'.

To put the question another way, Hume concluded the dedication by saying that *Douglas* is 'one of the most interesting and pathetic pieces that was ever exhibited on any theater', superior to the work of Voltaire and even Shakespeare. The reader might well

[21] Letter 465, January 1772, *Letters*, II:253.

ask what justifies a critic such as Hume in making this claim. 'Of the Standard of Taste' provides a defence for the superiority of Hume's own judgements.

Hume defends the privileged nature of certain aesthetic sensibilities by isolating four conditions which allow us to distinguish the sentiment of some critics above that of others. The first is what Hume calls that '*delicacy* of imagination, which is requisite to convey a sensibility of those finer emotions' (p. 216). Those who lack this fine discrimination judge works of art 'without any distinction ... the finer touches pass unnoticed and disregarded' (p. 228). A second element is practice and the 'frequent survey or contemplation of a particular species of beauty' (p. 221). A third necessity is a wide range of '*comparisons* between the several species and degrees of excellency' (p. 223). Hume believes that someone 'who has had no opportunity of comparing the different kinds of beauty, is indeed totally unqualified to pronounce an opinion with regard to any object presented to him' (p. 223). Finally, according to Hume, we must rely most on those critics who are free from prejudice. This might seem to be a touchy point for Hume, since his judgements of *Douglas* might be thought to be tainted by the fact that the author was his friend and cousin. Significantly, Hume defines freedom from prejudice not as the absence of personal connections, but in terms of an *ability* to transcend personal considerations. True critics must be able to abstract themselves from their personal situations and place themselves in the 'same situation as the audience'.

While the theoretical significance of the essay on taste cannot be denied, the essay thus takes on an additional meaning in its original context. The qualities that Hume isolates are as much a characterization of Hume himself as they are of an abstract ideal critic. 'Of the Standard of Taste' is, as much as anything else, a description of Hume as critic. As such the essay points out a stark contrast between the violent passions of fear and hope which undergird religious superstition and the calm and delicate passions of the man of letters. Just as the gloomiest passages of 'The Natural History' are barely veiled portraits of religious fanatics such as Warburton, 'Of the Standard of Taste' provides a contrasting picture of Hume himself.

'Of the Standard of Taste' was to be Hume's last significant philosophical essay, specifically written as the concluding essay of his last philosophical book. As such, it can be seen as an intellectual self-portrait of the mature Hume. Just as 'My Own Life' sums up Hume's literary career, 'Of the Standard of Taste' shows us a vision of Hume at his mature prime.

John Immerwahr
Villanova University, 1995

FOUR

DISSERTATIONS.

Written by the fame AUTHOR,
and Printed for A. MILLAR.

I. Eſſays and Treatiſes on ſeveral Subjects. In 4 Volumes, Duodecimo.

Containing in

VOL. I. Eſſays Moral and Political.

VOL. II. Philoſophical Eſſays concerning Human Underſtanding.

VOL. III. An Enquiry concerning the Principles of Morals.

VOL. IV. Political Diſcourſes.

II. The Hiſtory of *Great Britain*. In 2 Vol. Quarto.

Containing in

VOL. I. The Reigns of *James* I, and *Charles* I.

VOL. II. The Commonwealth, and the Reigns of *Charles* II. and *James* II.

FOUR
DISSERTATIONS.

I. THE NATURAL HISTORY OF RELIGION.
II. OF THE PASSIONS.
III. OF TRAGEDY.
IV. OF THE STANDARD OF TASTE.

BY

DAVID HUME, Efq.

LONDON,
Printed for A. Millar, in the Strand.
MDCCLVII.

TO

The Reverend Mr. Hume,

Author of DOUGLAS, a Tragedy.

MY DEAR SIR,

IT was the practice of the antients to addrefs their compofitions
only to friends and equals, and to render their dedications monuments of
regard and affection, not of fervility
and flattery. In thofe days of inge-
nuous and candid liberty, a dedication
did honour to the perfon to whom it

a   was

was addreſſed, without degrading the author. If any partiality appeared towards the patron, it was at leaſt the partiality of friendſhip and affection.

ANOTHER inſtance of true liberty, of which antient times can alone afford us an example, is the liberty of thought, which engaged men of letters, however different in their abſtract opinions, to maintain a mutual friendſhip and regard; and never to quarrel about principles, while they agreed in inclinations and manners. Science was often the ſubject of diſputation, never of animoſity. *Cicero*, an academic, addreſſed his philoſophical treatiſes, ſometimes to *Brutus*, a ſtoic; ſometimes to *Atticus*, an epicurean.

I HAVE

I HAVE been feized with a ftrong defire of renewing thefe laudable practices of antiquity, by addreffing the following differtations to you, my good friend: For fuch I will ever call and efteem you, notwithftanding the oppofition, which prevails between us, with regard to many of our fpeculative tenets. Thefe differences of opinion I have only found to enliven our converfation; while our common paffion for fcience and letters ferved as a cement to our friendfhip. I ftill admired your genius, even when I imagined, that you lay under the influence of prejudice; and you fometimes told me, that you excufed my errors, on account of the candor and fincerity, which, you thought, accompanied them.

BUT

But to tell truth, it is leſs my admiration of your fine genius, which has engaged me to make this addreſs to you, than my eſteem of your character and my affection to your perſon. That generoſity of mind which ever accompanies you; that cordiality of friendſhip, that ſpirited honour and integrity, have long intereſted me ſtrongly in your behalf, and have made me deſirous, that a monument of our mutual amity ſhould be publicly erected, and, if poſſible, be preſerved to poſterity.

I own too, that I have the ambition to be the firſt who ſhall in public expreſs his admiration of your noble tragedy of Douglas; one of the moſt inter-

interesting and pathetic pieces, that
was ever exhibited on any theatre.
Should I give it the preference to the
Merope of *Maffei*, and to that of *Voltaire*, which it resembles in its subject;
should I affirm, that it contained more
fire and spirit than the former, more
tenderness and simplicity than the latter;
I might be accused of partiality: And
how could I entirely acquit myself,
after the professions of friendship,
which I have made you? But the unfeigned tears which flowed from every
eye, in the numerous representations
which were made of it on this theatre;
the unparalleled command, which
you appeared to have over every affection of the human breast: These
are incontestible proofs, that you possess the true theatric genius of *Shakespear*

and

and *Otway*, refined from the unhappy barbarifm of the one, and licentioufnefs of the other.

MY enemies, you know, and, I own, even fometimes my friends, have reproached me with the love of paradoxes and fingular opinions; and I expect to be expofed to the fame imputation, on account of the character, which I have here given of your DOUGLAS. I fhall be told, no doubt, that I had artfully chofen the only time, when this high efteem of that piece could be regarded as a paradox, to wit, before its publication ; and that not being able to contradict in this particular the fentiments of the public, I have, at leaft, refolved to go before them.   But I fhall be amply compenfated

penſated for all theſe pleaſantries, if
you accept this teſtimony of my regard,
and believe me to be, with the greateſt
ſincerity,

DEAR SIR,

Your moſt affectionate Friend,

and humble Servant,

EDINBURGH, 3,
Jan. 1757.

DAVID HUME.

DISSERTATION I.

NATURAL HISTORY

OF

RELIGION.

DISSERTATION I.

The Natural History of Religion.

INTRODUCTION.

AS every enquiry, which regards Religion, is of the utmoſt importance, there are two queſtions in particular, which challenge our principal attention, to wit, that concerning it's foundation in reaſon, and that concerning its origin in human nature. Happily, the firſt queſtion, which is the moſt important, admits of the moſt obvious, at leaſt, the cleareſt ſolution. The whole frame of nature beſpeaks an intelligent author; and no rational enquirer can, after ſerious reflexion, ſuſpend his belief a moment with regard to the primary principles of genuine Theiſm and Religion. But the other queſtion, concerning the origin of religion in human nature, admits of ſome more difficulty. The belief of inviſible, intelligent power has been very generally diffuſed over the human race, in all places and in all ages; but it has neither perhaps been ſo univerſal as to admit of no ex-

ceptions,

ceptions, nor has it been, in any degree, uniform in the ideas, which it has fuggefted. Some nations have been difcovered, who entertained no fentiments of Religion, if travellers and hiftorians may be credited ; and no two nations, and fcarce any two men, have ever agreed precifely in the fame fentiments. It would appear, therefore, that this preconception fprings not from an original inftinct or primary impreffion of nature, fuch as gives rife to felf-love, affection betwixt the fexes, love of progeny, gratitude, refentment; fince every inftinct of this kind has been found abfolutely univerfal in all nations and ages, and has always a precife, determinate object, which it inflexibly purfues. The firft religious principles muft be fecondary ; fuch as may eafily be perverted by various accidents and caufes, and whofe operation too, in fome cafes, may, by an extraordinary concurrence of circumftances, be altogether prevented. What thofe principles are, which give rife to the original belief, and what thofe accidents and caufes are, which direct its operation, is the fubject of our prefent enquiry.

I. It

I.

IT appears to me, that if we confider the improvement of human fociety, from rude beginnings to a ftate of greater perfection, polytheifm or idolatry was, and neceffarily muft have been, the firft and moft antient religion of mankind. This opinion I fhall endeavour to confirm by the following arguments.

'Tis a matter of fact unconteftable, that about 1700 years ago all mankind were idolaters. The doubtful and fceptical principles of a few philofophers, or the theifm, and that too not entirely pure, of one or two nations, form no objection worth regarding. Behold then the clear teftimony of hiftory. The farther we mount up into antiquity, the more do we find mankind plunged into idolatry. No marks, no fymptoms of any more perfect religion. The moft antient records of human race ftill prefent us with polytheifm as the popular and eftablifhed fyftem. The north, the fouth, the eaft, the weft, give their unanimous teftimony to the fame fact. What can be oppofed to fo full an evidence?

As

As far as writing or hiftory reaches, mankind, in antient times, appear univerfally to
have been polytheifts. Shall we affert, that,
in more antient times, before the knowledge
of letters, or the difcovery of any art or fcience,
men entertained the principles of pure theifm?
That is, while they were ignorant and barbarous, they difcovered truth: But fell into error,
as foon as they acquired learning and polite-
nefs.

But in this affertion you not only contradict
all appearance of probability, but alfo our prefent experience concerning the principles and
opinions of barbarous nations. The favage
tribes of *America*, *Africa*, and *Afia* are all idolaters. Not a fingle exception to this rule.
Infomuch, that, were a traveller to tranfport
himfelf into any unknown region; if he found
inhabitants cultivated with arts and fciences,
tho' even upon that fuppofition there are odds
againft their being theifts, yet could he not fafely,
till farther enquiry, pronounce any thing on
that head: But if he found them ignorant
and barbarous, he might beforehand declare
them idolaters; and there fcarce is a poffibility
of his being miftaken.

It

2

I⟨T⟩ feems certain, that, according to the natural progrefs of human thought, the ignorant multitude muſt firſt entertain ſome groveling and familiar notion of ſuperior powers, before they ſtretch their conception to that perfect being, who beſtowed order on the whole frame of nature. We may as reaſonably imagine, that men inhabited palaces before huts and cottages, or ſtudied geometry before agriculture; as aſſert that the deity appeared to them a pure ſpirit, omniſcient, omnipotent, and omnipreſent, before he was apprehended to be a powerful, tho' limited being, with human paſſions and appetites, limbs and organs. The mind riſes gradually, from inferior to ſuperior: By abſtracting from what is imperfect, it forms an idea of perfection: And ſlowly diſtinguiſhing the nobler parts of its frame from the groſſer, it learns to transfer only the former, much elevated and refined, to its divinity. Nothing could diſturb this natural progreſs of thought, but ſome obvious and invincible argument, which might immediately lead the mind into the pure principles of theiſm, and make it overleap, at one bound, the vaſt interval, which is interpoſed betwixt the human and the divine na-

B 3   ture.

ture. But tho' I allow, that the order and frame of the univerfe, when accurately examined, affords fuch an argument ; yet I can never think that this confideration could have an influence on mankind, when they formed their firft, rude notions of religion.

The caufes of objects, which are quite familiar to us, never ftrike our attention or curiofity ; and however extraordinary or furprizing thefe objects may be in themfelves, they are paft over, by the raw and ignorant multitude, without much examination or enquiry. *Adam*, rifing at once, in paradife, and in the full perfection of his faculties, would naturally, as reprefented by *Milton*, be aftonifhed at the glorious appearances of nature, the heavens, the air, the earth, his own organs and members ; and would be led to afk, whence this wonderful fcene arofe. But a barbarous, neceffitous animal (fuch as man is on the firft origin of fociety) preffed by fuch numerous wants and paffions, has no leifure to admire the regular face of nature, or make enquiries concerning the caufe of objects, to which, from his infancy, he has been gradually accuftomed. On the contrary, the more regular and uniform, that is, the more

perfect

perfect, nature appears, the more is he familiarized to it, and the lefs inclined to fcrutinize and examine it. A monftrous birth excites his curiofity, and is deemed a prodigy. It alarms him from its novelty; and immediately fets him a trembling, and facrificing, and praying. But an animal compleat in all its limbs and organs, is to him an ordinary fpectacle, and produces no religious opinion or affection. Afk him, whence that animal arofe; he will tell you, from the copulation of its parents. And thefe, whence? From the copulation of theirs. A few removes fatisfy his curiofity, and fets the objects at fuch a diftance, that he entirely lofes fight of them. Imagine not, that he will fo much as ftart the queftion, whence the firft animal; much lefs, whence the whole fyftem or united fabric of the univerfe arofe. Or, if you ftart fuch a queftion to him, expect not, that he will employ his mind with any anxiety about a fubject, fo remote, fo uninterefting, and which fo much exceeds the bounds of his capacity.

BUT farther, if men were at firft led into the belief of one fupreme being, by reafoning from the frame of nature, they could never poffibly

leave

leave that belief, in order to embrace idolatry; but the same principles of reasoning, which at first produced, and diffused over mankind, so magnificent an opinion, must be able, with greater facility, to preserve it. The first invention and proof of any doctrine is infinitely more difficult than the supporting and retaining it.

THERE is a great difference betwixt historical facts and speculative opinions; nor is the knowledge of the one propagated in the same manner with that of the other. An historical fact, while it passes by oral tradition from eye-witnesses and contemporaries, is disguised in every successive narration, and may at last retain but very small, if any, resemblance of the original truth, on which it was founded. The frail memories of men, their love of exaggeration, their supine carelessness; these principles, if not corrected by books and writing, soon pervert the account of historical events; where argument or reasoning has little or no place, nor can ever recal the truth, which has once escaped those narrations. 'Tis thus the fables of *Hercules*, *Theseus*, *Bacchus* are supposed to have been originally founded in true history, corrupted by tradition. But with regard to specu-

lative

lative opinions, the cafe is far otherwife. If thefe opinions be founded in arguments fo clear and obvious as to carry conviction with the generality of mankind, the fame arguments, which at firft diffufed the opinions, will ftill preferve them in their original purity. If the arguments be more abftrufe, and more remote from vulgar apprehenfions, the opinions will always be confined to a few perfons ; and as foon as men leave the contemplation of the arguments, the opinions will immediately be loft and buried in oblivion. Which ever fide of this dilemma we take, it muft appear impoffible, that theifm could, from reafoning, have been the primary religion of human race, and have afterwards, by its corruption, given birth to'idolatry and to all the various fuperftitions of the heathen world. Reafon, when very obvious, prevents thefe corruptions : When abftrufe, it keeps the principles entirely from the knowledge of the vulgar, who are alone liable to corrupt any principles, or opinions.

II.

IF we would, therefore, indulge our curiosity, in enquiring concerning the origin of religion, we muſt turn our thoughts towards idolatry or polytheiſm, the primitive Religion of uninſtructed mankind.

WERE men led into the apprehenſion of inviſible, intelligent power by a contemplation of the works of nature, they could never poſſibly entertain any conception but of one ſingle being, who beſtowed exiſtence and order on this vaſt machine, and adjuſted all its parts, according to one regular plan or connected ſyſtem. For tho', to perſons of a certain turn of mind, it may not appear altogether abſurd, that ſeveral independent beings, endowed with ſuperior wiſdom, might conſpire in the contrivance and execution of one regular plan; yet is this a mere arbitrary ſuppoſition, which, even if allowed poſſible, muſt be confeſſed neither to be ſupported by probability nor neceſſity. All things in the univerſe are evidently of a piece. Every thing is adjuſted to every thing. One

deſign

defign prevails thro' the whole. And this uniformity leads the mind to acknowledge one author; becaufe the conception of different authors, without any diftinction of attributes or operations, ferves only to give perplexity to the imagination, without beftowing any fatisfaction on the underftanding [a].

On the other hand, if, leaving the works of nature, we trace the footfteps of invifible power in the various and contrary events of human life, we are neceffarily led into polytheifm, and to the acknowledgment of feveral limited and imperfect deities. Storms and tempefts ruin what is nourifhed by the fun. The fun deftroys what is foftered by the moifture of dews and rains. War may be favourable to a nation, whom the inclemency of the feafons afflicts with famine. Sicknefs and peftilence may depopulate a kingdom, amidft the moft profufe plenty. The fame nation is not, at the

[a] The ftatue of *Laocoon*, as we learn from *Pliny*, was the work of three artifts : But 'tis certain, that, were we not told fo, we fhould never have concluded, that a groupe of figures, cut from one ftone, and united in one plan, was not the work and contrivance of one ftatuary. To afcribe any fingle effect to the combination of feveral caufes, is not furely a natural and obvious fuppofition.

B 6   fame

fame time, equally fuccefsful by fea and by land.
And a nation, which now triumphs over its
enemies, may anon fubmit to their more prof-
perous arms. In fhort, the conduct of events
or what we call the plan of a particular providence, is fo full of variety and uncertainty, that,
if we fuppofe it immediately ordered by any intelligent beings, we muft acknowledge a contrariety in their defigns and intentions, a conftant combat of oppofite powers, and a repentance or change of intention in the fame power,
from impotence or levity. Each nation has its
tutelar deity. Each element is fubjected to its
invifible power or agent. The province of
each god is feparate from that of another. Nor
are the operations of the fame god always certain and invariable. To day, he protects : To
morrow, he abandons us. Prayers and facrifices, rites and ceremonies, well or ill performed, are the fources of his favour or enmity,
and produce all the good or ill fortune, which
are to be found amongft mankind.

We may conclude, therefore, that, in all
nations, which have embraced polytheifm or
idolatry, the firft ideas of religion arofe not
from a contemplation of the works of nature,
but

but from a concern with regard to the events of life, and from the inceſſant hopes and fears, which actuate the human mind. Accordingly, we find, that all idolaters, having ſeparated the provinces of their deities, have recourſe to that inviſible agent, to whoſe authority they are immediately ſubjected, and whoſe province it is to ſuperintend that courſe of actions, in which they are, at any time, engaged. *Juno* is invoked at marriages; *Lucina* at births. *Neptune* receives the prayers of ſeamen; and *Mars* of warriors. The huſbandman cultivates his field under the protection of *Ceres*; and the merchant acknowledges the authority of *Mercury*. Each natural event is ſuppoſed to be governed by ſome intelligent agent; and nothing proſperous or adverſe can happen in life, which may not be the ſubject of peculiar prayers or thankſgivings [b].

---

[b] *Fragilis et laborioſa mortalitas in partes iſta digeſſit, infirmitatis ſuæ memor, ut portionibus quiſquis coleret, quo maxime indigeret.* Plin. lib. ii. cap. 7. So early as *Heſiod's* time there were 30,000 deities. *Oper. & Dier.* lib. i. ver. 250. But the taſk to be performed by theſe, ſeems ſtill too great for their number. The provinces of the deities were ſo ſubdivided, that there was even a God of *Sneezing*, See *Ariſt. Probl.* Sect. 33. cap. 7. The province of copulation, ſuitable to the importance and dignity of it, was divided amongſt ſeveral deities.

IT

IT muſt neceſſarily, indeed, be allowed, that, in order to carry men's attention beyond the viſible courſe of things, or lead them into any inference concerning inviſible intelligent power, they muſt be actuated by ſome paſſion, which prompts their thought and reflection; ſome motive, which urges their firſt enquiry. But what paſſion ſhall we here have recourſe to, for explaining an effect of ſuch mighty conſequence? Not ſpeculative curioſity ſurely, or the pure love of truth. That motive is too refined for ſuch groſs apprehenſions, and would lead men into enquiries concerning the frame of nature; a ſubject too large and comprehenſive for their narrow capacities. No paſſions, therefore, can be ſuppoſed to work upon ſuch barbarians, but the ordinary affections of human life; the anxious concern for happineſs, the dread of future miſery, the terror of death, the thirſt of revenge, the appetite for food and other neceſſaries. Agitated by hopes and fears of this nature, eſpecially the latter, men ſcrutinize, with a trembling curioſity, the courſe of future cauſes, and examine the various and

4

contrary

contrary events of human life. And in this difordered fcene, with eyes ftill more difordered and aftonifhed, they fee the firft obfcure traces of divinity.

III. We

III.

WE are placed in this world, as in a great theatre, where the true springs and causes of every event, are entirely unknown to us; nor have we either sufficient wisdom to foresee, or power to prevent those ills, with which we are continually threatened. We hang in perpetual suspense betwixt life and death, health and sickness, plenty and want; which are distributed amongst the human species by secret and unknown causes, whose operation is oft unexpected, and always unaccountable. These *unknown causes*, then, become the constant object of our hope and fear ; and while the passions are kept in perpetual alarm by an anxious expectation of the events, the imagination is equally employed in forming ideas of those powers, on which we have so entire a dependance. Could men anatomize nature, according to the most probable, at least the most intelligible philosophy, they would find, that these causes are nothing but the particular fabric and structure of the minute parts of their own bodies and of external objects ; and that, by a regular and constant machinery, all the events are produced,

duced, about which they are fo much concerned. But this philofophy exceeds the comprehenfion of the ignorant multitude, who can only conceive the *unknown caufes* in a general and confufed manner; tho' their imagination, perpetually employed on the fame fubject, muft labour to form fome particular and diftinct idea of them. The more they confider thefe caufes themfelves, and the uncertainty of their operation, the lefs fatisfaction do they meet with in their refearch; and, however unwilling, they muft at laft have abandoned fo arduous an attempt, were it not for a propenfity in human nature, which leads into a fyftem, that gives them fome feeming fatisfaction.

THERE is an univerfal tendency amongft mankind to conceive all beings like themfelves, and to transfer to every object thofe qualities, with which they are familiarly acquainted, and of which they are intimately confcious. We find human faces in the moon, armies in the clouds; and by a natural propenfity, if not corrected by experience and reflection, afcribe malice and good-will to every thing, that hurts or pleafes us. Hence the frequency and beauty of the *profopopœia* in poetry, where trees,

mountains,

mountains and ftreams are perfonified, and the
inanimate parts of nature acquire fentiment and
paffion. And tho' thefe poetical figures and
expreffions gain not on the belief, they may
ferve, at leaft, to prove a certain tendency in
the imagination, without which they could neither be beautiful nor natural. Nor is a river-
god or hama-dryad always taken for a mere
poetical or imaginary perfonage ; but may fometimes enter into the real creed of the ignorant
vulgar ; while each grove or field is reprefented
as poffeft of a particular *genius* or invifible power,
which inhabits and protects it. Nay, philofophers cannot entirely exempt themfelves from
this natural frailty ; but have oft afcribed to inanimate matter the horror of a *vacuum*, fym-
pathies, antipathies, and other affections of
human nature. The abfurdity is not lefs,
while we caft our eyes upwards ; and transfer-
ring, as is too ufual, human paffions and infirmities to the deity, reprefent him as jealous and
revengeful, capricious and partial, and, in fhort,
a wicked and foolifh man in every refpect, but
his fuperior power and authority. No wonder,
then, that mankind, being placed in fuch an
abfolute ignorance of caufes, and being at the
fame time fo anxious concerning their future
fortunes,

fortunes, fhould immediatly acknowledge a dependence on invifible powers, poffeft of fentiment and intelligence. The *unknown caufes*, which continually employ their thought, appearing always in the fame afpect, are all apprehended to be of the fame kind or fpecies. Nor is it long before we afcribe to them thought, and reafon, and paffion, and fometimes even the limbs and figures of men, in order to bring them nearer to a refemblance with ourfelves.

In proportion as any man's courfe of life is governed by accident, we always find, that he encreafes in fuperftition; as may particularly be obferved of gamefters and failors, who, tho', of all mankind, the leaft capable of ferious meditation, abound moft in frivolous and fuperftitious apprehenfions. The gods, fays *Coriolanus* in *Dionyfius* *, have an influence in every affair; but above all, in war; where the event is fo uncertain. All human life, efpecially before the inftitution of order and good government, being fubject to fortuitous accidents; it is natural, that fuperftition fhould prevail every where in barbarous ages, and put men on the moft

* Lib. viii.

earneft

earneſt enquiry concerning thoſe inviſible powers, who diſpoſe of their happineſs or miſery. Ignorant of aſtronomy and the anatomy of plants and animals, and too little curious to obſerve the admirable adjuſtment of final cauſes; they remain ſtill unacquainted with a firſt and ſupreme creator, and with that infinitely perfect ſpirit, who alone, by his almighty will, beſtowed order on the whole frame of nature. Such a magnificent idea is too big for their narrow conceptions, which can neither obſerve the beauty of the work, nor comprehend the grandeur of its author. They ſuppoſe their deities, however potent and inviſible, to be nothing but a ſpecies of human creatures, perhaps raiſed from among mankind, and retaining all human paſſions and appetites, along with corporeal limbs and organs. Such limited beings, tho' maſters of human fate, being, each of them, incapable of extending his influence every where, muſt be vaſtly multiplied, in order to anſwer that variety of events, which happen over the whole face of nature. Thus every place is ſtored with a crowd of local deities; and thus idolatry has prevailed, and ſtill prevails, among the greateſt part of uninſtructed mankind *.

* The following lines of *Euripides* are ſo much to the preſent purpoſe that I cannot forbear quoting them :

ANY

ANY of the human affections may lead us into the notion of invifible, intelligent power; hope as well as fear, gratitude as well as affliction: But if we examine our own hearts, or obferve what paffes around us, we fhall find, that men are much oftener thrown on their knees by the melancholy than by the agreeable paffions. Profperity is eafily received as our due, and few queftions are afked concerning its caufe or author. It engenders cheerfulnefs and activity and alacrity and a lively enjoyment of every focial and fenfual pleafure: And during this ftate of mind, men have little leifure or inclination to think of the unknown, invifible regions. On the other hand, every difaftrous accident alarms us, and fets us on enquiries concerning the principles whence it arofe: Apprehenfions fpring up with regard to futurity: And the mind, funk into diffidence, terror, and melancholy, has recourfe to every

Ουκ εςιν ꙟδεν ϖιςον, ꙟτ ευδ᾽ξια,
Ουτ᾽ αν καλως ϖραϛοντα μη πραξειν κακως.
Φυρꙟσι δ᾽αυθ᾽οι Θεοι ϖαλιν τε και ϖροσω,
Ταραγμον εντιθεντες, ως αγνωσια
Σεβωμεν αυτꙟς.   HECUBA.

There is nothing fecure in the world; no glory, no profperity. The gods tofs all life into confufion; mix every thing with its reverfe; that all of us, from our ignorance and uncertainty, may pay them the more worfhip and reverence.

method

method of appeafing thofe fecret, intelligent powers, on whom our fortune is fuppofed entirely to depend.

No topic is more ufual with all popular divines than to difplay the advantages of affliction, in bringing men to a due fenfe of religion; by fubduing their confidence and fenfuality, which, in times of profperity, make them forgetful of a divine providence. Nor is this topic confined merely to modern religions. The ancients have alfo employed it. *Fortune has never liberally, without envy,* fays a *Greek* hiftorian [a], *beftowed an unmixt happinefs on mankind; but with all her gifts has ever conjoined fome difaftrous circumftance, in order to chaftize men into a reverence for the gods, whom, in a continued courfe of profperity, they are apt to neglect and forget.*

WHAT age or period of life is the moft addicted to fuperftition? The weakeft and moft timid. What fex? The fame anfwer muft be given. *The leaders and examples of every kind of fuperftition,* fays *Strabo* [b], *are the women. Thefe excite the men to devotion and fupplications, and the obfervance of religious days. It is rare to meet*

[a] Diod. Sic. Lib. iii.   [b] Lib. vii.

with

with one, that lives apart from the females, and yet is addicted to such practises. And nothing can, for this reason, be more improbable, than the account given of an order of men amongst the Getes, *who practised celibacy, and were notwithstanding the most religious fanatics.* A method of reasoning, which would lead us to entertain a very bad idea of the devotion of monks; did we not know by an experience, not so common, perhaps, in *Strabo's* days, that one may practice celibacy, and profess chastity; and yet maintain the closest connexions and most entire sympathy with that timorous and pious sex.

IV. THE

IV.

THE only point of theology, in which we
shall find a confent of mankind almost univerfal, is, that there is invifible, intelligent
power in the world: But whether this power be
fupreme or fubordinate, whether confined to
one being or diftributed amongft feveral, what
attributes, qualities, connexions or principles
of action ought to be afcribed to thofe beings;
concerning all thefe points, there is the wideft
difference in the popular fyftems of theology.
Our anceftors in *Europe*, before the revival of letters, believed, as we do at prefent, that there
was one fupreme God, the author of nature,
whofe power, tho', in itfelf, uncontrolable,
yet was often exerted by the interpofition of his
angels and fubordinate minifters, who executed
his facred purpofes. But they alfo believed,
that all nature was full of other invifible powers;
fairies, goblins, elves, fprights; beings, ftronger
and mightier than men, but much inferior to
the celeftial natures, who furround the throne of
God. Now fuppofe, that any one, in thofe
ages, had denied the exiftence of God and of
his angels; would not his impiety juftly have

deferved

deferved the appellation of atheifm, even tho'
he had ftill allowed, by fome odd capricious
reafoning, that the popular ftories of elves and
fairies were juft and well-grounded ? The difference, on the one hand, betwixt fuch a perfon
and a genuine theift is infinitely greater, than
that, on the other, betwixt him and one, that
abfolutely excludes all invifible, intelligent
power. And it is a fallacy, merely from the
cafual refemblance of names, without any conformity of meaning, to rank fuch oppofite opinions under the fame denomination.

To any one, who confiders juftly of the
matter, it will appear, that the gods of all
polytheifts or idolaters are no better than the
elves or fairies of our anceftors, and merit as
little any pious worfhip or veneration. Thefe
pretended religionifts are really a kind of fuperftitious atheifts, and acknowledge no being, that
correfponds to our idea of a deity. No firft
principle of mind or thought: No fupreme government and adminiftration : No divine contrivance or intention in the fabric of the world.

THE

THE *Chinese*, when [a] their prayers are not answered, beat their idols. The deities of the *Laplanders* are any large stone which they meet with of an extraordinary shape [b]. The *Egyptian* mythologists, in order to account for animal worship, said, that the gods, pursued by the violence of earth-born men, who were their enemies, had formerly been obliged to disguise themselves under the semblance of beasts [c]. The *Caunii*, a nation in the lesser *Asia*, resolving to admit no strange gods amongst them, regularly, at certain seasons, assembled themselves compleatly armed, beat the air with their lances, and proceeded in that manner to their frontiers ; in order, as they said, to expel the foreign deities [d]. *Not even the immortal gods*, said some *German* nations to *Cæsar*, *are a match for the Suevi* [e].

MANY ills, says *Dione* in *Homer* to *Venus* wounded by *Diomede*, many ills, my daughter, have the gods inflicted on men : And many ills, in return, have men inflicted on the gods [f]. We

---

[a] Pere le Comte.   [b] Regnard, Voïage de Lapponie.
[c] Diod. Sic. lib. i. Lucian. de Sacrificiis. *Ovid.* alludes to the same tradition, Metam. lib. v. l. 321. So also Manilius, lib. iv.   [d] Herodot. lib. i.   [e] Cæf. Comment. de bell. Gallico, lib. iv.   [f] Lib. ix. 382.

need

need but open any claffic author to meet with
thefe grofs reprefentations of the deities; and
Longinus [a] with reafon obferves, that fuch ideas
of the divine nature, if literally taken, contain
a true atheifm.

SOME writers [b] have been furprifed, that the
the impieties of *Ariflophanes* fhould have been
tolerated, nay publickly acted and applauded,
by the *Athenians*; a people fo fuperftitious and fo
jealous of the public religion, that, at that very
time, they put *Socrates* to death for his imagined incredulity. But thefe writers confider
not, that the ludicrous, familiar images, under
which the gods are reprefented by that comic
poet, inftead of appearing impious, were the
genuine lights, in which the ancients conceived
their divinities. What conduct can be more
criminal or mean, than that of *Jupiter* in the
Amphitryon? Yet that play, which reprefented
his gallant exploits, was fuppofed fo agreeable to
him, that it was always acted in *Rome* by public authority, when the State was threatened
with peftilence, famine, or any general calamity [c]. The *Romans* fuppofed, that, like all old

a Cap. ix.   b Pere Brumoy, Theatre des Grecs; &
Fontenelle, Hiftoire des Oracles.   c Arnob. lib vii.

letchers, he would be highly pleafed with the re-
hearfal of his former feats of activity and vigour,
and that no topic was fo proper, upon which to
flatter his pride and vanity.

THE *Lacedemonians*, fays *Xenophon* [a], always,
during war, put up their petitions very early in
the morning, in order to be beforehand with
their enemies, and by being the firft folicitors,
pre-engage the gods in their favour.   We
may gather from *Seneca* [b], that it was ufual for
the votaries in the temples, to make intereft
with the beadles or fextons, in order to have a
feat near the image of the deity, that they might
be the beft heard in their prayers and applications to him.   The *Tyrians*, when befieged by
Alexander, threw chains on the ftatue of *Hercules*, to prevent that deity from deferting to the
enemy [c].   *Auguftus*, having twice loft his fleet
by ftorms, forbad *Neptune* to be carried in pro-
ceffion along with the other gods ; and fancied,
that he had fufficiently revenged himfelf by that
expedient [d].   After *Germanicus's* death, the people
were fo enraged at their gods, that they ftoned

---

[a] De Laced. Rep.   [b] Epift. xli.   [c] Quint.
Curtius, lib. iv. cap. 3. Diod. Sic. lib. xvii.   [d] Sueton.
in vita Aug. cap. 16.

them

them in their temples; and openly renounced all allegiance to them [a].

To afcribe the origin and fabric of the univerfe to thefe imperfect beings never enters into the imagination of any polytheift or idolater. *Hefiod*, whofe writings, along with thofe of *Homer*, contained the canonical fyftem of the heathens [b]; *Hefiod*, I fay, fuppofes gods and men to have fprung equally from the unknown powers of nature [c]. And thro' the whole theogony of that author, *Pandora* is the only inftance of creation or a voluntary production; and fhe too was formed by the gods merely from defpight to *Prometheus*, who had furnifhed men with ftolen fire from the celeftial regions [d]. The ancient mythologifts, indeed, feem throughout to have rather embraced the idea of generation than that of creation, or formation; and to have thence accounted for the origin of this univerfe.

OVID, who lived in a learned age, and had been inftructed by philofophers in the principles of a

---

[a] Id. in vita Cal. cap. 5.   [b] Herodot. lib. ii. Lucian. *Jupiter confutatus, de luctu Saturn.* &c.   [c] Ὡς ομοθεν γεγαασι θεοι θνηλοι τ'ανθρωποι. Hef. Opera & Dies l. 108.   [d] Theog. l. 570.

     divine

divine creation or formation of the world; finding, that fuch an idea would not agree with the popular mythology, which he delivers, leaves it, in a manner, loofe and detached from his fyftem. *Quifquis fuit ille Deorum* [a] *:* Whichever of the gods it was, fays he, that diffipated the chaos, and introduced order into the univerfe. It could neither be *Saturn*, he knew, nor *Jupiter*, nor *Neptune*, nor any of the received deities of paganifm. His theological fyftem had taught him nothing upon that head, and he leaves the matter equally undetermined.

Diodorus Siculus [b], beginning his work with an enumeration of the moft reafonable opinions concerning the origin of the world, makes no mention of a deity or intelligent mind; tho' it is evident from his hiftory, that that author had a much greater pronenefs to fuperftition than to irreligion. And in another paffage [c], talking of the *Ichthyophages*, a nation in *India*, he fays, that there being fo great difficulty in accounting for their defcent, we muft conclude them to be *aborigines*, without any beginning of their generation, propagating their race from all eternity;

---

[a] Metamorph. lib. i, l. 32.   [b] Lib. i.
[c] Id. ibid.

as

as fome of the phyfiologers, in treating of the origin of nature, have juftly obferved. " But " in fuch fubjects as thefe," adds the hiftorian, " which exceed all human capacity, it may well " happen, that thofe, who difcourfe the moft, " know the leaft; reaching a fpecious appear- " ance of truth in their reafonings, while ex- " tremely wide of the real truth and matter of " fact. "

A ftrange fentiment in our eyes, to be em-braced by a profeft and zealous religionift [a] ! But it was merely by accident, that the queftion concerning the origin of the world did ever in antient times enter into religious fyftems, or was treated of by theologers. The philofo-phers alone made profeffion of delivering fyftems of this nature; and it was pretty late too before thefe bethought themfelves of having recourfe to a mind or fupreme intelligence, as the firft caufe of all. So far was it from being efteemed

[a] The fame author, who can thus account for the origin of the world without a Deity, efteems it impious to explain from phyfical caufes, the common accidents of life, earthquakes, inundations, and tempefts; and devoutly afcribes thefe to the anger of *Jupiter* or *Neptune*. A plain proof, whence he de-rived his ideas of religion. See lib. xv. pag. 364. Ex edit. Rhodomanni.

prophane

prophane in thofe days to account for the origin of things without a deity, that *Thales*, *Anaximenes*, *Heraclitus*, and others, who embraced that fyftem of cofmogony, paft unqueftioned ; while *Anaxagoras*, the firft undoubted theift among the philofophers, was perhaps the firft that ever was accufed of atheifm [a].

WE are told by *Sextus Empiricus* [b], that *Epicurus*, when a boy, reading with his preceptor thefe verfes of *Hefiod* :

Eldeft of beings, *chaos* firft arofe;

Next *earth*, wide-ftretcht, the *feat* of all.

the young fcholar firft betrayed his inquifitive genius, by afking, *And choas whence ?* But was

---

[a] It will be eafy to give a reafon, why *Thales*, *Anaximander*, and thofe early philofophers, who really were atheifts, might be very orthodox in the pagan creed ; and why *Anaxagoras* and *Socrates*, tho' real theifts, muft naturally, in antient times, be efteemed impious. The blind, unguided powers of nature, if they could produce men, might alfo produce fuch beings as *Jupiter* and *Neptune*, who being the moft powerful, intelligent exiftences in the world, would be proper objects of worfhip. But where a fupreme intelligence, the firft caufe of all, is admitted, thefe capricious beings, if they exift at all, muft appear very fubordinate and dependent, and confequently be excluded from the rank of deities. *Plato* (de Leg. lib. x.) affigns this reafon of the imputation thrown on *Anaxagoras*, viz. his denying the divinity of the ftars, planets, and other created objects. [b] Adverfus Mathem. lib. ix.

told

told by his preceptor, that he muft have recourfe to the philofophers for a folution of fuch queftions. And from this hint, *Epicurus* left philology and all other ftudies, in order to betake himfelf to that fcience, whence alone he expected fatisfaction with regard to thefe fublime fubjects.

THE common people were never likely to pufh their refearches fo far, or derive from reafoning their fyftems of religion; when philologers and mythologifts, we fee, fcarce ever difcovered fo much penetration. And even the philofophers, who difcourfed of fuch topics, readily affented to the groffeft theory, and admitted the joint origin of gods and men from night and chaos; from fire, water, air, or whatever they eftablifhed to be the ruling element.

NOR was it only on their firft origin, that the gods were fuppofed dependent on the powers of nature. Thro' the whole period of their exiftence, they were fubjected to the dominion of fate or deftiny. *Think of the force of neceffity*, fays *Agrippa* to the *Roman* people, *that force, to which even the gods muft fubmit* [a]. And

[a] Dionyf. Halic. lib. vi.

the

the younger *Pliny* [a], fuitable to this way of reafoning, tells us, that, amidſt the darkneſs, horror, and confuſion, which enſued upon the firſt
eruption of *Vefuvius*, feveral concluded, that all
nature was going to wrack, and that gods and
men were periſhing in one common ruin.

IT is great complaifance, indeed, if we dignify with the name of religion ſuch an imperfect
ſyſtem of theology, and put it on a level with
latter ſyſtems, which are founded on principles
more juſt and more ſublime. For my part,
I can ſcarce allow the principles even of *Marcus
Aurelius*, *Plutarch*, and ſome other *Stoics* and
Academics, tho' infinitely more refined than the
pagan fuperſtition, to be worthy of the honourable denomination of theiſm. For if the mythology of the heathens refemble the antient
European ſyſtem of ſpiritual beings, excluding
God and angels, and leaving only fairies and
fprights ; the creed of thefe philoſophers may
juſtly be faid to exclude a deity, and to leave
only angels and fairies.

[a] Epiſt. lib. vi.

V. BUT

V.

BUT it is chiefly our prefent bufinefs to confider the grofs polytheifm and idolatry of the vulgar, and to trace all its various appearances, in the principles of human nature, whence they are derived.

WHOEVER learns, by argument, the exiftence of invifible, intelligent power, muft reafon from the admirable contrivance of natural objects, and muft fuppofe the world to be the workmanfhip of that divine being, the original caufe of all things. But the vulgar polytheift, fo far from admitting that idea, deifies every part of the univerfe, and conceives all the confpicuous productions of nature to be themfelves fo many real divinities. The fun, moon, and ftars are all gods, according to his fyftem : Fountains are inhabited by nymphs, and trees by hamadryads : Even monkies, dogs, cats, and other animals often become facred in his eyes, and ftrike him with a religious veneration. And thus, however ftrong men's propenfity to believe invifible, intelligent power in nature, their propenfity is equally ftrong to reft their

C 6   attention

attention on fenfible, vifible objects; and in order to reconcile thefe oppofite inclinations, they are led to unite the invifible power with fome vifible object.

THE diftribution alfo of diftinct provinces to the feveral deities is apt to caufe fome allegory, both phyfical and moral, to enter into the vulgar fyftems of polytheifm. The god of war will naturally be reprefented as furious, cruel, and impetuous: The god of poetry as elegant, polite, and amiable: The god of merchandife, efpecially in early times, as thievifh and deceitful. The allegories, fuppofed in *Homer* and other mythologifts, I allow, have been often fo ftrained, that men of fenfe are apt entirely to reject them, and to confider them as the product merely of the fancy and conceit of critics and commentators. But that allegory really has place in the heathen mythology is undeniable even on the leaft reflection. *Cupid* the fon of *Venus*; the Mufes the daughters of memory; *Prometheus* the wife brother, and *Epimetheus* the foolifh; *Hygieia* or the goddefs of health defcended from *Æfculapius* or the god of phyfic: Who fees not, in thefe, and in many other inftances, the plain traces of allegory?

gory ? When a god is fuppofed to prefide over any paffion, event, or fyftem of actions; it is almoft unavoidable to give him a genealogy, attributes, and adventures, fuitable to his fuppofed powers and influence; and to carry on that fimilitude and comparifon, which is naturally fo agreeable to the mind of man.

ALLEGORIES, indeed, entirely perfect, we ought not to expect as the products of ignorance and fuperftition; there being no work of genius, that requires a nicer hand, or has been more rarely executed with fuccefs. That *Fear* and *Terror* are the fons of *Mars* is juft; but why by *Venus* a? That *Harmony* is the daughter of *Venus* is regular; but why by *Mars* b? That *Sleep* is the brother of *Death* is fuitable; but why defcribe him as enamoured of one of the Graces c? And fince the ancient mythologifts fall into miftakes fo grofs and obvious, we have no reafon furely to expect fuch refined and longfpun allegories, as fome have endeavoured to deduce from their fictions d.

---

a Hefiod. Theog. l. 935.   b Id. ibid. & Plut. in vita Pelop.   c Iliad. xiv. 267.

d *Lucretius* was plainly feduced by the ftrong appearance of allegory, which is obfervable in the pagan fictions. He firft addreffes himfelf to *Venus* as to that generating power, which

THE

THE deities of the vulgar are fo little fuperior to human creatures, that where men are affected with ftrong fentiments of veneration or gratitude for any hero or public benefactor; nothing can be more natural than to convert him into a god, and fill the heavens, after this manner, with continual recruits from amongft mankind. Moft of the divinities of the antient world are fuppofed to have once been men, and to have been beholden for their *apotheofis* to the admiration and affection of the people. And the real hiftory of their adventures, corrupted by tradition, and elevated by the marvellous, became a plentiful fource of fable; efpecially in paffing thro' the hands of poets, allegorifts, and priefts, who fucceffively improved upon the wonder and aftonifhment of the ignorant multitude.

PAINTERS too and fculptors came in for their fhare of profit in the facred myfteries; and furnifhing men with fenfible reprefentations of their

animates, renews, and beautifies the univerfe: But is foon betrayed by the mythology into incoherencies, while he prays to that allegorical perfonage to appeafe the furies of her lover, *Mars:* An idea not drawn from allegory, but from the popular religion, and which *Lucretius,* as an *Epicurean,* could not confiftently admit of.

divinities,

divinities, whom they cloathed in human figures, gave great encrease to the public devotion, and determined its object. It was probably for want of these arts in rude and barbarous ages, that men deified plants, animals, and even brute, unorganized matter; and rather than be without a sensible object of worship, affixed divinity to such ungainly forms. Could any statuary of *Syria*, in early times, have formed a just figure of *Apollo*, the conic stone, *Heliogabalus*, had never become the object of such profound adoration, and been received as a representation of the solar deity [a].

STILPO was banished by the council of *Areopagus* for affirming that the *Minerva* in the citadel was no divinity; but the workmanship of *Phidias*, the sculptor [b]. What degree of reason may we expect in the religious belief of the vulgar in other nations; when *Athenians* and *Areopagites* could entertain such gross conceptions?

---

[a] Herodian. lib. v. *Jupiter Ammon* is represented by *Curtius* as a deity of the same kind, lib. iv. cap. 7. The *Arabians* and *Pessinuntians* adored also shapeless, unformed stones as their deity. Arnob. lib. vi. So much did their folly exceed that of the *Egyptians*. [b] Diog. Laert. lib. ii.

THESE

I

THESE then are the general principles of polytheifm, founded in human nature, and little or nothing dependent on caprice and accident. As the *caufes*, which beftow on us happinefs or mifery, are, in general, very unknown and uncertain, our anxious concern endeavours to attain a determinate idea of them; and finds no better expedient than to reprefent them as intelligent, voluntary agents, like ourfelves; only fomewhat fuperior in power and wifdom. The limited influence of thefe agents, and their great proximity to human weaknefs, introduce the various diftribution and divifion of their authority; and thereby give rife to allegory. The fame principles naturally deify mortals, fuperior in power, courage, or underftanding, and produce hero-worfhip; along with fabulous hiftory and mythological tradition, in all its wild and unaccountable forms. And as an invifible fpiritual intelligence is an object too refined for vulgar apprehenfion, men naturally affix it to fome fenfible reprefentation; fuch as either the more confpicuous parts of nature, or the ftatues, images, and pictures, which a more refined age forms of its divinities.

ALMOST

ALMOST all idolaters, of whatever age or country, concur in thefe general principles and conceptions ; and even the particular characters and provinces, which they affign to their deities are not extremely different [a]. The *Greek* and *Roman* travellers and conquerors, without much difficulty, found their own deities every where ; and faid, this is *Mercury*, that *Venus*; this *Mars*, that *Neptune*; by whatever titles the ftrange gods may be denominated. The goddefs *Hertha* of our *Saxon* anceftors feems to be no other, according to *Tacitus* [b], than the *Mater Tellus* of the *Romans*; and his conjecture was evidently juft.

[a] See Cæfar of the religion of the Gauls, De bello Gallico, lib. vi. [b] De moribus Germ.

VI. THE

VI.

THE doctrine of one fupreme deity, the author of nature, is very antient, has fpread it-felf over great and populous nations, and among them has been embraced by all ranks and condition of perfons: But whoever thinks that it has owed its fuccefs to the prevalent force of thofe invincible reafons, on which it is undoubtedly founded, would fhow himfelf little acquainted with the ignorance and ftupidity of the people, and their incurable prejudices in favour of their particular fuperftitions. Even at this day, and in *Europe*, afk any of the vulgar, why he believes in an omnipotent creator of the world; he will never mention the beauty of final caufes, of which he is wholly ignorant: He will not hold out his hand, and bid you contemplate the fupplenefs and variety of joints in his fingers, their bending all one way, the counterpoife which they receive from the thumb, the foftnefs and flefhy parts of the infide of his hand, with all the other circumftances, which render that member fit for the ufe, to which it was deftined. To thefe he has been long accuftomed; and he beholds them with liftleffnefs

and

and unconcern. He will tell you of the fudden and unexpected death of fuch a one : The fall and bruife of fuch another : The exceffive drought of this feafon : The cold and rains of another. Thefe he afcribes to the immediate operation of providence : And fuch events, as, with good reafoners, are the chief difficulties in admitting a fupreme intelligence, are with him the fole arguments for it.

MANY theifts, even the moft zealous and refined, have denied a *particular* providence, and have afferted, that the Sovereign mind or firft principle of all things, having fixt general laws, by which nature is governed, gives free and uninterrupted courfe to thefe laws, and difturbs not, at every turn, the fettled order of events, by particular volitions. From the beautiful connexion, fay they, and rigid obfervance of eftablifhed rules, we draw the chief argument for theifm; and from the fame principles are enabled to anfwer the principal objections againft it. But fo little is this underftood by the generality of mankind, that, wherever they obferve any one to afcribe all events to natural caufes, and to remove the particular interpofal of a deity, they are apt to fufpect him of the groffeft infidelity.

delity. *A little philosophy*, says my Lord *Bacon*, *makes men atheists : A great deal reconciles them to religion.* For men, being taught, by superstitious prejudices, to lay the stress on a wrong place; when that fails them, and they discover, by a little reflection, that the course of nature is regular and uniform, their whole faith totters, and falls to ruin. But being taught, by more reflection, that this very regularity and uniformity is the strongest proof of design and of a supreme intelligence, they return to that belief, which they had deserted; and they are now able to establish it on a firmer and more durable foundation.

CONVULSIONS in nature, disorders, prodigies, miracles, tho' the most opposite to the plan of a wise superintendent, impress mankind with the strongest sentiments of religion; the causes of events seeming then the most unknown and unaccountable. Madness, fury, rage, and an inflamed imagination, tho' they sink men nearest the level of beasts, are, for a like reason, often supposed to be the only dispositions, in which we can have any immediate communication with the deity.

WE

WE may conclude, therefore, upon the whole, that since the vulgar, in nations, which have embraced the doctrine of theism, still build it upon irrational and superstitious opinions, they are never led into that opinion by any process of argument, but by a certain train of thinking, more suitable to their genius and capacity.

IT may readily happen, in an idolatrous nation, that, tho' men admit the existence of several limited deities, yet may there be some one god, whom, in a particular manner, they make the object of their worship and adoration. They may either suppose, that, in the distribution of power and territory among the gods, their nation was subjected to the jurisdiction of that particular deity; or reducing heavenly objects to the model of things below, they may represent one god as the prince or supreme magistrate of the rest, who, tho' of the same nature, rules them with an authority, like that which an earthly sovereign exercises over his subjects and vassals. Whether this god, therefore, be considered as their peculiar patron, or as the general sovereign of heaven, his votaries will endeavour, by every act, to insinuate themselves into his favour; and supposing him to be pleased, like

4

like themselves, with praise and flattery, there is no eulogy or exaggeration, which will be spared in their addresses to him. In proportion as men's fears or distresses become more urgent, they still invent new strains of adulation; and even he who out-does his predecessors, in swelling up the titles of his divinity, is sure to be out-done by his successors, in newer and more pompous epithets of praise. Thus they proceed; till at last they arrive at infinity itself, beyond which there is no farther progress: And it is well, if, in striving to get farther, and to represent a magnificent simplicity, they run not into inexplicable mystery, and destroy the intelligent nature of their deity; on which alone any rational worship or adoration can be founded. While they confine themselves to the notion of a perfect being, the creator of the world, they coincide, by chance, with the principles of reason and true philosophy; tho' they are guided to that notion, not by reason, of which they are in a great measure incapable, but by the adulation and fears of the most vulgar superstition.

We often find amongst barbarous nations, and even sometimes amongst civilized, that,
when

when every ftrain of flattery has been exhaufted towards arbitrary princes; when every human quality has been applauded to the utmoft; their fervile courtiers reprefent them, at laft, as real divinities, and point them out to the people as objeéts of adoration. How much more natural, therefore, is it, that a limited deity, who at firft is fuppofed only the immediate author of the particular goods and ills in life, fhould in the end be reprefented as fovereign maker and modifier of the univerfe?

EVEN where this notion of a fupreme deity is already eftablifhed; tho' it ought naturally to leffen every other worfhip, and abafe every objeét of reverence, yet if a nation has entertained the opinion of a fubordinate tutelar divinity, faint, or angel; their addreffes to that being gradually rife upon them, and encroach on the adoration due to their fupreme deity. The virgin *Mary*, ere checkt by the reformation, had proceeded, from being merely a good woman to ufurp many attributes of the Almighty [a]:

---

[a] The *Jacobins*, who denied the immaculate conception, have ever been very unhappy in their doétrine, even tho' political reafons have kept the Romifh church from condemning it. The *Cordeliers* have run away with all the popularity. But in

God

God and St. *Nicholas* go hand in hand, in all
the prayers and petitions of the *Muscovites*.

THUS the deity, who, from love, converted
himself into a bull, in order to carry off *Europa*;
and who, from ambition, dethroned his father,
Saturn, became the *Optimus Maximus* of the
heathens. Thus, notwithstanding the sublime
ideas suggested by *Moses* and the inspired writers,
many vulgar *Jews* seem still to have conceived the
supreme Being as a mere topical deity or national
protector.

RATHER than relinquish this propensity to
adulation, religionists, in all ages, have involved
themselves in the greatest absurdities and con-
tradictions.

HOMER, in one passage, calls *Oceanus* and
Tethys the original parents of all things, con-

the fifteenth Century, as we learn from *Boulainvilliers*, an
Italian Cordelier maintained, that, during the three days, when
Christ was interred, the hypostatic union was dissolved, and that
his human nature was not a proper object of adoration, during
that period. Without the art of divination, one might foretel,
that so gross and impious a blasphemy would not fail to be ana-
thematized by the people. It was the occasion of great insults.
on the part of the *Jacobins*; who now got some recompence for
their misfortunes in the war about the immaculate conception.
See *Histoire abregée*, pag. 499.

formable

NATURAL HISTORY OF RELIGION. 49

formable to the eſtabliſhed mythology and tradition of the *Greeks :* Yet, in other paſſages, he
could not forbear complimenting *Jupiter*, the
reigning deity, with that magnificent appellation ; and accordingly denominates him the father of gods and men. He forgets, that every
temple, every ſtreet was full of the anceſtors,
uncles, brothers, and ſiſters of this *Jupiter* ;
who was in reality nothing but an upſtart parricide and uſurper. A like contradiction is ob-
ſervable in *Heſiod* ; and is ſo much the leſs ex-
cuſable, that his profeſſed intention was to deliver
a true genealogy of the gods.

WERE there a religion (and we may ſuſpect
Mahometaniſm of this inconſiſtence) which ſometimes painted the deity in the moſt ſublime colours, as the creator of heaven and earth ; ſometimes degraded him nearly to a level with human creatures in his powers and faculties ; while
at the ſame time it aſcribed to him ſuitable infirmities, paſſions, and partialities of the moral
kind : That religion, after it was extinct, would
alſo be cited as an inſtance of thoſe contradic-
tions, which ariſe from the groſs, vulgar, natural conceptions of mankind, oppoſed to their
continual propenſity towards flattery and ex-

D   aggeration.

aggeration.　Nothing indeed would prove more
ftrongly the divine origin of any religion, than
to find (and happily this is the cafe with Chriftianity) that it is free from a contradiction, fo
incident to human nature.

VII.

IT appears certain, that, tho' the original notions of the vulgar reprefent the Divinity as a very limited being, and confider him only as the particular caufe of health or ficknefs; plenty or want; profperity or adverfity; yet when more magnificent ideas are urged upon them, they efteem it dangerous to refufe their affent. Will you fay, that your deity is finite and bounded in his perfections; may be overcome by a greater force; is fubject to human paffions, pains, and infirmities; has a beginning, and may have an end? This they dare not affirm; but thinking it fafeft to comply with the higher encomiums, they endeavour, by an affected ravifhment and devotion, to ingratiate them-felves with him. As a confirmation of this, we may obferve, that the affent of the vulgar is, in this cafe, merely verbal, and that they are in-capable of conceiving thofe fublime qualities, which they feemingly attribute to the deity. Their real idea of him, notwithftanding their pompous language, is ftill as poor and frivolous as ever.

THAT

THAT original intelligence, fay the *Magians*, who is the firft principle of all things, difcovers himfelf *immediately* to the mind and underftanding alone; but has placed the fun as his image in the vifible univerfe; and when that bright luminary diffufes its beams over the earth and the firmament, it is a faint copy of the glory, which refides in the higher heavens. If you would efcape the difpleafure of this divine being, you muft be careful never to fet your bare foot upon the ground, nor fpit into a fire, nor throw any water upon it, even tho' it were confuming a whole city [a]. Who can exprefs the perfections of the Almighty, fay the *Mahometans*? Even the nobleft of his works, if compared to him, are but duft and rubbifh. How much more muft human conception fall fhort of his infinite perfections? His fmile and favour renders men for ever happy; and to obtain it for your children, the beft method is to cut off from them, while infants, a little bit of fkin, about half the breadth of a farthing. Take two bits of cloath [b], fay the *Roman catholics*, about an inch or an inch and a half fquare, join them by the corners with two ftrings or pieces

a Hyde de Relig. veterum Perfarum.   b Called the
Scapulaire.

of

of tape about fixteen inches long, throw this over
your head, and make one of the bits of cloath
lie upon your breaft, and the other upon your
back, keeping them next your fkin. There is
not a better fecret for recommending yourfelf to
that infinite Being, who exifts from eternity to
eternity.

THE *Getes,* commonly called immortal, from
their fteddy belief of the foul's immortality,
were genuine theifts and unitarians. They affirmed *Zamolxis,* their deity, to be the only true
god; and afferted the worfhip of all other nations to be addreffed to mere fictions and chimeras.
But were their religious principles any more refined, on account of thefe magnificent pretenfions? Every fifth year they facrified a human
victim, whom they fent as a meffenger to their
deity, in order to inform him of their wants and
neceffities. And when it thundered, they were
fo provoked, that, in order to return the defi-
ance, they let fly arrows at him, and declined
not the combat as unequal. Such at leaft is
the account, which *Herodotus* gives of the theifm
of the immortal *Getes* [a].

[a] Lib. iv.

D 3   VIII. IT

VIII.

IT is remarkable, that the principles of religion have a kind of flux and reflux in the human mind, and that men have a natural tendency to rife from idolatry to theifm, and to fink again from theifm into idolatry. The vulgar, that is, indeed, all mankind, a few excepted, being ignorant and uninftructed, never elevate their contemplation to the heavens, or penetrate by their difquifitions into the fecret ftructure of vegetable or animal bodies; fo as to difcover a fupreme mind or original providence, which beftowed order on every part of nature. They confider thefe admirable works in a more confined and felfifh view; and finding their own happinefs and mifery to depend on the fecret influence and unforefeen concurrence of external objects, they regard, with perpetual attention, the *unknown caufes*, which govern all thefe natural events, and diftribute pleafure and pain, good and ill, by their powerful, but filent, operation. The unknown caufes are ftill appealed to, at every emergence; and in this general appearance or confufed image, are the perpetual objects of human hopes and fears₂ fears, wifhes and apprehenfions. By degrees, the active imagination of men, uneafy in this abftract conception of objects, about which it is inceffantly employed, begins to render them more particular, and to cloathe them in fhapes more fuitable to its natural comprehenfion. It reprefents them to be fenfible, intelligent beings, like mankind; actuated by love and hatred, and flexible by gifts and entreaties, by prayers and facrifices. Hence the origin of religion: And hence the origin of idolatry or polytheifm.

But the fame anxious concern for happinefs, which engenders the idea of thefe invifible, intelligent powers, allows not mankind to remain long in the firft fimple conception of them; as powerful, but limited beings; mafters of human fate, but flaves to deftiny and the courfe of nature. Men's exaggerated praifes and compliments ftill fwell their idea upon them; and elevating their deities to the utmoft bounds of perfection, at laft beget the attributes of unity and infinity, fimplicity and fpirituality. Such refined ideas, being fomewhat difproportioned to vulgar comprehenfion, remain not long in their original purity; but require to be fupported by the notion of inferior mediators or

fubordinate

fubordinate agents, which interpofe betwixt mankind and their fupreme deity. Thefe demi-gods or middle beings, partaking more of human nature, and being more familiar to us, become the chief objects of devotion, and gradually recal that idolatry, which had been formerly banifhed by the ardent prayers and panegyrics of timorous and indigent mortals. But as thefe idolatrous religions fall every day into groffer and more vulgar conceptions, they at laft deftroy themfelves, and, by the vile reprefentations, which they form of their deities, make the tide turn again towards theifm. But fo great is the propenfity, in this alternate revolution of human fentiments, to return back to idolatry, that the utmoft precaution is not able effectually to prevent it. And of this, fome theifts, particularly the *Jews* and *Mahometans*, have been fenfible; as appears by their banifhing all the arts of ftatuary and painting, and not allowing the reprefentations, even of human figures, to be taken by marble or colours; left the common infirmity of mankind fhould thence produce idolatry. The feeble apprehenfions of men cannot be fatisfied with conceiving their deity as a pure fpirit and perfect intelligence; and yet their natural terrors keep them from

imputing

imputing to him the leaft fhadow of limitation and imperfection. They fluctuate betwixt thefe oppofite fentiments. The fame infirmity ftill drags them downwards, from an omnipotent and fpiritual deity to a limited and corporeal one, and from a corporeal and limited deity to a ftatue or vifible reprefentation. The fame endeavour at elevation ftill pufhes them upwards, from the ftatue or material image to the invifible power; and from the invifible power to an infinitely perfect deity, the creator and fo--vereign of the univerfe.

IX. Po-

IX.

POLYTHEISM or idolatrous worſhip, being founded entirely in vulgar traditions, is liable to this great inconvenience, that any practice or opinion, however barbarous or corrupted, may be authorized by it; and full ſcope is left for knavery to impoſe on credulity, till morals and humanity be expelled from the religious ſyſtems of mankind. At the ſame time, idolatry is attended with this evident advantage, that, by limiting the powers and functions of its deities, it naturally admits the gods of other ſects and nations to a ſhare of divinity, and renders all the various deities, as well as rites, ceremonies, or traditions, compatible with each other [a]. Theiſm is oppoſite both in its advan-

---

[a] *Verrius Flaccus*, cited by *Pliny*, lib. xxviii. cap. 2. affirmed, that it was uſual for the *Romans*, before they laid ſiege to any town, to invocate the tutelar deity of the place, and by promiſing him equal or greater honours than thoſe he at preſent enjoyed, bribe him to betray his old friends and votaries. The name of the tutelar deity of *Rome* was for this reaſon kept a moſt religious myſtery ; leſt the enemies of the republic ſhould be able, in the ſame manner, to draw him over to their ſervice. For without the name, they thought, nothing of that kind could be practiſed. *Pliny* ſays, that the common form of invocation

tages

tages and difadvantages. As that fyftem fuppofes one fole deity, the perfection of reafon and
goodnefs, it fhould, if juftly profecuted, banifh
every thing frivolous, unreafonable, or inhuman
from religious worfhip, and fet before men the
moft illuftrious example, as well as the moft
commanding motives of juftice and benevolence.
Thefe mighty advantages are not indeed over-
ballanced, (for that is not poffible) but fomewhat diminifhed, by inconveniencies, which,
arife from the vices and prejudices of mankind.
While one fole object of devotion is acknowledged, the worfhip of other deities is regarded
as abfurd and impious. Nay, this unity of object feems naturally to require the unity of faith
and ceremonies, and furnifhes defigning men
with a pretext for reprefenting their adverfaries
as prophane, and the fubjects of divine as well
as human vengeance. For as each fect is pofitive, that its own faith and worfhip are entirely
acceptable to the deity, and as no one can conceive, that the fame being fhould be pleafed
with different and oppofite rites and principles;
the feveral fects fall naturally into animofity,

was preferved to his time in the ritual of the pontifs. And
Macrobius has tranfmitted a copy of it from the fecret things of
Sammonicus Serenus,

and

and mutually difcharge on each other, that facred zeal and rancour, the moft furious and implacable of all human paffions.

THE tolerating fpirit of idolaters both in antient and modern times, is very obvious to any
one, who is the leaft converfant in the writings
of hiftorians or travellers. When the oracle of
Delphi was afked, what rites or worfhip were
moft acceptable to the gods? Thofe legally
eftablifhed in each city, replied the oracle [a].
Even priefts, in thofe ages, could, it feems,
allow falvation to thofe of a different communion.
The *Romans* commonly adopted the gods of the
conquered people; and never difputed the attributes of thofe topical and national deities, in
whofe territories they refided. The religious
wars and perfecutions of the *Egyptian* idolaters
are indeed an exception to this rule; but are
accounted for by antient authors from reafons
very fingular and remarkable. Different fpecies
of animals were the deities of the different fects
of the *Egyptians*; and the deities being in continual war, engaged their votaries in the fame
contention. The worfhipers of dogs could
not long remain in peace with the adorers of

[a] Xenoph. Memor. lib. ii.

çats

cats or wolves [a]. And where that reafon took not place, the *Egyptian* fuperftition was not fo incompatible as is commonly imagined; fince we learn from *Herodotus* [b], that very large contributions were given by *Amafis* towards rebuilding the temple of *Delphi*.

THE intolerance of almoft all religions, which have maintained the unity of god, is as remarkable as the contrary principle in polytheifts. The implacable, narrow fpirit of the *Jews* is well known. *Mahometanifm* fet out with ftill more bloody principles; and even to this day, deals out damnation, tho' not fire and faggot, to all other fects. And if, amongft *Chriftians*, the *Englifh* and *Dutch* have embraced the principles of toleration, this fingularity has proceeded from the fteddy refolution of the civil magiftrate, in oppofition to the continued efforts of priefts and bigots.

THE difciples of *Zoroafter* fhut the doors of heaven againft all but the *Magians* [c]. Nothing could more obftruct the progrefs of the *Perfian* conquefts, than the furious zeal of that nation

[a] Plutarch. de Ifid. & Ofiride.　　[b] Lib, ii, fub fine.
[c] Hyde de Relig. vet, Perfarum,

againft

againſt the temples and images of the *Greeks*. And after the overthrow of that empire, we find *Alexander*, as a polytheiſt, immediately re-eſtabliſhing the worſhip of the *Babylonians*, which their former princes, as monotheiſts, had carefully aboliſhed [a]. Even the blind and devoted attachment of that conqueror to the *Greek* ſuperſtition hindered not but he himſelf ſacrificed according to the *Babyloniſh* rites and ceremonies [b].

So ſociable is polytheiſm, that the utmoſt fierceneſs and averſion, which it meets with in an oppoſite religion, is ſcarce able to diſguſt it, and keep it at a diſtance. *Auguſtus* praiſed extremely the reſerve of his grandſon, *Caius Cæſar*, when, paſſing by *Jeruſalem*, he deigned not to ſacrifice according to the *Jewiſh* law. But for what reaſon did *Auguſtus* ſo much approve of this conduct? Only, becauſe that religion was by the pagans eſteemed ignoble and barbarous [c].

I may venture to affirm, that few corruptions of idolatry and polytheiſm are more pernicious to political ſociety than this corruption of

---

[a] Arrian. de Exped. lib. iii. Id. lib. vii. [b] Id. ibid.
[c] Sueton. in vita Aug. c. 93.

theiſm,

theifm [a], when carried to the utmoft height. The human facrifices of the *Carthaginians*, *Mexicans*, and many barbarous nations [b], fcarce exceed the inquifition and perfecutions of *Rome* and *Madrid*. For befides, that the effufion of blood may not be fo great in the former cafe as in the latter; befides this, I fay, the human victims, being chofen by lot or by fome exterior figns, affect not, in fo confiderable a degree, the reft of the fociety. Whereas virtue, knowledge, love of liberty, are the qualities, which call down the fatal vengeance of inquifitors; and when expelled, leave the fociety in the moft fhameful ignorance, corruption, and bondage. The illegal murder of one man by a tyrant is more pernicious than the death of a thoufand by peftilence, famine, or any undiftinguifhing calamity.

[a] *Corruptio optimi peffima.*

[b] Moft nations have fallen into this guilt; tho' perhaps, that impious fuperftition has never prevailed very much in any civilized nation, unlefs we except the *Carthaginians.* For the *Tyrians* foon abolifhed it. A facrifice is conceived as a prefent; and any prefent is delivered to the deity by deftroying it and rendering it ufelefs to men; by burning what is folid, pouring out the liquid, and killing the animate. For want of a better way of doing him fervice, we do ourfelves an injury; and fancy that we thereby exprefs, at leaft, the heartinefs of our good will and adoration. Thus our mercenary devotion deceives ourfelves, and imagines it deceives the deity.

In

IN the temple of *Diana* at *Aricia* near *Rome*, whoever murdered the prefent prieft, was legally entitled to be inftalled his fucceffor [a]. A very fingular inftitution! For, however barbarous and bloody the common fuperftitions often are to the laity, they ufually turn to the advantage of the holy order.

[a] Strabo, lib. v. Sueton. in vita Cal.

X. FROM

X.

FROM the comparifon of theifm and idolatry, we may form fome other obfervations,
which will alfo confirm the vulgar obfervation,
that the corruption of the beft things gives rife
to the worft.

WHERE the deity is reprefented as infinitely
fuperior to mankind, this belief, tho' altogether
juft, is apt, when joined with fuperftitious terrors, to fink the human mind into the loweft
fubmiffion and abafement, and to reprefent the
monkifh virtues of mortification, pennance, humility and paffive fuffering, as the only qualities, which are acceptable to him. But where
the gods are conceived to be only a little fuperior to mankind, and to have been, many of
them, advanced from that inferior rank, we are
more at our eafe in our addreffes to them, and
may even, without profanenefs, afpire fometimes to a rivalfhip and emulation of them.
Hence activity, fpirit, courage, magnanimity,
love of liberty, and all the virtues, which ag-
grandize a people.

THE

THE heroes in paganifm correfpond exactly to the faints in popery and holy dervifes in *Mahometanifm.* The place of *Hercules, Thefeus, Hector, Romulus,* is now fupplied by *Dominic, Francis, Anthony,* and *Benedict.* And inftead of the deftruction of monfters, the fubduing tyrants, the defence of our native country; celeftial honours are obtained by whippings and faftings, by cowardice and humility, by abject fubmiffion and flavifh obedience.

ONE great incitement to the pious *Alexander* in his warlike expeditions was his rivalfhip of *Hercules* and *Bacchus,* whom he juftly pretended to have excelled [a]. *Brafidas,* that generous and noble *Spartan,* after falling in battle, had heroic honours paid him by the inhabitants of *Amphipolis,* whofe defence he had embraced [b]. And in general, all founders of ftates and colonies amongft the *Greeks* were raifed to this inferior rank of divinity, by thofe who reaped the benefit of their labours.

THIS gave rife to the obfervation of *Machiavel* [c], that the doctrines of the *Chriftian* reli-

---

[a] Arrian. paffim.   [b] Thucyd. lib. v.
[c] Difcorfi, lib. vi.

gion

gion (meaning the catholic; for he knew no other) which recommend only paffive courage and fuffering, had fubdued the fpirit of mankind, and had fitted them for flavery and fubjection. And this obfervation would certainly be juft, were there not many other circumftances in human fociety, which controul the genius and character of a religion.

BRASIDAS feized a moufe, and being bit by it, let it go. *There is nothing fo contemptible,* fays he, *but what may be fafe, if it has but courage to defend itfelf* [a]. *Bellarmine,* patiently and humbly allowed the fleas and other odious vermin to prey upon him. *We fhall have heaven,* fays he, *to reward us for our fufferings: But thefe poor creatures have nothing but the enjoyment of the prefent life* [b]. Such difference is there betwixt the maxims of a *Greek* hero and a *Catholic* faint.

[a] Plut. Apophth.　　[b] Bayle, Article BELLARMINE.

XI. HERE

XI.

HERE is another obfervation to the fame purpofe, and a new proof that the corruption of the beft things begets the worft. If we examine, without prejudice, the antient heathen mythology, as contained in the poets, we fhall not difcover in it any fuch monftrous abfurdity, as we may be apt at firft to apprehend. Where is the difficulty of conceiving, that the fame powers or principles, whatever they were, which formed this vifible world, men and animals, produced alfo a fpecies of intelligent creatures, of more refined fubftance and greater authority than the reft? That thefe creatures may be capricious, revengeful, paffionate, voluptuous, is eafily conceived; nor is any circumftance more apt, amongft ourfelves, to engender fuch vices, than the licence of abfolute authority. And in fhort, the whole mythological fyftem is fo natural, that, in the vaft variety of planets and worlds, contained in this univerfe, it feems more than probable, that, fomewhere or other, it is really carried into execution.

THE

THE chief objection to it with regard to this planet, is, that it is not afcertained by any juft reafon or authority. The antient tradition, infifted on by the heathen priefts and theologers, is but a weak foundation; and tranfmitted alfo fuch a number of contradictory reports, fupported, all of them, by equal authority, that it became abfolutely impoffible to fix a preference amongft them. A few volumes, therefore, muft contain all the polemical writings of pagan priefts. And their whole theology muft confift more of traditional ftories and fuperftitious practices than of philofophical argument and controverfy.

BUT where theifm forms the fundamental principle of any popular religion, that tenet is fo conformable to found reafon, that philofophy is apt to incorporate itfelf with fuch a fyftem of theology. And if the other dogmas of that fyftem be contained in a facred book, fuch as the Alcoran, or be determined by any vifible authority, like that of the Roman pontif, fpeculative reafoners naturally carry on their affent, and embrace a theory, which has been inftilled into them by their earlieft education, and which alfo poffeffes fome degree of confiftence and uniformity.

uniformity. But as thefe appearances do often, all of them, prove deceitful, philofophy will foon find herfelf very unequally yoaked with her new affociate; and inftead of regulating each principle, as they advance together, fhe is at every turn perverted to ferve the purpofes of fuperftition. For befides the unavoidable incoherencies, which muft be reconciled and adjufted; one may fafely affirm, that all popular theology, efpecially the fcholaftic, has a kind of appetite for abfurdity and contradiction. If that theology went not beyond reafon and common fenfe, her doctrines would appear too eafy and familiar. Amazement muft of neceffity be raifed: Myftery affected: Darknefs and obfcurity fought after: And a foundation of merit afforded the devout votaries, who defire an opportunity of fubduing their rebellious reafon, by the belief of the moft unintelligible fophifms,

ECCLESIASTICAL hiftory fufficiently confirms thefe reflections. When a controverfy is ftarted, fome people pretend always with certainty to conjecture the iffue. Which ever opinion, fay they, is moft contrary to plain fenfe is fure to prevail; even where the general intereft of the fyftem requires not that decifion. Tho' the
reproach

reproach of herefy may, for fome time, be bandied about amongſt the diſputants, it always reſts at laſt on the ſide of reaſon. Any one, it is pretended, that has but learning enough of this kind to know the definition of *Arian*, *Pelagian*, *Eraſtian*, *Socinian*, *Sabellian*, *Eutychian*, *Neſtorian*, *Monothelite*, &c. not to mention *Proteſtant*, whoſe fate is yet uncertain, will be convinced of the truth of this obſervation. And thus a ſyſtem becomes more abſurd in the end, merely from its being reaſonable and philoſophical in the beginning.

To oppoſe the torrent of ſcholaſtic religion by ſuch feeble maxims as theſe, that *it is impoſſible for the ſame thing to be and not to be*, that *the whole is greater than a part*, that *two and three make five*; is pretending to ſtop the ocean with a bull-ruſh. Will you ſet up profane reaſon againſt ſacred myſtery? No puniſhment is great enough for your impiety. And the ſame fires, which were kindled for heretics, will ſerve alſo for the deſtruction of philoſophers.

XII. WE

XII.

WE meet every day with people fo fceptical
with regard to hiftory, that they affert it impoffible for any nation ever to believe fuch abfurd
principles as thofe of *Greek* and *Egyptian* paganifm; and at the fame time fo dogmatical
with regard to religion, that they think the
fame abfurdities are to be found in no other
communions. *Cambyfes* entertained like prejudices; and very impioufly ridiculed, and even
wounded, *Apis*, the great god of the *Egyptians*,
who appeared to his profane fenfes nothing but
a large fpotted bull. But *Herodotus* [a] judicioufly
afcribes this fally of paffion to a real madnefs or
diforder of the brain: Otherwife, fays the hiftorian, he would never have openly affronted
any eftablifhed worfhip. For on that head,
continues he, every nation are beft fatisfied with
their own, and think they have the advantage
over every other nation.

IT muft be allowed, that the *Roman* catholics are a very learned fect; and that no one

---

a Lib. iii. c. 38.

communion,

communion, but that of the church of *England*, can dispute their being the most learned of all the christian churches : Yet *Averroes*, the famous *Arabian*, who, no doubt, had heard of the *Egyptian* superstitions, declares, that, of all religions, the most absurd and non-sensical is that, whose votaries eat, after having created, their deity.

I BELIEVE, indeed, that there is no tenet in all paganism, which would give so fair a scope to ridicule as this of the *real presence :* For it is so absurd, that it eludes the force of almost all argument. There are even some pleasant stories of that kind, which, tho' somewhat profane, are commonly told by the Catholics themselves. One day, a priest, it is said, gave inadvertently, instead of the sacrament, a counter, which had by accident fallen among the holy wafers. The communicant waited patiently for some time, expecting it would dissolve on his tongue : But finding, that it still remained entire, he took it off. *I wish*, cries he to the priest, *you have not committed some mistake : I wish you have not given me God the Father : He is so hard and tough there is no swallowing him.*

E   A FAMOUS

A FAMOUS general, at that time in the *Muf-covite* fervice, having come to *Paris* for the recovery of his wounds, brought along with him a young *Turk*, whom he had taken prifoner. Some of the doctors of the *Sorbonne* (who are altogether as pofitive as the *Dervifes* of *Conftan-tinople*) thinking it a pity, that the poor *Turk* fhould be damned for want of inftruction, fol-licited *Muftapha* very hard to turn Chriftian, and promifed him, for his encouragement, plenty of good wine in this world, and paradife in the next. Thefe allurements were too powerful to be refifted; and therefore, having been well in-ftructed and catechized, he at laft agreed to re-ceive the facraments of baptifm and the Lord's fupper. The prieft, however, to make every thing fure and folid, ftill continued his inftruc-tions; and began his catechifm next day with the ufual queftion, *How many Gods are there? None at all*, replies *Benedict*; for that was his new name. *How! None at all!* cries the prieft. *To be fure*, faid the honeft profelyte. *You have told me all along that there is but one God: And yefterday I eat him.*

SUCH

Such are the doctrines of our brethren, the Catholics. But to these doctrines we are so accustomed, that we never wonder at them: Tho', in a future age, it will probably become difficult to persuade some nations, that any human, two-legged creature, could ever embrace such principles. And it is a thousand to one, but these nations themselves shall have something full as absurd in their own creed, to which they will give a most implicite and most religious assent.

I lodged once at *Paris* in the same *hotel* with an ambassador from *Tunis*, who, having past some years at *London*, was returning home that way. One day, I observed his *Moorish* excellency diverting himself under the porch, with surveying the splendid equipages that drove along; when there chanced to pass that way some *Capucin* friars, who had never seen a *Turk*; as he, on his part, tho' accustomed to the *European* dresses, had never seen the grotesque figure of a *Capucin*: And there is no expressing the mutual admiration, with which they inspired each other. Had the chaplain of the embassy entered into a dispute with these *Franciscans*, their reciprocal surprize had been of the same nature. And

E 2   thus

thus all mankind ſtand ſtaring at one another; and there is no beating it out of their heads, that the turban of the *African* is not juſt as good or as bad a faſhion as the cowl of the *European*. *He is a very honeſt man*, ſaid the prince of *Sallee*, ſpeaking of *de Ruyter*, *It is a pity he were a Chriſtian*.

How can you worſhip leeks and onions, we ſhall ſuppoſe a *Sorbonniſt* to ſay to a prieſt of *Sais ?* If we worſhip them, replies the latter ; at leaſt, we do not, at the ſame time, eat them. But what ſtrange objeĉts of adoration are cats and monkies, ſays the learned doĉtor ? They are at leaſt as good as the reliĉts or rotten bones of martyrs, anſwers his no leſs learned antagoniſt. Are you not mad, inſiſts the Catholic, to cut one another's throat about the preference of a cabbage or a cucumber. Yes, ſays the pagan ; I allow it, if you will confeſs, that all thoſe are ſtill madder, who fight about the preference among volumes of ſophiſtry, ten thouſand of which are not equal in value to one cabbage or cucumber [a].

[a] It is ſtrange that the *Egyptian* religion, tho' ſo abſurd, ſhould yet have borne ſo great a reſemblance to the *Jewiſh*, that antient writers even of the greateſt genius were not able to

EVERY

EVERY by-ftander will eafily judge (but unfortunately the by-ftanders are very few) that, if nothing were requifite to eftablifh any popular fyftem, but the expofing the abfurdities of other fyftems, every votary of every fuperftition could give a fufficient reafon for his blind and bigotted attachment to the principles, in which he has been educated. But without fo extenfive a knowledge, on which to ground this affurance, (and perhaps, better without it) there is not wanting a fufficient ftock of religious zeal and faith amongft mankind. *Diodorus Siculus* b gives

---

obferve any difference betwixt them. For it is very remarkable, that both *Tacitus* and *Suetonius,* when they mention that decree of the fenate, under *Tiberius,* by which the *Egyptian* and *Jewifh* profelytes were banifhed from *Rome,* exprefsly treat thefe religions as the fame ; and it appears, that even the decree itfelf was founded on that fuppofition. *Actum & de facris* Ægyptiis, Judaicifque *pellendis ; factumque patrum confultum, ut quatuor millia libertini generis* ea fuperftitione *infecta, quis idonea ætas, in infulam Sardiniam veherentur, coercendis illic latrociniis ; & fi ob gravitatem cœli interiffent,* vile damnum: *Ceteri cederent Italia, nifi certam ante diem profanos ritus exuiffent. Tacit. Ann.* lib. ii. c. 85. *Externas cæremonias,* Ægyptios, Judaicofque *ritus compefcuit ; coactis qui* fuperftitione ea *tenebantur, religiofas veftes cum inftrumento omni comburere,* &c. *Sueton. Tiber.* c. 36. Thefe wife heathens, obferving fomething in the general air, and genius, and fpirit of the two religions to be the fame, efteemed the differences of their dogmas too frivolous to deferve any attention.

b *Lib.* i.

E 3

a rea remarkable inftance to this purpofe, of which he was himfelf an eye-witnefs. While *Egypt* lay under the greateft terror of the *Roman* name, a legionary fo'dier having inadvertently been guilty of the facrilegious impiety of killing a cat, the whole people rofe upon him with the ut-moft fury; and all the efforts of their prince were not able to fave him. The fenate and people of *Rome*, I am perfuaded, would not, then, have been fo delicate with regard to their national deities. They very frankly, a little after that time, voted *Auguftus* a place in the celeftial manfions; and would have dethroned every god in heaven, for his fake, had he feemed to defire it. *Præfens divus habebitur Auguftus*, fays *Horace*. That is a very impor-tant point: And in other nations and other ages, the fame circumftance has not been efteemed altogether indifferent [a].

NOTWITHSTANDING the fanctity of our holy religion, fays *Tully* [b], no crime is more

---

[a] When *Louis* the XIVth took on himfelf the protection of the Jefuites college of *Clermont*, the fociety ordered the king's arms to be put up over their gate, and took down the crofs, in order to make way for it: Which gave occafion to the follow-ing epigram:

Suftulit hinc Chrifti, pofuitque infignia Regis:
Impia gens, alium nefcit habere Deum.

[b] De nat. Deor. l. i.

common

common with us than facrilege: But was it ever heard, that an *Egyptian* violated the temple of a cat, an ibis, or a crocodile? There is no torture, an *Egyptian* would not undergo, fays the fame author in another place [a], rather than injure an ibis, an afpic, a cat, a dog, or a crocodile. Thus it is ftrictly true, what *Dryden* obferves

    " Of whatfoe'er defcent their godhead be,
    " Stock, ftone, or other homely pedigree,
    " In his defence his fervants are as bold,
    " As if he had been born of beaten gold."
             ABSALOM and ACHITOPHEL.

Nay, the bafer the materials are, of which the divinity is compofed, the greater devotion is he likely to excite in the breafts of his deluded votaries. They exult in their fhame, and make a merit with their deity, in braving, for his fake, all the ridicule and contumely of his enemies. Ten thoufand *Croifes* inlift themfelves under the holy banners, and even openly triumph in thofe parts of their religion, which their adverfaries regard as the moft reproachful.

THERE occurs, I own, a difficulty in the *Egyptian* fyftem of theology; as indeed, few

[a] Tufc. Quæft. lib. v.

E 4   fyftems

fyftems are entirely free from difficulties. It is evident, from their method of propagation, that a couple of cats, in fifty years, would ftock a whole kingdom; and if that religious veneration were ftill paid them, it would, in twenty more, not only be eafier in *Egypt* to find a god than a man, which *Petronius* fays was the cafe in fome parts of *Italy*; but the gods muft at laft entirely ftarve the men, and leave themfelves neither priefts nor votaries remaining. It is probable, therefore, that that wife nation, the moft celebrated in antiquity for prudence and found policy, forefeeing fuch dangerous confequences, referved all their worfhip for the full-grown divinities, and ufed the freedom to drown the holy fpawn or little fucking gods, without any fcruple or remorfe. And thus the practice of warping the tenets of religion, in order to ferve temporal interefts, is not, by any means, to be regarded as an invention of thefe latter ages.

THE learned, philofophical *Varro*, difcourfing of religion, pretends not to deliver any thing beyond probabilities and appearances : Such was his good fenfe and moderation! But the paffionate, the zealous *Auguftin*, infults the noble *Roman* on his fcepticifm and referve, and profeffes the

the moſt thorough belief and aſſurance [a]. A heathen poet, however, contemporary with the ſaint, abſurdly eſteems the religious ſyſtem of the latter ſo falſe, that even the credulity of children, he ſays, could not engage them to believe it [b].

Is it ſtrange, when miſtakes are ſo common, to find every one poſitive and dogmatical? And that the zeal often riſes in proportion to the error? *Moverunt,* ſays *Spartian, & ea tempeſtate Judæi bellum quod vetabantur mutilare genitalia* [c].

If ever there was a nation or a time, in which the public religion loſt all authority over mankind, we might expect, that infidelity in *Rome,* during the *Ciceronian* age, would openly have erected its throne, and that *Cicero* himſelf, in every ſpeech and action, would have been its moſt declared abettor. But it appears, that, whatever ſceptical liberties that great man might uſe, in his writings or in philoſophical converſation; he yet avoided, in the common conduct of life, the imputation of deiſm and profaneneſs. Even in his own family, and to his wife, *Terentia,* whom he highly truſted, he

---

[a] De civitate Dei, l. iii. c. 17. Numitiani iter, lib. i. l. 386.   [b] Claudii Rutilii
[c] In vita Adriani.

was

was willing to appear a devout religionist; and
there remains a letter, addrest to her, in which
he seriously desires her to offer sacrifice to *Apollo*
and *Æsculapius*, in gratitude for the recovery of his health [a].

POMPEY's devotion was much more sincere:
In all his conduct, during the civil wars, he
paid a great regard to auguries, dreams, and
prophesies [b]. *Augustus* was tainted with superstition of every kind. As it is reported of *Milton*, that his poetical genius never flowed with
ease and abundance in the spring; so *Augustus*
observed, that his own genius for dreaming
never was so perfect during that season, nor was
so much to be relied on, as during the rest of
the year. That great and able emperor was
also extremely uneasy when he happened to
change his shoes, and put the right foot shoe on
the left foot [c]. In short, it cannot be doubted,
but the votaries of the established superstition of
antiquity were as numerous in every state, as
those of the modern religion are at present. Its
influence was as universal; tho' it was not so

---

[a] Lib. xiv. epist. 7.   [b] Cicero de Divin. lib. ii. c. 24.
[c] Sueton. Aug. cap. 90, 91, 92.   Plin. lib. ii. cap. 7.

great.

great. As many people gave their aſſent to it; tho' that aſſent was not ſeemingly ſo ſtrong, pre-ciſe, and affirmative.

WE may obſerve, that, notwithſtanding the dogmatical, imperious ſtyle of all ſuperſtition, the conviction of the religioniſts, in all ages, is more affected than real, and ſcarce ever ap-proaches, in any degree, to that ſolid belief and perſuaſion, which governs us in the common affairs of life. Men dare not avow, even to their own hearts, the doubts, which they enter-tain on ſuch ſubjects: They make a merit of implicite faith; and diſguiſe to themſelves their real infidelity, by the ſtrongeſt aſſeverations and moſt poſitive bigotry. But nature is too hard for all their endeavours, and ſuffers not the ob-ſcure, glimmering light, afforded in thoſe ſha-dowy regions, to equal the ſtrong impreſſions, made by common ſenſe and by experience. The uſual courſe of men's conduct belies their words, and ſhows, that the aſſent in theſe mat-ters is ſome unaccountable operation of the mind betwixt diſbelief and conviction, but ap-proaching much nearer the former than the latter.

SINCE,

SINCE, therefore, the mind of man appears of fo loofe and unfteddy a contexture, that, even at prefent, when fo many perfons find an intereft in continually employing on it the chiffel and the hammer, yet are they not able to engrave theological tenets with any lafting impreffion; how much more muft this have been the cafe in antient times, when the retainers to the holy function were fo much fewer in comparifon? No wonder, that the appearances were then very inconfiftent, and that men, on fome occafions, might feem determined infidels, and enemies to the eftablifhed religion, without being fo in reality; or at leaft, without knowing their own minds in that particular.

ANOTHER caufe, which rendered the antient religions much loofer than the modern, is, that the former were *traditional* and the latter are *fcriptural*; and the tradition in the former was complex, contradictory, and, on many occafions, doubtful; fo that it could not poffibly be reduced to any ftandard and canon, or afford any determinate articles of faith. The ftories of the gods were numberlefs like the popifh legends; and tho' every one, almoft, believed a part of thefe ftories, yet no one could believe or know the

the whole: While, at the fame time, all muft have acknowledged, that no one part ftood on a better foundation than the reft. The traditions of different cities and nations were alfo, on many occafions, directly oppofite; and no reafon could be found for preferring one to the other. And as there was an infinite number of ftories, with regard to which tradition was no way pofitive; the gradation was infenfible, from the moft fundamental articles of faith, to thofe loofe and precarious fictions. The pagan religion, therefore, feemed to vanifh like a cloud, whenever one approached to it, and examined it piecemeal. It could never be afcertained by any fixt dogmas and principles. And tho' this did not convert the generality of mankind from fo abfurd a faith; for when will the people be reafonable? yet it made them faulter and hefitate more in maintaining their principles, and was even apt to produce, in certain difpofitions of mind, fome practices and opinions, which had the appearance of determined infidelity.

To which we may add, that the fables of the pagan religion were, of themfelves, light, eafy, and familiar; without devils or feas of brimftone, or any objects, that could much terrify
the

the imagination.   Who could forbear fmiling,
when he thought of the loves of *Mars* and
Venus, or the amorous frolics of *Jupiter* and
Pan? In this refpect, it was a true poetical religion; if it had not rather too much levity for the
graver kinds of poetry.   We find that it has
been adopted by modern bards ; nor have thefe
talked with greater freedom and irreverence of
the gods, whom they regarded as fictions, than
the antient did of the real objects of their
devotion.

THE inference is by no means juft, that, becaufe a fyftem of religion has made no deep impreffion on the minds of a people, it muft therefore have been pofitively rejected by all men of
common fenfe, and that oppofite principles, in
fpite of the prejudices of education, were generally eftablifhed by argument and reafoning.
I know not, but a contrary inference may be
more probable. The lefs importunate and affuming any fpecies of fuperftition appears, the lefs
will it provoke men's fpleen and indignation, or
engage them into enquiries concerning its foundation and origin.   This in the mean time
is obvious, that the empire of all religious
faith over the underftanding is wavering and
uncertain,

uncertain, fubject to all varieties of humour, and dependent on the prefent incidents, which ftrike the imagination. The difference is only in the degrees. An antient will place a ftroke of impiety and one of fuperftition alternately, thro' a whole difcourfe [a] : A modern often thinks in the fame way, tho' he may be more guarded in his expreffions.

LUCIAN tells us exprefsly [b], that whoever believed not the moft ridiculous fables of paganifm was efteemed by the people profane and impious. To what purpofe, indeed, would that agreeable author have employed the whole force of his wit and fatyr againft the national religion, had not that religion been generally believed by his countrymen and contemporaries?

[a] Witnefs this remarkable paffage of *Tacitus: Præter multi-plices rerum humanarum cafus, cœlo terraque prodigia, & fulmi-num monitus, & futurorum præfagia, læta, triftia, ambigua, manifefta. Nec enim umquam atrocioribus populi Romani cladi-bus, magifque juftis judiciis approbatum eft, non effe curæ Diis fecuritatem noftram, effe ultionem, Hift.* lib. i. *Auguftus's* quarrel with *Neptune* is an inftance of the fame kind. Had not the emperor believed *Neptune* to be a real being and to have do-minion over the fea ; where had been the foundation of his anger ? And if he believed it, what madnefs to provoke ftill far-ther that deity ? The fame obfervation may be made upon *Quinctilian's* exclamations, on account of the death of his children, lib. vi. Præf.   [b] Philopfeudes.

LIVY

LIVY [a] acknowledges as frankly, as any divine would at prefent, the common incredulity of his age ; but then he condemns it as feverely. And who can imagine, that a national fuperftition, which could delude fo great a man, would not alfo impofe on the generality of the people?

THE *Stoics* beftowed many magnificent and even impious epithets on their fage; that he alone was rich, free, a king, and equal to the immortal gods. They forgot to add, that he was not inferior in prudence and underftanding to an old woman. For furely nothing can be more pitiful than the fentiments, which that fect entertained with regard to all popular fuperftitions ; while they very ferioufly agree with the common augurs, that, when a raven croaks from the left, it is a good omen; but a bad one, when a rook makes a noife from the fame quarter. *Panætius* was the only *Stoic*, amongft the *Greeks*, who fo much as doubted with regard to auguries and divinations [b]. *Marcus Antoninus* [c] tells us, that he himfelf had received many admonitions from the gods in his fleep. It is true ; *Epictetus* [d] forbids us to regard the

[a] Lib. x. cap. 40.   [b] Cicero de Divin. lib. i. cap. 3.
& 7.   [c] Lib. i. § 17.   [d] Ench. § 17.

4   language

language of rooks and ravens; but it is not, that they do not speak truth : It is only, becauſe they can fortel nothing but the breaking of our neck or the forfeiture of our eſtate; which are cir-cumſtances, ſays he, that no way concern us. Thus the *Stoics* join a philoſophical enthuſiaſm to a religious ſuperſtition. The force of their mind, being all turned to the ſide of morals, unbent itſelf in that of religion [a].

PLATO [b] introduces *Socrates* affirming, that the accuſation of impiety raiſed againſt him was owing entirely to his rejecting ſuch fables, as thoſe of *Saturn's* caſtrating his father, *Uranus*, and *Jupiter's* dethroning *Saturn :* Yet in a ſub-ſequent dialogue [c], *Socrates* confeſſes, that the doctrine of the mortality of the ſoul was the re-ceived opinion of the people. Is there here any contradiction ? Yes, ſurely: But the contradiction is not in *Plato*; it is in the people, whoſe reli-gious principles in general are always compoſed of the moſt diſcordant parts; eſpecially in an

[a] The *Stoics*, I own, were not quite orthodox in the eſta-bliſhed religion; but one may ſee, from theſe inſtances, that they went a great way: And the people undoubtedly went every length.

[b] Eutyphro.   [c] Phædo.

age,

age, when superstition sate so easy and light upon them [a].

[a] *Xenophon's* conduct, as related by himself, is, at once, an incontestable proof of the general credulity of mankind in those ages, and the incoherencies, in all ages, of men's opinions in religious matters. That great captain and philosopher, the disciple of *Socrates*, and one who has delivered some of the most refined sentiments with regard to a deity, gave all the following marks of vulgar, pagan superstition. By *Socrates's* advice, he consulted the oracle of *Delphi*, before he would engage in the expedition of *Cyrus*. De exped. lib. iii. p. 294. ex edit. Leuncl. Sees a dream the night after the generals were seized; which he pays great regard to, but thinks ambiguous. Id. p. 295. He and the whole army regard sneezing as a very lucky omen. Id. p. 300. Has another dream, when he comes to the river *Centrites*, which his fellow general, *Chirosophus*, also pays great regard to. Id. lib. iv. p. 323. The *Greeks* suffering from a cold north wind, sacrifice to it, and the historian observes, that it immediately abated. Id. p. 329. *Xenophon* consults the sacrifices in secret, before he would form any resolution with himself about settling a colony. Lib. v. p. 359. He himself a very skilful augur. Id. p. 361. Is determined by the victims to refuse the sole command of the army, which was offered him. Lib. vi. p. 273. *Cleander*, the *Spartan*, tho' very desirous of it, refuses it for the same reason. Id. p. 392. *Xenophon* mentions an old dream with the interpretation given him, when he first joined *Cyrus*. P. 373. Mentions also the place of *Hercules's* descent into hell as believing it, and says the marks of it are still remaining. Id. p. 375. Had almost starved the army rather than lead to the field against the auspices. Id. p. 382, 383. His friend, *Euclides*, the augur, would not believe that he had brought no money from the expedition; till he (*Euclides*) sacrificed, and then he saw the matter clearly in the *Exta*. Lib. vii. p. 425. The same philosopher, proposing a project of mines for the encrease of the *Athenian* revenues, advises them first to

THE

THE fame *Cicero*, who affeeted, in his own family, to appear a devout religionift, makes no fcruple, in a public court of judicature, of treating the doctrine of a future ftate as a moft ridiculous fable, to which no body could give any attention [a]. *Salluft* [b] reprefents *Cæfar* as fpeaking the fame language in the open fenate [c].

BUT that all thefe freedoms implied not a total and univerfal infidelity and fcepticifm

consult the oracle. De rat. red. p. 932. That all this devotion was not a farce, in order to ferve a political purpofe, appears both from the facts themfelves, and from the genius of that age, when little or nothing could be gained by hypocrify. Befides, *Xenophon*, as appears from his *Memorabilia*, was a kind of heretic in thofe times, which no political devotee ever is. It is for the fame reafon, I maintain, that *Newton*, *Locke*, *Clarke*, &c. being *Arians* or *Socinians*, were very fincere in the creed they profeft: And I always oppofe this argument to fome libertines, who will needs have it, that it was impoffible, but that thefe great philofophers muft have been hypocrites.

[a] Pro Cluentio, cap. 61.   [b] De bello Catilin.

[c] *Cicero* (Tufc. Quæft. lib. i. cap. 5, 6.) and *Seneca* (Epift. 24.) as alfo *Juvenal* (Satyr. 2.) maintain that there is no boy or old woman fo ridiculous as to believe the poets in their accounts of a future ftate. Why then does *Lucretius* fo highly exalt his mafter for freeing us from thefe terrors? Perhaps the generality of mankind were then in the difpofition of *Cephalus* in *Plato* (de Rep. lib. i.) who while he was young and healthful could ridicule thefe ftories; but as foon as he became old and infirm, began to entertain apprehenfions of their truth. This, we may obferve, not to be unufual even at prefent.

amongft

amongst the people, is too apparent to be denied. Tho' fome parts of the national religion hung loofe upon the minds of men, other parts adhered more clofely to them: And it was the great bufinefs of the fceptical philofophers to fhow, that there was no more foundation for one than for the other. This is the artifice of *Cotta* in the dialogues concerning *the nature of the gods*. He refutes the whole fyftem of mythology by leading the orthodox, gradually, from the more momentous ftories, which were believed, to the more frivolous, which every one ridiculed: From the gods to the goddeffes; from the goddeffes to the nymphs; from the nymphs to the fawns and fatyrs. His mafter, *Carneades*, had employed the fame method of reafoning [a].

UPON the whole, the greateft and moft obfervable differences betwixt a *traditional*, *mythological* religion, and a *fyftematical*, *fcholaftic* one, are two: The former is often more reafonable, as confifting only of a multitude of ftories, which, however groundlefs, imply no exprefs abfurdity and demonftrative contradic-

[a] Sext. Empir. adverf. Mathem. lib. viii.

tion;

tion; and fits alfo fo eafy and light on men's minds, that tho' it may be as univerfally received, it makes no fuch deep impreffion on the affections and underftanding.

XIII. THE

XIII.

THE primary religion of mankind arifes chiefly from an anxious fear of future events; and what ideas will naturally be entertained of invifible, unknown powers, while men lie under difmal apprehenfions of any kind, may eafily be conceived. Every image of vengeance, feverity, cruelty, and malice muft occur and augment the ghaftlinefs and horror, which oppreffes the amazed religionift. A panic having once feized the mind, the active fancy ftill farther multiplies the objects of terror; while that profound darknefs, or, what is worfe, that glimmering light, with which we are invironed, reprefents the fpectres of divinity under the moft dreadful appearances imaginable. And no idea of perverfe wickednefs can be framed, which thofe terrified devotees do not readily, without fcruple, apply to their deity.

THIS appears the natural ftate of religion, when furveyed in one light. But if we confider, on the other hand, that fpirit of praife and eulogy, which neceffarily has place in all religions, and which is the confequence of thefe very terrors,

terrors, we muſt expeçt a quite contrary fyſtem of theology to prevail. Every virtue, every ex-cellence muſt be aſcribed to the divinity, and no exaggeration be eſteemed ſufficient to reach thoſe perfeçtions, with which he is endowed. Whatever ſtrains of panegyric can be invented, are immediately embraced, without conſulting any arguments or phænomena. And it is eſteemed a ſufficient confirmation of them, that they give us more magnificent ideas of the divine objeçt of our worſhip and adoration.

HERE therefore is a kind of contradiçtion be-twixt the different principles of human nature, which enter into religion. Our natural terrors preſent the notion of a deviliſh and malicious deity: Our propenſity to praiſe leads us to ac-knowledge an excellent and divine. And the influence of theſe oppoſite principles are vari-ous, according to the different ſituation of the human underſtanding.

IN very barbarous and ignorant nations, ſuch as the *Africans* and *Indians*, nay even the *Ja-poneſe*, who can form no extenſive ideas of power and knowledge, worſhip may be paid to a being, whom they confeſs to be wicked and de-teſtable ;

teftable ; tho' they may be cautious, perhaps, of pronouncing this judgment of him in public, or in his temple, where he may be fuppofed to hear their reproaches.

Such rude, imperfect ideas of the divinity ad-here long to all idolaters ; and it may fafely be affirmed, that the *Greeks* themfelves never got entirely rid of them. It is remarked by *Xeno-phon* [a], in praife of *Socrates*, that that philofo-pher affented not to the vulgar opinion, which fuppofed the gods to know fome things, and be ignorant of others : He maintained that they knew every thing ; what was done, faid, or even thought. But as this was a ftrain of phi-lofophy [b] much above the conception of his countrymen, we need not be furprized, if very frankly, in their books and converfation, they blamed the deities, whom they worfhiped in their temples. It is obfervable, that *Hero-dotus* in particular fcruples not, in many paffages, to afcribe *envy* to the gods ; a fentiment, of all

[a] Mem. lib. i.

[b] It was confidered among the antients, as a very extraordi-nary, philofophical paradox, that the prefence of the gods was not confined to the heavens, but was extended every where ; as we learn from *Lucian.* *Hermotimus five De fectis.*

others,

others, the moſt ſuitable to a mean and deviliſh nature. The pagan hymns however, ſung in public worſhip, contained nothing but epithets of praiſe ; even while the actions aſcribed to the gods were the moſt barbarous and deteſtable. When *Timotheus*, the poet, recited a hymn to *Diana*, where he enumerated, with the greateſt eulogies, all the actions and attributes of that cruel, capricious goddeſs: *May your daughter*, ſaid one preſent, *become ſuch as the deity whom you celebrate* [a].

But as men farther exalt their idea of their divinity ; it is often their notion of his power and knowledge only, not of his goodneſs, which is improved. On the contrary, in proportion to the ſuppoſed extent of his ſcience and authority, their terrors naturally augment ; while they believe, that no ſecrecy can conceal them from his ſcrutiny, and that even the inmoſt receſſes of their breaſt lie open before him. They muſt then be careful not to form expreſsly any ſentiment of blame and diſapprobation. All muſt be applauſe, raviſhment, extacy. And while their gloomy apprehenſions make them

[a] Plutarch. de Superſt.

F

aſcribe

afcribe to him meafures of conduct, which, in human creatures, would be highly blamed, they muft ftill affect to praife and admire thefe meafures in the object of their devotional addreffes. And thus it may fafely be affirmed, that many popular religions are really, in the conception of their more vulgar votaries, a fpecies of dæmonifm; and the higher the deity is exalted in power and knowledge, the lower of courfe is he frequently depreft in goodnefs and benevolence; whatever epithets of praife may be beftowed on him by his amazed adorers. Amongft idolaters, the words may be falfe, and belie the fecret opinion: But amongft more exalted religionifts, the opinion itfelf often contracts a kind of falfhood, and belies the inward fentiment. The heart fecretly detefts fuch meafures of cruel and implacable vengeance; but the judgment dares not but pronounce them perfect and adorable. And the additional mifery of this inward ftruggle aggravates all the other terrors, by which thefe unhappy victims to fuperftition are for ever haunted.

LUCIAN [a] obferves, that a young man, who reads the hiftory of the gods in *Homer* or *He-*

---

[a] Necyomantia.

fiod,

ſiod, and finds their factions, wars, injuſtice, inceſt, adultery, and other immoralities ſo highly celebrated, is much ſurprized afterwards, when he comes into the world, to obſerve, that puniſhments are by law inflicted on the ſame actions, which he had been taught to aſcribe to ſuperior beings. The contradiction is ſtill perhaps ſtronger betwixt the repreſentations given us by ſome latter religions and our natural ideas of generoſity, lenity, impartiality, and juſtice; and in proportion to the multiplied terrors of theſe religions, the barbarous conceptions of the divinity are multiplied upon us [a]. Nothing can

[a] *Bacchus,* a divine being, is repreſented by the heathen mythology as the inventor of dancing and the theatre. Plays were antiently, even a part of public worſhip on the moſt ſolemn occaſions, and often employed in times of peſtilence, to appeaſe the offended deities. But they have been zealouſly preſcribed by the godly in latter ages; and the play-houſe, according to a learned divine, is the porch of hell.

But in order to ſhow more evidently, that it is poſſible for a religion to repreſent the divinity in ſtill a more immoral unamiable light than the antient, we ſhall cite a long paſſage from an author of taſte and imagination, who was ſurely no enemy to Chriſtianity. It is the chevalier *Ramſay,* a writer, who had ſo laudable an inclination to be orthodox, that his reaſon never found any difficulty, even in the doctrines which freethinkers ſcruple the moſt, the trinity, incarnation, and ſatisfaction: His humanity alone, of which he ſeems to have had a great ſtock, rebelled againſt the doctrines of eternal reprobation and predeſtination. He expreſſes himſelf thus: ' What ſtrange ideas, ſays he, would an Indian

preſerve

preferve untainted the genuine principles of
morals in our judgment of human conduct,

' or a Chinese philofopher have of our holy religion, if they
' judged by the fchemes given of it by our modern freethinkers,
' and pharifaical doctors of all fects? According to the odious and
' too *vulgar* fyftem of thefe incredulous fcoffers and credulous
' fcriblers, "The God of the Jews is a moft cruel, unjuft, par-
" tial and fantaftical being. He created, about 6000 years
" ago, a man and a woman, and placed them in a fine garden
" of Afia, of which there are no remains. This garden was
" furnifhed with all forts of trees, fountains, and flowers. He
" allowed them the ufe of all the fruits of this beautiful garden,
" except of one, that was planted in the midft thereof, and
" that had in it a fecret virtue of preferving them in continual
" health and vigor of body and mind, of exalting their natural
" powers and making them wife. The devil entered into the
" body of a ferpent, and folicited the firft woman to eat of this
" forbidden fruit; fhe engaged her hufband to do the fame. To
" punifh this flight curiofity and natural defire of life and know-
" ledge, God not only threw our firft parents out of paradife,
" but he condemned all their pofterity to temporal mifery, and
" the greateft part of them to eternal pains, tho' the fouls of
" thefe innocent children have no more relation to that of Adam
" than to thofe of Nero and Mahomet; fince, according to the
" fcholaftic drivellers, fabulifts, and mythologifts, all fouls
" are created pure, and infufed immediately into mortal bodies,
" fo foon as the fœtus is formed. To accomplifh the barbarous,
" partial decree of predeftination and reprobation, God aban-
" doned all nations to darknefs, idolatry and fuperftition, with-
" out any faving knowledge or falutary graces; unlefs it was
" one particular nation, whom he chofe as his peculiar people.
" This chofen nation was, however, the moft ftupid, ungrateful,
" rebellious, and perfidious of all nations. After God had thus
" kept the far greater part of all the human fpecies, during

but

but the abfolute neceffity of thefe principles to the exiftence of fociety. If common concep-

" near 4000 years, in a reprobate ftate, he changed all of a
" fudden, and took a fancy for other nations, befide the Jews.
" Then he fent his only begotten Son to the world, under a
" human form, to appeafe his wrath, fatisfy his vindictive ju-
" ftice, and die for the pardon of fin. Very few nations, how-
" ever, have heard of this gofpel; and all the reft, tho' left in
" invincible ignorance, are damned without exception or any
" poffibility of remiffion. The greateft part of thofe, who
" have heard of it, have changed only fome fpeculative notions
" about God, and fome external forms in worfhip: For, in
" other refpects, the bulk of Chriftians have continued as cor-
" rupt, as the reft of mankind in their morals; yea, fo much
" the more perverfe and criminal, that their lights were greater.
" Unlefs it be a very fmall felect number, all other Chriftians, like
" the pagans, will be for ever damned; the great facrifice of-
" fered up for them will become void and of no effect. God
" will take delight for ever in their torments and blafphemies;
. " and tho' he can, by one *fiat*, change their hearts, yet they will
" remain for ever unconverted and unconvertible, becaufe he will
" be for ever unappeafeable and irreconcileable. It is true, that
" all this makes God odious, a hater of fouls, rather than a
" lover of them; a cruel, vindictive tyrant, an impotent or a
" wrathful dæmon, rather than an all-powerful, beneficent Fa-
" ther of fpirits: Yet all this is a myftery. He has fecret rea-
" fons for his conduct, that are impenetrable; and tho' he ap-
" pears unjuft and barbarous; yet we muft believe the contrary,
" becaufe what is injuftice, crime, cruelty, and the blackeft
" malice in us, is in him juftice, mercy, and fovereign goodnefs."
' Thus the incredulous freethinkers, the judaizing Chriftians, and
' the fataliftic doctors, have disfigured and difhonoured the fublime
' myfteries of our holy faith; thus, they have confounded the nature
' of good and evil; transformed the moft monftrous paffions into
' divine attributes, and furpaffed the pagans in blafphemy, by

tion

tion can indulge princes in a fyftem of ethics, fomewhat different from that which fhould regulate private perfons ; how much more thofe fuperior beings, whofe attributes, views, and nature are fo totally unknown to us ? *Sunt fuperis fua jura* [a]; The gods have maxims of juftice peculiar to themfelves.

' afcribing to the eternal nature, as perfections, what makes the ' moft horrid crimes amongft men. The groffer pagans contented ' themfelves with divinizing luft, inceft, and adultry ; but the pre- ' deftinarian doctors have divinized cruelty, wrath, fury, venge- ' ance, and all the blackeft vices.' See the chevalier Ramfay's philofophical principles of natural and revealed religion, Part II. p. 401.

The fame author afferts, in other places, that the *Arminian* and *Molinift* fchemes ferve very little to mend the matter : And having thus thrown himfelf out of all received fects of Chriftianity, he is obliged to advance a fyftem of his own, which is a kind of *Origenifm*, and fuppofes the pre-exiftence of the fouls both of men and beafts, and the eternal falvation and converfion of all men, beafts, and devils. But this notion, being quite peculiar to himfelf, we need not treat of. I thought the opinions of this ingenious author very curious ; but I pretend not to warrant the juftnefs of them.

a Ovid. Metam. lib. ix. 501.

XIV. HERE

XIV.

HERE I cannot forbear obferving a fact, which may be worth the attention of thofe, who make human nature the object of their enquiry. It is certain, that, in every religion, however fublime the verbal definition, which it gives of its divinity, many of the votaries, perhaps the greateft number, will ftill feek the divine favour, not by virtue and good morals, which alone can be acceptable to a perfect being, but either by frivolous obfervances, by intemperate zeal, by rapturous extafies, or by the belief of myfterious and abfurd opinions. The leaft part of the *Sadder*, as well as of the *Pentateuch*, confifts in precepts of morality ; and we may be affured, that that part was always the leaft obferved and regarded. When the old *Romans* were attacked with a peftilence, they never afcribed their fufferings to their vices, or dreamed of repentance and amendment. They never thought that they were the general robbers of the world, whofe ambition and avarice made defolate the earth, and reduced opulent nations to want and beggary. They only created a dictator [a], in

---

[a] Called Dictator clavis figendæ caufa. T. Livii, l. vii. c. 3.

F 4 order

order to drive a nail into a door; and by that means, they thought that they had sufficiently appeased their incensed deity.

In *Ægina*, one faction entering into a conspiracy, barbarously and treacherously assassinated seven hundred of their fellow-citizens; and carried their fury so far, that, one miserable fugitive having fled to the temple, they cut off his hands, by which he clung to the gates, and carrying him out of holy ground, immediately murdered him. *By this impiety*, says *Herodotus* [a], (not by the other many cruel assassinations) *they offended the gods, and contracted an inexpiable guilt.*

Nay, if we should suppose, what seldom happens, that a popular religion were found, in which it was expressly declared, that nothing but morality could gain the divine favour; if an order of priests were instituted to inculcate this opinion, in daily sermons, and with all the arts of persuasion; yet so inveterate are the people's prejudices, that for want of some other superstition, they would make the very attendance on these sermons the essentials of religion, rather

[a] Lib. vi.

than

than place them in virtue and good morals. The fublime prologue of *Zaleucus's* laws [a] infpired not the *Locrians*, fo far as we can learn, with any founder notions of the meafures of acceptance with the deity, than were familiar to the other *Greeks*.

THIS obfervation, then, holds univerfally: But ftill one may be at fome lofs to account for it. It is not fufficient to obferve, that the people, every where, degrade their deities into a fimilitude with themfelves, and confider them merely as a fpecies of human creatures, fomewhat more potent and intelligent. This will not remove the difficulty. For there is no *man* fo ftupid, as that, judging by his natural reafon, he would not efteem virtue and honefty the moft valuable qualities, which any perfon could poffefs. Why not afcribe the fame fentiment to his deity? Why not make all religion, or the chief part of it, to confift in thefe attainments?

NOR is it fatisfactory to fay, that the practice of morality is more difficult than that of fuperftition; and is therefore rejected. For,

[a] To be found in Diod. Sic. lib. xii,

not

not to mention the exceffive pennances of the *Brahmans* and *Talapoins* ; it is certain, that the *Rhamadan* of the *Turks*, during which the poor wretches, for many days, often in the hotteft months of the year, and in fome of the hotteft climates of the world, remain without eating or drinking from the rifing to the fetting of the fun ; this *Rhamadan*, I fay, muft be more fevere, than the practice of any moral duty, even to the moft vicious and depraved of mankind. The four lents of the *Mufcovites*, and the aufterities of fome *Roman Catholics*, appear more difagreable than meeknefs and benevolence. In fhort, all virtue, when men are reconciled to it by ever fo little practice, is agreeable : All fuperftition is for ever odious and burthenfome.

PERHAPS, the following account may be received as a true folution of the difficulty. The duties, which a man performs as a friend or parent, feem merely owing to his benefactor or children ; nor can he be wanting to thefe duties, without breaking thro' all the ties of nature and morality. A ftrong inclination may prompt him to the performance : A fentiment of order and moral beauty joins its force to thefe natural tyes : And the whole man, if truly virtuous,

is

is drawn to his duty, without any effort or
endeavour. Even with regard to the virtues,
which are more auftere, and more founded on
reflection, fuch as public fpirit, filial duty, temperance, or integrity; the moral obligation, in
our apprehenfion, removes all pretence to religious merit; and the virtuous conduct is
efteemed no more than what we owe to fociety
and to ourfelves. In all this, a fuperftitious
man finds nothing, which he has properly performed for the fake of his deity, or which can
peculiarly recommend him to the divine favour
and protection. He confiders not, that the moft
genuine method of ferving the divinity is by
promoting the happinefs of his creatures. He
ftill looks out for fome more immediate fervice
of the fupreme being, in order to allay thofe
terrors, with which he is haunted. And any
practice recommended to him, which either
ferves to no purpofe in life, or offers the
ftrongeft violence to his natural inclinations;
that practice he will the more readily embrace,
on account of thofe very circumftances, which
fhould make him abfolutely reject it. It feems
the more purely religious, that it proceeds from
no mixture of any other motive or confideration. And if, for its fake, he facrifices much

of

of his eafe and quiet, his claim of merit appears ftill to rife upon him, in proportion to the zeal and devotion, which he difcovers. In reftoring a loan, or paying a debt, his divinity is no way beholden to him ; becaufe thefe acts of juftice are what he was bound to perform, and what many would have performed, were there no god in the univerfe. But if he faft a day, or give himfelf a found whipping ; this has a direct reference, in his opinion, to the fervice of God. No other motive could engage him to fuch aufterities. By thefe diftinguifhed marks of devotion, he has now acquired the divine favour ; and may expect, in recompence, protection and fafety in this world, and eternal happinefs in the next.

HENCE the greateft crimes have been found, in many inftances, compatible with a fuperftitious piety and devotion : Hence it is juftly regarded as unfafe to draw any certain inference in favour of a man's morals from the fervor or ftrictnefs of his religious exercifes, even tho' he himfelf believe them fincere. Nay, it has been obferved, that enormities of the blackeft dye, have been rather apt to produce fuperftitious terrors, and encreafe the religious paffion. *Bomilcar,*

milcar, having formed a confpiracy for affaffi-
nating at once the whole fenate of *Carthage*,
and invading the liberties of his country, loft the
opportunity, from a continual regard to omens
and prophefies. *Thofe who undertake the moft criminal and moft dangerous enterprizes are commonly
the moft fuperftitious*; as an antient hiftorian [a]
remarks on this occafion. Their devotion and
fpiritual faith rife with their fears. *Catiline*
was not contented with the eftablifhed deities,
and received rites of his national religion : His
anxious terrors made him feek new inventions
of this kind [b]; which he never probably had
dreamed of, had he remained a good citizen,
and obedient to the laws of his country.

To which we may add, that, even after the
commiffion of crimes, there arife remorfes and
fecret horrors, which give no reft to the mind,
but make it have recourfe to religious rites and
ceremonies, as expiations of its offences. Whatever weakens or diforders the internal frame
promotes the interefts of fuperftition : And nothing is more deftructive to them than a manly,

[a] Diod. Sic. lib. xx.
[b] Cic. Catil. i. Salluft. de bello Catil.

ft-eddy

fteddy virtue, which either preferves us from difaftrous, melancholy accidents, or teaches us to bear them. During fuch calm funfhine of the mind, thefe fpectres of falfe divinity never make their appearance. On the other hand, while we abandon ourfelves to the natural, undifciplined fuggeftions of our timid and anxious hearts, every kind of barbarity is afcribed to the fupreme being, from the terrors, with which we are agitated; and every kind of caprice, from the methods which we embrace, in order to appeafe him. *Barbarity, caprice*; thefe qualities, however nominally difguifed, we may univerfally obferve, to form the ruling character of the deity, in popular religions. Even priefts, inftead of correcting thefe depraved ideas of mankind, have often been found ready to fofter and encourage them. The more tremendous the divinity is reprefented, the more tame and fubmiffive do men become to his minifters: And the more unaccountable the meafures of acceptance required by him, the more neceffary does it become to abandon our natural reafon, and yield to their ghoftly guidance and direction. And thus it may be allowed, that the artifices of men aggravate our natural infirmities

2

firmities and follies of this kind, but never originally beget them. Their root ftrikes deeper into the mind, and fprings from the effential and univerfal properties of human nature.

XV. THO'

XV.

THO' the ftupidity of men, barbarous and uninftructed, be fo great, that they may not fee a fovereign author in the more obvious works of nature, to which they are fo much familiarized; yet it fcarce feems poffible, that any one of good underftanding fhould reject that idea, when once it is fuggefted to him. A purpofe, an intention, a defign is evident in every thing; and when our comprehenfion is fo far enlarged as to contemplate the firft rife of this vifible fyftem, we muft adopt, with the ftrongeft conviction, the idea of fome intelligent caufe or author. The uniform maxims too, which prevail thro' the whole frame of the univerfe, naturally, if not neceffarily, lead us to conceive this intelligence as fingle and undivided, where the prejudices of education oppofe not fo reafonable a theory. Even the contrarieties of nature, by difcovering themfelves every where, become proofs of fome confiftent plan, and eftablifh one fingle purpofe or intention, however inexplicable and incomprehenfible.

λ   GOOD

GOOD and ill are univerfally intermingled and confounded; happinefs and mifery, wifdom and folly, virtue and vice. Nothing is pure and entirely of a piece. All advantages are attended with difadvantages. An univerfal compenfation prevails in all conditions of being and exiftence. And it is fcarce poffible for us, by our moft chimerical wifhes, to form the idea of a ftation or fituation altogether defirable. The draughts of life, according to the poet's fiction, are always mixed from the veffels on each hand of *Jupiter*: Or if any cup be prefented altogether pure, it is drawn only, as the fame poet tells us, from the left-handed veffel.

THE more exquifite any good is, of which a fmall fpecimen is afforded us, the fharper is the evil, allied to it; and few exceptions are found to this uniform law of nature. The moft fprightly wit borders on madnefs; the higheft effufions of joy produce the deepeft melancholy; the moft ravifhing pleafures are attended with the moft cruel laffitude and difguft; the moft flattering hopes make way for the fevereft difappointments. And in general, no courfe of life has fuch fafety (for happinefs is not to be dreamed of) as the temperate and moderate, which

which maintains, as far as poffible, a medio-
crity, and a kind of infenfibility, in every thing.

As the good, the great, the fublime, the
ravifhing are found eminently in the genuine
principles of theifm; it may be expected, from
the analogy of nature, that the bafe, the abfurd,
the mean, the terrifying will be difcovered
equally in religious fictions and chimeras.

THE univerfal propenfity to believe in invifible, intelligent power, if not an original inftinct, being at leaft a general attendant of
human nature, it may be confidered as a kind of
mark or ftamp, which the divine workman has
fet upon his work; and nothing furely can more
dignify mankind, than to be thus felected from
all the other parts of the creation, and to bear
the image or impreffion of the univerfal Creator.
But confult this image, as it commonly appears
in the popular religions of the world. How is
the deity disfigured in our reprefentations of
him! What caprice, abfurdity, and immorality
are attributed to him! How much is he degraded even below the character which we
fhould naturally, in common life, afcribe to a
man of fenfe and virtue!

WHAT

WHAT a noble privilege is it of human reason to attain the knowledge of the supreme being; and, from the visible works of nature, be enabled to infer so sublime a principle as its supreme Creator? But turn the reverse of the medal. Survey most nations and most ages. Examine the religious principles, which have, in fact, prevailed in the world. You will scarcely be persuaded, that they are other than sick men's dreams: Or perhaps will regard them more as the playsome whimsies of monkeys in human shape, than the serious, positive, dogmatical asseverations of a being, who dignifies himself with the name of rational.

HEAR the verbal protestations of all men: Nothing they are so certain of as their religious tenets. Examine their lives: You will scarcely think that they repose the smallest confidence in them.

THE greatest and truest zeal gives us no security against hypocrisy: The most open impiety is attended with a secret dread and compunction.

No theological abfurdities fo glaring as have not, fometimes, been embraced by men of the greateft and moft cultivated underftanding. No religious precepts fo rigorous as have not been adopted by the moft voluptuous and moft abandoned of men.

IGNORANCE *is the mother of Devotion:* A maxim, that is proverbial, and confirmed by general experience. Look out for a people, entirely devoid of religion: If you find them at all, be affured, that they are but few degrees removed from brutes.

WHAT fo pure as fome of the morals, included in fome theological fyftems? What fo corrupted as fome of the practices, to which thefe fyftems give rife?

THE comfortable views, exhibited by the belief of futurity, are ravifhing and delightful. But how quickly vanifh, on the appearance of its terrors, which keep a more firm and durable poffeffion of the human mind?

THE whole is a riddle, an ænigma, an inexplicable myftery. Doubt, uncertainty, fufpence

of

of judgment appear the only refult of our moft accurate fcrutiny, concerning this fubject. But fuch is the frailty of human reafon, and fuch the irrefiftible contagion of opinion, that even this deliberate doubt could fcarce be upheld; did we not enlarge our view, and oppofing one fpecies of fuperftition to another, fet them a quarreling; while we ourfelves, during their fury and contention, happily make our efcape, into the calm, tho' obfcure, regions of philofophy.

DISSERTATION II.

OF THE

PASSIONS.

DISSERTATION II.

Of the Passions.

SECT. I.

1. SOME objects produce immediately an agreeable fenfation, by the original ftructure of our organs, and are thence denominated GOOD; as others, from their immediate difagreeable fenfation, acquire the appellation of EVIL. Thus moderate warmth is agreeable and good; exceffive heat painful and evil.

SOME objects again, by being naturally conformable or contrary to paffion, excite an agreeable or painful fenfation; and are thence called *Good* or *Evil*. The punifhment of an adverfary, by gratifying revenge, is good; the ficknefs of a companion, by affecting friendfhip, is evil.

2. ALL

2. ALL good or evil, whence-ever it arises, produces various passions and affections, according to the light, in which it is surveyed.

WHEN good is certain or very probable, it produces JOY: When evil is in the same situation, there arises GRIEF or SORROW.

WHEN either good or evil is uncertain, it gives rise to FEAR or HOPE, according to the degrees of uncertainty on one side or the other.

DESIRE arises from good considered simply; and AVERSION, from evil. The WILL exerts itself, when either the presence of the good or absence of the evil may be attained by any action of the mind or body.

3. NONE of these passions seem to contain any thing curious or remarkable, except *Hope* and *Fear*, which, being derived from the probability of any good or evil, are mixt passions, that merit our attention.

PROBA-

PROBABILITY arifes from an oppofition of contrary chances or caufes, by which the mind is not allowed to fix on either fide; but is inceffantly toft from one to another, and in one moment is determined to confider an object as exiftent, and in another moment as the contrary. The imagination or underftanding, call it which you pleafe, fluctuates betwixt the oppofite views; and tho' perhaps it may be oftener turned to one fide than the other, it is impoffible for it, by reafon of the oppofition of caufes or chances, to reft on either. The *pro* and *con* of the queftion alternately prevail; and the mind, furveying the objects in their oppofite caufes, finds fuch a contrariety as utterly deftroys all certainty or eftablifhed opinion.

SUPPOSE, then, that the object, concerning which we are doubtful, produces either defire or averfion; it is evident, that, according as the mind turns itfelf to one fide or the other, it muft feel a momentary impreffion of joy or forrow. An object, whofe exiftence we defire, gives fatisfaction, when we think of thofe caufes, which produce it; and for the fame reafon, excites grief or uneafinefs, from the oppofite confideration. So that, as the underftanding,

in

in probable queftions, is divided betwixt the contrary points of view, the heart muft in the fame manner be divided betwixt oppofite emo-, tions.

Now, if we confider the human mind, we fhall obferve, that, with regard to the paffions, it is not like a wind-inftrument of mufic, which, in running over all the notes, immediately lofes the found when the breath ceafes; but rather refembles a ftring-inftrument, where, after each ftroke, the vibrations ftill retain fome found, which gradually and infenfibly decays. The imagination is extremely quick and agile; but the paffions, in comparifon, are flow and reftive: For which reafon, when any object is prefented, which affords a variety of views to the one and emotions to the other; tho' the fancy may change its views with great celerity; each ftroke will not produce a clear and diftinct note of paffion, but the one paffion will always be mixt and confounded with the other. According as the probability inclines to good or evil, the paffion of grief or joy predominates in the compofition; and thefe paffions, being intermingled by means of the

contrary

contrary views of the imagination, produce by the union the paffions of hope or fear.

4. As this theory feems to carry its own evidence along with it, we fhall be more concife in our proofs.

THE paffions of fear and hope may arife, when the chances are equal on both fides, and no fuperiority can be difcovered in one above the other. Nay, in this fituation the paffions are rather the ftrongeft, as the mind has then the leaft foundation to reft upon, and is toft with the greateft uncertainty. Throw in a fuperior degree of probability to the fide of grief, you immediately fee that paffion diffufe itfelf over the compofition, and tincture it into fear. Encreafe the probability, and by that means the grief; the fear prevails ftill more and more, till at laft it runs infenfibly, as the joy continually diminifhes, into pure grief. After you have brought it to this fituation, diminifh the grief, by a contrary operation to that, which encreafed it, to wit, by diminifhing the probability on the melancholy fide; and you will fee the paffion clear every moment, till it changes infenfibly

G 3

into

into hope; which again runs, by flow degrees, into joy, as you encreafe that part of the compofition, by the encreafe of the probability. Are not thefe as plain proofs, that the paffions of fear and hope are mixtures of grief and joy, as in optics it is a proof, that a coloured ray of the fun, paffing thro' a prifm, is a compofition of two others, when, as you diminifh or encreafe the quantity of either, you find it prevail proportionably, more or lefs, in the compofition?

5. PROBABILITY is of two kinds; either whan the object is itfelf uncertain, and to be determined by chance; or when, tho' the object be already certain, yet is it uncertain to our judgment, which finds a number of proofs or prefumptions on each fide of the queftion. Both thefe kinds of probability caufe fear and hope; which muft proceed from that property, in which they agree; to wit, the uncertainty and fluctuation which they beftow on the paffion, by that contrariety of views, which is common to both.

6. IT

6. It is a probable good or evil, which commonly caufes hope or fear; becaufe probability, producing an inconftant and wavering furvey of an object, occafions naturally a like mixture and uncertainty of paffion. But we may obferve, that, wherever, from other caufes, this mixture can be produced, the paffions of fear and hope will arife, even tho' there be no probability.

An evil, conceived as barely *poffible*, fometimes produces fear; efpecially if the evil be very great. A man cannot think of exceffive pain and torture without trembling, if he runs the leaft rifque of fuffering them. The fmallnefs of the probability is compenfated by the greatnefs of the evil.

But even *impoffible* evils caufe fear; as when we tremble on the brink of a precipice, tho' we know ourfelves to be in perfect fecurity, and have it in our choice, whether we will advance a ftep farther. The immediate prefence of the evil influences the imagination and produces a fpecies of belief; but being oppofed by the reflection on our fecurity, that belief is im-

G 4   mediately

mediately retracted, and caufes the fame kind of paffion, as when, from a contrariety of chances, contrary paffions are produced.

EVILS, which are *certain*, have fometimes the fame effect as the poffible or impoffible. A man, in a ftrong prifon, without the leaft means of efcape, trembles at the thoughts of the rack, to which he is fentenced. The evil is here fixed in itfelf; but the mind has not courage to fix upon it; and this fluctuation gives rife to a paffion of a fimilar appearance with fear.

7. BUT it is not only where good or evil is uncertain as to its *exiftence*, but alfo as to its *kind*, that fear or hope arifes. If any one were told, that one of his fons is fuddenly killed; the paffion, occafioned by this event, would not fettle into grief, till he got certain information, which of his fons he had loft. Tho' each fide of the queftion produces here the fame paffion; that paffion cannot fettle, but receives from the imagination, which is unfixt, a tremulous, unfteddy motion, refembling the mixture and contention of grief and joy.

8. THUS

8. Thus all kinds of uncertainty have a strong connexion with fear, even tho' they do not caufe any oppofition of paffions, by the oppofite views, which they prefent to us. Should I leave a friend in any malady, I fhould feel more anxiety upon his account, than if he were prefent; tho' perhaps I am not only incapable of giving him affiftance, but likewife of judging concerning the event of his ficknefs. There are a thoufand little circumftances of his fituation and condition, which I defire to know; and the knowledge of them would prevent that fluctuation and uncertainty, fo nearly allied to fear. *Horace* has remarked this phænomenon:

> *Ut affidens implumibus pullus avis*
> *Serpentûm allapfus timet,*
> *Magis relictis; non, ut adfit, auxili*
> *Latura plus præfentibus.*

A virgin on her bridal-night goes to bed full of fears and apprehenfions, tho' fhe expects nothing but pleafure. The confufion of wifhes and joys, the newnefs and greatnefs of the unknown event, fo embarrafs the mind, that it knows not in what image or paffion to fix itfelf.

G 5   9. Con-

9. CONCERNING the mixture of affections, we may remark, in general, that when contrary paſſions ariſe from objects no way connected together, they take place alternately. Thus when a man is afflicted for the loſs of a law-ſuit, and joyful for the birth of a ſon, the mind, running from the agreeable to the calamitous object; with whatever celerity it may perform this motion, can ſcarcely temper the one affection with the other, and remain betwixt them in a ſtate of indifference.

IT more eaſily attains that calm ſituation, when the *ſame* event is of a mixt nature, and contains ſomething adverſe and ſomething proſperous in its different circumſtances. For in that caſe, both the paſſions, mingling with each other by means of the relation, often become mutually deſtructive, and leave the mind in perfect tranquillity.

BUT ſuppoſe, that the object is not a compound of good and evil, but is conſidered as probable or improbable in any degree; in that caſe, the contrary paſſions will both of them be preſent at once in the ſoul, and inſtead of ballancing

lancing and tempering each other, will fubfift together, and by their union, produce a third impreffion or affection, fuch as hope or fear.

THE influence of the relations of ideas (which we fhall afterwards explain more fully) is plainly feen in this affair. In contrary paffions, if the objects be *totally different*, the paffions are like two oppofite liquors in different bottles, which have no influence on each other. If the objects be intimately *connected*, the paffions are like an *alcali* or an *acid*, which, being mingled, deftroy each other. If the relation be more imperfect, and confifts in the *contradictory* views of the *fame* object, the paffions are like oil and vinegar, which, however mingled, never perfectly unite and incorporate.

THE effect of a mixture of paffions, when one of them is predominant and fwallows up the other, fhall be explained afterwards.

SECT.

SECT. II.

1. BESIDES thofe paffions abovemen-tioned, which arife from a direct purfuit of good and averfion to evil, there are others of a more complicated nature, and imply more than one view or confideration. Thus *Pride* is a certain fatisfaction in ourfelves, on account of fome ac-complifhment or poffeffion, which we enjoy: *Humility*, on the other hand, is a diffatisfaction with ourfelves, on account of fome defect or infirmity.

LOVE or *Friendfhip* is a complacency in an-other, on account of his accomplifhments or fer-vices: *Hatred*, the contrary.

2. IN thefe two fets of paffions, there is an obvious diftinction to be made betwixt the *ob-ject* of the paffion and its *caufe*. The object of pride and humility is felf: The caufe of the paffion is fome excellence in the former cafe; fome fault, in the latter. The object of love and hatred is fome other perfon: The caufes,
in

in like manner, are either excellencies or faults.

WITH regard to all thefe paffions, the caufes are what excite the emotion; the object is what the mind directs its view to when the emotion is excited. Our merit, for inftance, raifes pride; and it is effential to pride to turn our view on ourfelf with complacency and fatisfaction.

Now as the caufes of thefe paffions are very numerous and various, tho' their object be uniform and fimple; it may be a fubject of curiofity to confider, what that circumftance is, in which all thefe various caufes agree; or, in other words, what is the real, efficient caufe of the paffion. We fhall begin with pride and humility.

3. IN order to explain the caufes of thefe paffions, we muft reflect on certain properties, which, tho' they have a mighty influence on every operation, both of the underftanding and paffions, are not commonly much infifted on by philofophers. The firft of thefe is the *affo-ciation* of ideas, or that principle, by which we make

make an eafy tranfition from one idea to another. However uncertain and changeable our thoughts may be, they are not entirely without rule and method in their changes. They ufually pafs with regularity, from one object, to what refembles it, is contiguous to it, or produced by it [a]. When one idea is prefent to the imagination; any other, united by thefe relations, naturally follows it, and enters with more facility, by means of that introduction.

THE *fecond* property, which I fhall obferve in the human mind, is a like affociation of impreffions or emotions. All *refembling* impreffions are connected together; and no fooner one arifes, than the reft naturally follow. Grief and difappointment give rife to anger, anger to envy, envy to malice, and malice to grief again. In like manner, our temper, when elevated with joy, naturally throws itfelf into love, generofity, courage, pride, and other refembling affections.

IN the *third* place, it is obfervable of thefe two kinds of affociation, that they very much

[a] See philofophical Effays. Effay iii.

affift

affift and forward each other, and that the
tranfition is more eafily made, where they both
concur in the fame object. Thus, a man, who,
by any injury from another, is very much dif-
compofed and ruffled in his temper, is apt to
find a hundred fubjects of hatred, difcontent,
impatience, fear, and other uneafy paffions;
efpecially, if he can difcover thefe fubjects in
or near the perfon, who was the object of his
firft emotion. Thofe principles, which forward
the tranfition of ideas, here concur with thofe,
which operate on the paffions; and both, unit-
ing in one action, beftow on the mind a double
impulfe.

UPON this occafion, I may cite a paffage from
an elegant writer, who expreffes himfelf in the
following manner [a]. " As the fancy delights
" in every thing, that is great, ftrange, or
" beautiful, and is ftill the more pleafed the
" more it finds of thefe perfections in the *fame*
" object, fo it is capable of receiving new fatis-
" faction by the affiftance of another fenfe.
" Thus, any continued found, as the mufic of
" birds, or a fall of waters, awakens every

---

[a] Addifon, Spectator, N° 412.

" moment

" moment the mind of the beholder, and makes
" him more attentive to the feveral beauties of
" the place, that lie before him. Thus, if
" there arifes a fragrancy of fmells or perfumes,
" they heighten the pleafure of the imagination,
" and make even the colours and verdure of
" the landfcape appear more agreeable; for the
" ideas of both fenfes recommend each other,
" and are pleafanter together than where they
" enter the mind feparately : As the different
" colours of a picture, when they are well dif-
" pofed, fet off one another, and receive an
" additional beauty from the advantage of the
" fituation." In thefe phænomena, we may
remark the affociation both of impreffions and
ideas ; as well as the mutual affiftance thefe af-
fociations lend to each other.

4. It feems to me, that both thefe fpecies
of relation have place in producing *Pride* or
Humility, and are the real, efficient caufes of
the paffion.

With regard to the firft relation, that of
ideas, there can be no queftion. Whatever
we are proud of, muft, in fome manner, belong

long to us. It is always *our* knowledge, *our*
fenfe, beauty, poffeffions, family, on which we
value ourfelves. Self, which is the *object* of
the paffion, muft ftill be related to that quality
or circumftance, which *caufes* the paffion.
There muft be a connexion betwixt them; an
eafy tranfition of the imagination; or a facility
of the conception in paffing from one to the
other. Where this connexion is wanting, no
object can either excite pride or humility; and
the more you weaken the connexion, the more
you weaken the paffion.

5. THE only fubject of enquiry is, whether
there be a like relation of impreffions or fentiments, wherever pride or humility is felt;
whether the circumftance, which caufes the paffion, produces antecedently a fentiment fimilar
to the paffion; and whether there be an eafy
transfufion of the one into the other.

THE feeling or fentiment of pride is agreeable; of humility, painful. An agreeable fenfation is, therefore, related to the former; a
painful, to the latter. And if we find, after
examination, that every object, which produces
pride,

pride, produces alfo a feparate pleafure; and every object, that caufes humility, excites in like manner a feparate uneafinefs; we muſt allow, in that cafe, that the prefent theory is fully proved and afcertained. The double relation of ideas and fentiments will be acknowledged inconteſtible.

6. To begin with perfonal merit and demerit, the moſt obvious caufes of thefe paffions; it would be entirely foreign to our prefent purpofe to examine the foundation of moral diſtinctions. It is fufficient to obferve, that the foregoing theory concerning the origin of the paffions may be defended on any hypothefis. The moſt probable fyſtem, which has been advanced to explain the difference betwixt vice and virtue, is, that either from a primary conſtitution of nature, or from a fenfe of public or private intereſt, certain characters, upon the very view and contemplation, produce uneafinefs; and others, in like manner, excite pleafure. The uneafinefs and fatisfaction, produced in the fpectator, are effential to vice and virtue. To approve of a character, is to feel a delight upon its appearance. To difapprove of it, is to be fenfible

fible of an uneafinefs. The pain and pleafure, therefore, being, in a manner, the primary fource of blame or praife, muft alfo be the caufes of all their effects; and confequently, the caufes of pride and humility, which are the un-avoidable attendants of that diftinction.

But fuppofing this theory of morals fhould not be received; it is ftill evident, that pain and pleafure, if not the fources of moral diftinctions, are at leaft infeparable from them. A gene-rous and noble character affords a fatisfaction even in the furvey; and when prefented to us, tho' only in a poem or fable, never fails to charm and delight us. On the other hand, cruelty and treachery difpleafe from their very nature; nor is it poffible ever to reconcile us to thefe qualities, either in ourfelves or others. Virtue, therefore, produces always a pleafure diftinct from the pride or felf fatisfaction, which attends it: Vice, an uneafinefs feparate from the humility or remorfe.

But a high or low conceit of ourfelves arifes not from thofe qualities alone of the mind, which, according to common fyftems of ethics, have been defined parts of moral duty; but from any other,

other, which have a connexion with pleasure
or uneasiness. Nothing flatters our vanity more
than the talent of pleasing by our wit, good
humour, or any other accomplishment; and
nothing gives us a more sensible mortification,
than a disappointment in any attempt of that
kind. No one has ever been able to tell precisely, what *wit* is, and to shew why such a
system of thought must be received under that
denomination, and such another rejected. It is
by taste alone we can decide concerning it; nor
are we possest of any other standard, by which
we can form a judgment of this nature. Now
what is this *taste*, from which true and false wit
in a manner receive their being, and without
which no thought can have a title to either of
these denominations? It is plainly nothing but
a sensation of pleasure from true wit, and of dif-
gust from false, without our being able to tell
the reasons of that satisfaction or uneasiness.
The power of exciting these opposite sensations
is, therefore, the very essence of true or false
wit; and consequently, the cause of that vanity
or mortification, which arises from one or the
other.

7. BEAUTY

7. BEAUTY of all kinds gives us a peculiar delight and ſatisfaction; as deformity produces pain, upon whatever ſubject it may be placed, and whether ſurveyed in an animate or inanimate object. If the beauty or deformity belong to our own face, ſhape, or perſon, this pleaſure or uneaſineſs is converted into pride or humility; as having in this caſe all the circumſtances requiſite to produce a perfect tranſition, according to the preſent theory.

IT would ſeem, that the very eſſence of beauty conſiſts in its power of producing pleaſure. All its effects, therefore, muſt proceed from this circumſtance: And if beauty is ſo univerſally the ſubject of vanity, it is only from its being the cauſe of pleaſure.

CONCERNING all other bodily accompliſhments, we may obſerve in general, that whatever in ourſelves is either uſeful, beautiful, or ſurprizing, is an object of pride; and the contrary, of humility. Theſe qualities agree in producing a ſeparate pleaſure; and agree in nothing elſe.

WE

WE are vain of the furprizing adventures which we have met with, the efcapes which we have made, the dangers to which we have been expofed; as well as of our furprifing feats of vigour and activity. Hence the origin of vulgar lying; where men, without any intereft, and merely out of vanity, heap up a number of extraordinary events, which are either the fictions of their brain; or, if true, have no connexion with themfelves. Their fruitful invention fupplies them with a variety of adventures; and where that talent is wanting, they appropriate fuch as belong to others, in order to gratify their vanity: For betwixt that paffion, and the fentiment of pleafure, there is always a clofe connexion.

8. BUT tho' pride and humility have the qualities of our mind and body, that is, of felf, for their natural and more immediate caufes; we find by experience, that many other objects produce thefe affections. We found vanity upon houfes, gardens, equipage, and other external objects; as well as upon perfonal merit and accomplifhments. This happens when external objects acquire any particular relation to ourfelves,

ourfelves, and are affociated or connected with us. A beautiful fifh in the ocean, a well proportioned animal in a foreft, and indeed any thing, which neither belongs nor is related to us, has no manner of influence on our vanity; whatever extraordinary qualities it may be endowed with, and whatever degree of furprize and admiration it may naturally occafion. It muft be fomeway affociated with us, in order to touch our pride. It's idea muft hang, in a manner, upon that of ourfelves; and the tranfition from one to the other muft be eafy and natural.

MEN are vain of the beauty either of *their* country, or *their* county, or even of *their* parifh. Here the idea of beauty plainly produces a pleafure. This pleafure is related to pride. The object or caufe of this pleafure is, by the fuppofition, related to felf, the object of pride. By this double relation of fentiments and ideas, a tranfition is made from one to the other.

MEN are alfo vain of the temperature of the climate, in which they are born; of the fertility of their native foil; of the goodnefs of the wines, fruits, or victuals, produced by it; of the foftnefs or force of their language, with

2   other

other particulars of that kind. Thefe objects
have plainly a reference to the pleafures of the
fenfes, and are originally confidered as agreeable to the feeling, tafte, or hearing. How
could they become caufes of pride, except by
means of that tranfition above explained?

THERE are fome, who difcover a vanity of
an oppofite kind, and affect to depreciate their
own country, in comparifon of thofe, to which
they have travelled. Thefe perfons find, when
they are at home, and furrounded with their
countrymen, that the ftrong relation betwixt
them and their own nation is fhar'd with fo
many, that it is in a manner loft to them;
whereas, that diftant relation to a foreign country, which is formed by their having feen it,
and lived in it, is augmented by their confidering how few have done the fame. For this reafon, they always admire the beauty, utility,
and rarity of what they have met with abroad,
above what they find at home.

SINCE we can be vain of a country, climate,
or any inanimate object, which bears a relation
to us; it is no wonder we fhould be vain of the
qualities of thofe, who are connected with us

I   by

by blood or friendſhip. Accordingly we find, that any qualities, which, when belonging to our-ſelf, produce pride, produce alſo, in a leſs degree, the ſame affection, when diſcovered in perſons, related to us. The beauty, addreſs, merit, credit, and honours of their kindred are care-fully diſplayed by the proud, and are conſider-able ſources of their vanity.

As we are proud of riches in ourſelves, we deſire, in order to gratify our vanity, that every one, who has any connexion with us, ſhould likewiſe be poſſeſt of them, and are aſhamed of ſuch as are mean or poor among our friends and relations. Our forefathers being conceived as our neareſt relations; every one naturally affects to be of a good family, and to be deſcended from a long ſucceſſion of rich and honourable anceſtors.

THOSE, who boaſt of the antiquity of their fa-milies, are glad when they can join this circum-ſtance, that their anceſtors, for many generations, have been uinnterrupted proprietors of the *ſame* portion of land, and that their family has never changed its poſſeſſions, or been tranſplanted into any other county or province. It is an additional

H   ſubject

subject of vanity, when they can boast, that thefe poffeffions have been tranfmitted thro' a defcent, compofed entirely of males, and that the honours and fortune have never paft thro' any female. Let us endeavour to explain thefe phænomena from the foregoing theory.

WHEN any one values himfelf on the antiquity of his family, the fubjects of his vanity are not merely the extent of time and number of anceftors (for in that refpect all mankind are alike) but thefe circumftances, joined to the riches and credit of his anceftors, which are fuppofed to reflect a luftre on himfelf, upon account of his connexion with them. Since therefore the paffion depends on the connexion, whatever ftrengthens the connexion muft alfo encreafe the paffion, and whatever weakens the connexion muft diminifh the paffion. But it is evident, that the famenefs of the poffeffions muft ftrengthen the relation of ideas, arifing from blood and kindred, and convey the fancy with greater facility from one generation to another; from the remoteft anceftors to their pofterity, who are both their heirs and their defcendants. By this facility, the fentiment is tranfmitted more entire, and excites a greater degree of pride and vanity.

THE

THE case is the same with the transmission of the honours and fortune, thro' a succession of males, without their passing thro' any female. It is an obvious quality of human nature, that the imagination naturally turns to whatever is important and considerable; and where two objects are presented, a small and a great, it usually leaves the former, and dwells entirely on the latter. This is the reason, why children commonly bear their fathers name, and are esteemed to be of a nobler or meaner birth, according to *his* family. And tho' the mother should be possest of superior qualities to the father, as often happens, the *general rule* prevails, notwithstanding the exception, according to the doctrine, which shall be explained afterwards. Nay, even when a superiority of any kind is so great, or when any other reasons have such an effect, as to make the children rather represent the mother's family than the father's, the general rule still retains an efficacy, sufficient to weaken the relation, and make a kind of breach in the line of ancestors. The imagination runs not along them with the same facility, nor is able to transfer the honour and credit of the ancestors to their posterity of the same name and family so readily, as when the

transition

transition is conformable to the general rules, and passes thro' the male line, from father to son, or from brother to brother.

9. BUT *property*, as it gives us the fulleft power and authority over any object, is the relation, which has the greatest influence on thefe paffions.

EVERY thing, belonging to a vain man, is the beft that is any where to be found. His houfes, equipage, furniture, cloaths, horfes, hounds, excel all others in his conceit; and it is eafy to obferve, that, from the leaft advantage in any of thefe, he draws a new fubject of pride and vanity. His wine, if you will believe him, has a finer flavour than any other; his cookery is more exquifite; his table more orderly; his fervants more expert; the air, in which he lives, more healthful; the foil, which he cultivates, more fertile; his fruits ripen earlier, and in greater perfection : Such a thing is remarkable for it's novelty; fuch another for it's antiquity: This is the workmanfhip of a famous artift; that belonged once to fuch a prince or great man. All objects, in a word, which are
ufeful,

useful, beautiful, or surprizing, or are related to such, may, by means of property, give rise to this passion. These all agree in giving pleasure. This alone is common to them; and therefore must be the quality, that produces the passion, which is their common effect. As every new instance is a new argument, and as the instances are here without number; it would seem, that this theory is sufficiently confirmed by experience.

RICHES imply the power of acquiring whatever is agreeable; and as they comprehend many particular objects of vanity, necessarily become one of the chief causes of that passion.

10. OUR opinions of all kinds are strongly affected by society and sympathy, and it is almost impossible for us to support any principle or sentiment, against the universal consent of every one, with whom we have any friendship or correspondence. But of all our opinions, those, which we form in our own favour; however lofty or presuming; are, at bottom, the frailest, and the most easily shaken by the con-

H 3   tradiction

tradiction and oppofition of others. Our great concern, in this cafe, makes us foon alarmed, and keeps our paffions upon the watch: Our confcioufnefs of partiality ftill makes us dread a miftake: And the very difficulty of judging concerning an object, which is never fet at a due diftance from us, nor is feen in a proper point of view, makes us hearken anxioufly to the opinions of others, who are better qualified to form juft opinions concerning us. Hence that ftrong love of fame, with which all mankind are poffeft. It is in order to fix and confirm their favourable opinion of themfelves, not from any original paffion, that they feek the applaufes of others. And when a man defires to be praifed, it is for the fame reafon, that a beauty is pleafed with furveying herfelf in a favorable looking-glafs, and feeing the reflexion of her own charms.

Tho' it be difficult in all points of fpeculation to diftinguifh a caufe, which encreafes an effect, from one, which folely produces it; yet in the prefent cafe the phænomena feem pretty ftrong and fatisfactory in confirmation of the foregoing principle.

WE

WE receive a much greater fatisfaction from the approbation of thofe, whom we ourfelves efteem and approve of, than of thofe, whom we contemn and defpife.

WHEN efteem is obtained after a long and intimate acquaintance, it gratifies our vanity in a peculiar manner.

THE fuffrage of thofe, who are fhy and backward in giving praife, is attended with an additional relifh and enjoyment, if we can obtain it in our favour.

WHERE a great man is nice in his choice of favourites, every one courts with greater earneftnefs his countenance and protection.

PRAISE never gives us much pleafure, unlefs it concur with our own opinion, and extol us for thofe qualities, in which we chiefly excel.

THESE phænomena feem to prove, that the favourable opinions of others are regarded only as authorities, or as confirmations of our own opinion. And if they have more influence in this fubject than in any other, it is

H 4   eafily

eafily accounted for from the nature of the
fubject.

11. THUS few objects, however related to
us, and whatever pleafure they produce, are
able to excite a great degree of pride or felf-fatisfaction; unlefs they be alfo obvious to others,
and engage the approbation of the fpectators.
What difpofition of mind fo defirable as the
peaceful, refigned, contented; which readily
fubmits to all the difpenfations of providence,
and preferves a conftant ferenity amidft the
greateft misfortunes and difappointments? Yet
this difpofition, tho' acknowledged to be a virtue or excellence, is feldom the foundation of
great vanity or felf-applaufe; having no brilliant
or exterior luftre, and rather cheering the heart,
than animating the behaviour and converfation.
The cafe is the fame with many other qualities
of the mind, body, or fortune; and this circumftance, as well as the double relations above
mentioned, muft be admitted to be of confequence in the production of thefe paffions.

A SECOND circumftance, which is of confequence in this affair, is the conftancy and duration

tion of the object. What is very cafual and inconftant, beyond the common courfe of human affairs, gives little joy, and lefs pride. We are not much fatisfied with the thing itfelf; and are ftill lefs apt to feel any new degree of felf-fatisfaction upon its account. We forefee and anticipate its change; which makes us little fatisfied with the thing itfelf: We compare it to ourfelves, whofe exiftence is more durable; by which means its inconftancy appears ftill greater. It feems ridiculous to make ourfelves the object of a paffion, on account of a quality or poffeffion, which is of fo much fhorter duration, and attends us during fo fmall a part of our exiftence.

A THIRD circumftance, not to be neglected, is, that the objects, in order to produce pride or felf-value, muft be peculiar to us, or at leaft, common to us with a few others. The advantages of fun-fhine, weather, climate, &c. diftinguifh us not from any of our companions, and give us no preference or fuperiority. The comparifon, which we are every moment apt to make, prefents no inference to our advantage; and we ftill remain, notwithftanding thefe en-

joyments,

joyments, on a level with all our friends and acquaintance.

As health and ſickneſs vary inceſſantly to all men, and there is no one, who is ſolely or certainly fixed in either; theſe accidental bleſſings and calamities are in a manner ſeparated from us, and are not conſidered as a foundation for vanity or humiliation. But wherever a malady of any kind is ſo rooted in our conſtitution, that we no longer entertain any hopes of recovery, from that moment it damps our ſelf-conceit; as is evident in old men, whom nothing mortifies more than the conſideration of their age and infirmities. They endeavour, as long as poſſible, to conceal their blindneſs and deafneſs, their rheums and gouts; nor do they ever avow them without reluctance and uneaſineſs. And tho' young men are not aſhamed of every head-ach or cold which they fall into; yet no topic is more proper to mortify human pride, and make us entertain a mean opinion of our nature, than this, that we are every moment of our lives ſubject to ſuch infirmities. This proves, that bodily pain and ſickneſs are in themſelves proper cauſes of humility; tho' the cuſtom of eſtimating every thing, by compariſon, more than by

I   its

its intrinfic worth and value, makes us over-look thofe calamities, which we find incident to every one, and caufes us to form an idea of our merit and character, independent of them.

WE are afhamed of fuch maladies as affect others, and are either dangerous or difagreeable to them. Of the epilepfy; becaufe it gives a horror to every one prefent: Of the itch; be-caufe it is infectious: Of the king's evil; be-caufe it often goes to pofterity. Men al-ways confider the fentiments of others in their judgment of themfelves.

A FOURTH circumftance, which has an in-fluence on thefe paffions, is *general rules*; by which we form a notion of different ranks of men, fuitable to the power or riches of which they are poffeft; and this notion is not changed by any peculiarities of the health or temper of the perfons, which may deprive them of all enjoyment in their poffeffions. Cuftom rea-dily carries us beyond the juft bounds in our paffions, as well as in our reafonings.

IT may not be amifs to obferve on this occa-fion, that the influence of general rules and

maxims

maxims on the paffions very much contributes to facilitate the effects of all the principles or internal mechanifm, which we here explain. For it feems evident, that, if a perfon full-grown, and of the fame nature with ourfelves, were on a fudden tranfported into our world, he would be very much embarraffed with every object, and would not readily determine what degree of love or hatred, of pride or humility, or of any other paffion fhould be excited by it. The paffions are often varied by very inconfiderable principles; and thefe do not always play with perfect regularity, efpecially on the the firft tryal. But as cuftom or practice has brought to light all thefe principles, and has fettled the juft value of every thing; this muft certainly contribute to the eafy production of the paffions, and guide us, by means of general eftablifhed rules, in the proportions, which we ought to obferve in prefering one object to another. This remark may, perhaps, ferve to obviate difficulties, that may arife concerning fome caufes, which we here afcribe to particular paffions, and which may be efteemed too refined to operate fo univerfally and certainly, as they are found to do.

SECT.

SECT. III.

1. IN running over all the caufes, which produce the paffion of pride or that of humility; it would readily occur, that the fame circumftance, if transferred from ourfelf to another perfon, would render him the objeɕt of love or hatred, efteem or contempt. The virtue, genius, beauty, family, riches, and authority of others beget favourable fentiments in their behalf; and their vice, folly, deformity, poverty, and meannefs excite the contrary fentiments. The double relation of impreffions and ideas ftill operates on thefe paffions of love and hatred; as on the former of pride and humility. Whatever gives a feparate pleafure or pain, and is related to another perfon or conneɕted with him, makes him the objeɕt of our affeɕtion or difguft.

HENCE too injury or contempt is one of the greateft fources of hatred; fervices or efteem of friendfhip.

2. SOMETIMES a relation to ourſelf excites affection towards any perſon. But there is always here implied a relation of ſentiments, without which the other relation would have no influence [a].

A PERSON, who is related to us, or connected with us, by blood, by ſimilitude of fortune, of adventures, profeſſion, or country, ſoon becomes an agreeable companion to us; becauſe we enter eaſily and familiarly into his ſentiments and conceptions: Nothing is ſtrange or new to us: Our imagination, paſſing from ſelf, which is ever intimately preſent to us, runs ſmoothly along the relation or connexion, and conceives with a full ſympathy the perſon, who is nearly related to ſelf. He renders himſelf immediately acceptable, and is at once on an eaſy footing with us: No diſtance, no reſerve has place, where the perſon introduced is ſuppoſed ſo cloſely connected with us.

RELATION has here the ſame influence as cuſtom or acquaintance, in exciting affection;

[a] The affection of parents to children ſeems founded on an original inſtinct. The affection towards other relations depends on the principles here explained.

and from like caufes. The eafe and fatisfaction, which, in both cafes, attend our intercourfe or commerce, is the fource of the friendfhip.

3. THE paffions of love and hatred are always followed by, or rather conjoined with, benevolence and anger. It is this conjunction, which chiefly diftinguifhes thefe affections from pride and humility. For pride and humility are pure emotions in the foul, unattended with any defire, and not immediately exciting us to action. But love and hatred are not compleat within themfelves, nor reft in that emotion, which they produce; but carry the mind to fomething farther. Love is always followed by a defire of happinefs to the perfon beloved, and an averfion to his mifery: As hatred produces a defire of the mifery, and an averfion to the happinefs of the perfon hated. Thefe oppofite defires feem to be originally and primarily conjoined with the paffions of love and hatred. It is a conftitution of nature, of which we can give no farther explication.

4. COM-

4. COMPASSION frequently arifes, where there is no preceding efteem or friendfhip; and compaffion is an uneafinefs in the fufferings of another. It feems to fpring from the intimate and ftrong conception of his fufferings; and our imagination proceeds by degrees, from the lively idea, to the real feeling of another's mifery.

MALICE and envy alfo arife in the mind without any preceding hatred or injury; tho' their tendency is exactly the fame with that of anger and ill-will. The comparifon of ourfelves. with others feems the fource of envy and malice. The more unhappy another is, the more happy do we ourfelves appear in our own conception.

5. THE fimilar tendency of compaffion to that of benevolence, and of envy to anger, forms a very clofe relation betwixt thefe two fets of paffions; tho' of a different kind from that in-fifted on above. It is not a refemblance of feel-ing or fentiment, but a refemblance of tendency or direction. Its effect, however, is the fame, in producing an affociation of paffions. Com-

paffion

passion is seldom or never felt without some mixture of tenderness or friendship; and envy is naturally accompanied with anger or ill-will. To desire the happiness of another, from whatever motive, is a good preparative to affection: And to delight in another's misery almost unavoidably begets aversion towards him.

EVEN where interest is the source of our concern, it is commonly attended with the same consequences. A partner is a natural object of friendship; a rival of enmity.

6. POVERTY, meanness, disappointment, produce contempt and dislike: But when these misfortunes are very great, or are represented to us in very strong colours, they excite compassion, and tenderness, and friendship. How is this contradiction to be accounted for? The poverty and meanness of another, in their common appearance, gives us uneasiness, by a species of imperfect sympathy; and this uneasiness produces aversion or dislike, from the resemblance of sentiment. But when we enter more intimately into another's concerns, and wish for his happiness, as well as feel his misery, friend-

ship

ſhip or good-will ariſes, from the ſimilar tendency of the inclinations.

7. In reſpect, there is a mixture of humility,
along with the eſteem or affection: In contempt, a mixture of pride.

THE amorous paſſion is uſually compounded
of complacency in beauty, a bodily appetite, and
friendſhip or affection. The cloſe relation of
theſe ſentiments is very obvious, as well as their
origin from each other, by means of that relation. Were there no other phænomenon to
reconcile as to the preſent theory, this alone,
methinks, were ſufficient.

SECT.

SECT. IV.

1. THE prefent theory of the paffions depends entirely on the double relations of fentiments and ideas, and the mutual affiftance, which
thefe relations lend to each other. It may not,
therefore, be improper to illuftrate thefe principles by fome farther inftances.

2. THE virtues, talents, accomplifhments,
and poffeffions of others make us love and efteem
them : Becaufe thefe objects excite a pleafant
fenfation, which is related to love; and having
alfo a relation or connexion with the perfon,
this union of ideas forwards the union of fentiments, according to the foregoing reafoning.

BUT fuppofe, that the perfon, whom we
love, is alfo related to us, by blood, country,
or friendfhip; it is evident, that a fpecies of
pride muft alfo be excited by his accomplifhments and poffeffions; there being the fame
double relation, which we have all along infifted on. The perfon is related to us, or there
is

is an eafy tranfition of thought from him to us;
and the fentiments, excited by his advantages
and virtues, are agreeable, and confequently
related to pride. Accordingly we find, that
people are naturally vain of the good qualities
or high fortune of their friends and countrymen.

3. But it is obfervable, that, if we reverfe
the order of the paffions, the fame effect does
not follow. We pafs eafily from love and affection to pride and vanity; but not from the
latter paffions to the former, tho' all the relations be the fame. We love not thofe related
to us on account of our own merit; tho' they
are naturally vain on account of our merit.
What is the reafon of this difference? The
tranfition of the imagination to ourfelves, from
objects related to us, is always very eafy; both
on account of the relation, which facilitates the
tranfition, and becaufe we there pafs from re-
moter objects to thofe which are contiguous.
But in paffing from ourfelves to objects, related
to us; tho' the former principle forwards the
tranfition of thought, yet the latter oppofes it;
and confequently there is not the fame eafy
transfufion

transfusion of paffions from pride to love as from love to pride.

4. THE virtues, fervices, and fortune of one man infpire us readily with efteem and affection for another related to him. The fon of our friend is naturally entitled to our friendfhip: The kindred of a very great man value them-felves, and are valued by others, on account of that relation. The force of the double relation is here fully difplayed.

5. THE following are inftances of another kind, where the operation of thefe principles may ftill be difcovered. Envy arifes from a fu-periority in others; but it is obfervable, that it is not the great difproportion betwixt us, which excites that paffion, but on the contrary, our proximity. A great difproportion cuts off the relation of the ideas, and either keeps us from comparing ourfelves with what is remote from us, or diminifhes the effects of the comparifon.

A POET is not apt to envy a philofopher or a poet of a different kind, of a different nation, or or of a different age. All thefe differences, if they do not prevent, at leaft weaken the comparifon, and confequently the paffion.

THIS too is the reafon, why all objects appear great or little, merely by a comparifon with thofe of the fame fpecies. A mountain neither magnifies nor diminifhes a horfe in our eyes: But when a *Flemifh* and a *Welch* horfe are feen together, the one appears greater and the other lefs, than when viewed apart.

FROM the fame principle we may account for that remark of hiftorians, that any party, in a civil war, or even factious divifion, always choofe to call in a foreign enemy at any hazard rather than fubmit to their fellow-citizens. *Guicciardin* applies this remark to the wars in *Italy*; where the relations betwixt the different ftates are, properly fpeaking, nothing but of name, language, and contiguity. Yet even thefe relations, when joined with fuperiority, by making the comparifon more natural, make it likewife more grievous, and caufe men to fearch for fome other fuperiority, which may be attended with no relation, and by that means, may have a lefs fenfible influence on the imagination.

imagination. When we cannot break the affociation, we feel a ftronger defire to remove the fuperiority. This feems to be the reafon, why travellers, tho' commonly lavifh of their praifes to the *Chinefe* and *Perfians*, take care to depreciate thofe neighbouring nations, which may ftand upon a footing of rivalfhip with their native country.

6. THE fine arts afford us parallel inftances. Should an author compofe a treatife, of which one part was ferious and profound, another light and humourous; every one would condemn fo ftrange a mixture, and would blame him for the neglect of all rules of art and criticifm. Yet we accufe not *Prior* for joining his *Alma* and *Solomon* in the fame volume; tho' that amiable poet has fucceeded perfectly in the gaiety of the one, as well as in the melancholy of the other. Even fuppofe the reader fhould perufe thefe two compofitions without any interval, he would feel little or no difficulty in the change of the paffions. Why? but becaufe he confiders thefe performances as entirely different; and by that break in the ideas, breaks the progrefs

of

of the affections, and hinders the one from in-
fluencing or contradicting the other.

An heroic and burlesque design, united in one
picture, would be monstrous; tho' we place
two pictures of so opposite a character in the
same chamber, and even close together, without any scruple.

7. It needs be no matter of wonder, that the
easy transition of the imagination should have
such an influence on all the passions. It is this
very circumstance, which forms all the relations and connexions amongst objects. We
know no real connexion betwixt one thing
and another. We know only, that the idea of
one thing is associated with that of another, and
that the imagination makes an easy transition
betwixt them. And as the easy transition of
ideas, and that of sentiments mutually assist each
other; we might beforehand expect, that this
principle must have a mighty influence on all
our internal movements and affections. And
experience sufficiently confirms the theory.

For

FOR, not to repeat all the foregoing inftances : Suppofe, that I were travelling with a companion thro' a country, to which we are both utter ftrangers; it is evident, that, if the profpects be beautiful, the roads agreeable, and the fields finely cultivated ; this may ferve to put me in good humour, both with myfelf and fellow-traveller. But as the country has no connexion with myfelf or friend, it can never be the immediate caufe either of felf-value or of regard to him : And therefore, if I found not the paffion on fome other object, which bears to one of us a clofer relation, my emotions are rather to be confidered as the overflowings of an elevated or humane difpofition, than as an eftablifhed paffion. But fuppofing the agreeable profpect before us to be furveyed either from his country-feat or from mine ; this new connexion of ideas gives a new direction to the fentiment of pleafure, proceeding from the profpect, and raifes the emotion of regard or vanity, according to the nature of the connexion. There is not here, methinks, much room for doubt or difficulty.

I   SECT.

SECT. V.

1. IT feems evident, that reafon, in a ftrict fenfe, as meaning the judgment of truth and falfhood, can never, of itfelf, be any motive to the will, and can have no influence but fo far as it touches fome paffion or affection. *Abftract relations* of ideas are the object of curiofity, not of volition. And *matters of fact*, where they are neither good nor evil, where they neither excite defire nor averfion, are totally indifferent; and whether known or unknown, whether miftaken or rightly apprehended, cannot be regarded as any motive to action.

2. WHAT is commonly, in a popular fenfe, called reafon, and is fo much recommended in moral difcourfes, is nothing but a general and a calm paffion, which takes a comprehenfive and diftant view of its object, and actuates the will, without exciting any fenfible emotion. A man, we fay, is diligent in his profeffion from reafon; that is, from a calm defire of riches and a fortune. A man adheres to juftice from reafon;

that

that is, from a calm regard to a character with himfelf and others.

3. THE fame objects, which recommend themfelves to reafon in this fenfe of the word, are alfo the objects of what we call paffion, when they are brought near to us, and acquire fome other advantages, either of external fituation, or congruity to our internal temper; and by that means, excite a turbulent and fenfible emotion. Evil, at a great diftance, is avoided, we fay, from reafon: Evil, near at hand, produces averfion, horror, fear, and is the object of paffion.

4. THE common error of metaphyficians has lain in afcribing the direction of the will entirely to one of thefe principles, and fuppofing the other to have no influence. Men often act knowingly againft their intereft: It is not therefore the view of the greateft poffible good which always influences them. Men often counteract a violent paffion, in profecution of their diftant interefts and defigns: It is not therefore the prefent uneafinefs alone, which determines them.

I 2

In

In general, we may obferve, that both thefe principles operate on the will; and where they are contrary, that either of them prevails, according to the general character or prefent difpofition of the perfon. What we call *ftrength of mind* implies the prevalence of the calm paffions above the violent; tho' we may eafily obferve, that there is no perfon fo conftantly poffeft of this virtue, as never, on any occafion, to yield to the follicitation of violent affections and defires. From thefe variations of temper proceeds the great difficulty of deciding concerning the future actions and refolutions of men, where there is any contrariety of motives and paffions.

SECT.

S E C T. VI.

1. WE fhall here enumerate fome of thofe circumftances, which render a paffion calm or violent, which heighten or diminifh any emotion.

IT is a property in human nature, that any emotion, which attends a paffion, is eafily converted into it; tho' in their natures they be originally different from, and even contrary to each other. It is true, in order to caufe a perfect union amongft paffions, and make one produce the other, there is always required a double relation, according to the theory above delivered. But when two paffions are already produced by their feparate caufes, and are both prefent in the mind, they readily mingle and unite; tho' they have but one relation, and fometimes without any. The predominant paffion fwallows up the inferior, and converts it into itfelf. The fpirits, when once excited, eafily receive a change in their direction; and it is natural to imagine, that this change will come from the prevailing affection. The con-

I 3   nexion

nexion is in many cafes clofer betwixt any two paffions, than betwixt any paffion and indifference.

WHEN a perfon is once heartily in love, the little faults and caprices of his miftrefs, the jealoufies and quarrels, to which that commerce is fo fubject ; however unpleafant they be, and rather connected with anger and hatred ; are yet found, in many inftances, to give additional force to the prevailing paffion. It is a common artifice of politicians, when they would affect any perfon very much by a matter of fact, of which they intend to inform him, firft to excite his curiofity ; delay as long as poffible the fatiffying it ; and by that means raife his anxiety and impatience to the utmoft, before they give him a full infight into the bufinefs. They know, that his curiofity will precipitate him into the paffion, which they purpofe to raife, and will affift the object in its influence on the mind. A foldier, advancing to battle, is naturally infpired with courage and confidence, when he thinks on his friends and fellow-foldiers ; and is ftruck with fear and terror, when he reflects on the enemy. Whatever new emotion, therefore, proceeds from the former naturally encreafes the

the courage; as the fame emotion proceeding from the latter, augments the fear. Hence in martial difcipline, the uniformity and luftre of habit, the regularity of figures and motions, with all the pomp and majefty of war, encourage ourfelves and our allies; while the fame objects in the enemy ftrike terror into us, tho' agreeable and beautiful in themfelves.

Hope is, in itfelf, an agreeable paffion, and allied to friendfhip and benevolence; yet is it able fometimes to blow up anger, when that is the predominant paffion. *Spes addita fufcitat iras.* Virg.

2. Since paffions, however independent, are naturally transfufed into each other, if they are both prefent at the fame time; it follows, that when good or evil is placed in fuch a fituation as to caufe any particular emotion, befides its direct paffion of defire or averfion, that latter paffion muft acquire new force and violence.

3. This often happens, when any object excites contrary paffions. For it is obfervable,

I 4   that

that an oppofition of paffions commonly caufes a new emotion in the fpirits and produces more diforder than the concurrence of any two affections of equal force. This new emotion is eafily converted into the predominant paffion, and in many inftances, is obferved to encreafe its violence, beyond the pitch, at which it would have arrived, had it met with no oppofition. Hence we naturally defire what is forbid, and often take a pleafure in performing actions, merely becaufe they are unlawful. The notion of duty, when oppofite to the paffions, is not always able to overcome them; and when it fails of that influence, is apt rather to encreafe and irritate them, by producing an oppofition in our motives and principles.

4. The fame effect follows, whether the oppofition arifes from internal motives or external obftacles. The paffion commonly acquires new force in both cafes. The efforts, which the mind makes to furmount the obftacle, excite the fpirits, and enliven the paffion.

5. Un-

5. UNCERTAINTY has the fame effect as oppofition. The agitation of the thought, the quick turns which it makes from one view to another, the variety of paffions, which fucceed each other, according to the different views: All thefe produce an agitation in the mind; and this agitation transfufes itfelf into the predominant paffion.

SECURITY, on the contrary, diminifhes the paffions. The mind, when left to itfelf, immediately languifhes; and in order to preferve its ardour, muft be every moment fupported by a new flow of paffion. For the fame reafon, defpair, tho' contrary to fecurity, has a like influence.

6. NOTHING more powerfully excites any affection than to conceal fome part of its object, by throwing it into a kind of fhade, which, at the fame time, that it fhows enough to prepoffefs us in favour of the object, leaves ftill fome work for the imagination. Befides, that obfcurity is always attended with a kind of uncertainty; the effort, which the fancy makes to

I 5

compleat

compleat the idea, rouzes the fpirits, and gives an additional force to the paffion.

7. As defpair and fecurity, tho' contrary, produce the fame effects; fo abfence is obferved to have contrary effects, and in different circumftances, either encreafes or diminifhes our affection. *Rochefoucault* has very well remarked, that abfence deftroys weak paffions, but encreafes ftrong; as the wind extinguifhes a candle, but blows up a fire. Long abfence naturally weakens our idea, and diminifhes the paffion: But where the paffion is fo ftrong and lively as to fupport itfelf, the uneafinefs, arifing from abfence, encreafes the paffion, and gives it new force and influence.

8. WHEN the foul applies itfelf to the performance of any action, or the conception of any object, to which it is not accuftomed, there is a certain unpliablenefs in the faculties, and a difficulty of the fpirits moving in their new direction. As this difficulty excites the fpirits, it is the fource of wonder, furprize, and of all the emotions, which arife from novelty; and

and is in itſelf very agreeable, like every thing, which inlivens the mind to a moderate degree. But tho' ſurpriſe be agreeable in itſelf, yet as it puts the ſpirits in agitation, it not only augments our agreeable affections, but alſo our painful, according to the foregoing principle. Hence every thing, that is new, is moſt affecting, and gives us either more pleaſure or pain, than what, ſtrictly ſpeaking, ſhould naturally follow from it. When it often returns upon us, the novelty wears off; the paſſions ſubſide; the hurry of the ſpirits is over; and we ſurvey the object with greater tranquillity.

9. THE imagination and affections have a cloſe union together. The vivacity of the former, gives force to the latter. Hence the proſpect of any pleaſure, with which we are acquainted, affects us more than any other pleaſure, which we may own ſuperior, but of whoſe nature we are *wholly* ignorant. Of the one we can form a particular and determinate idea: The other, we conceive under the general notion of pleaſure.

I 6　　　　　　ANY

ANY satisfaction, which we lately enjoyed, and of which the memory is fresh and recent, operates on the will with more violence, than another of which the traces are decayed and almost obliterated.

A PLEASURE, which is suitable to the way of life, in which we are engaged, excites more our desires and appetites than another, which is foreign to it.

NOTHING is more capable of infusing any passion into the mind, than eloquence, by which objects are represented in the strongest and most lively colours. The bare opinion of another, especially when inforced with passion, will cause an idea to have an influence upon us, tho' that idea might otherwise have been entirely neglected.

IT is remarkable, that lively passions commonly attend a lively imagination. In this respect, as well as others, the force of the passion depends as much on the temper of the person, as on the nature or situation of the object.

WHAT

WHAT is diſtant, either in place or time, has not equal influence with what is near and contiguous.

.   .*.   *.*

I PRETEND not here to have exhauſted this ſubject. It is ſufficient for my purpoſe, if I have made it appear, that, in the production and con-duct of the paſſions, there is a certain regular mechaniſm, which is ſuſceptible of as accurate a diſquiſition, as the laws of motion, optics, hydroſtatics, or any part of natural philoſophy.

DISSERTATION III.

OF

TRAGEDY.

DISSERTATION III.

Of Tragedy.

IT feems an unaccountable pleafure, which the fpectators of a well-wrote tragedy receive from forrow, terror, anxiety, and other paffions, which are in themfelves difagreeable and uneafy. The more they are touched and affected, the more are they delighted with the fpectacle, and as foon as the uneafy paffions ceafe to operate, the piece is at an end. One fcene of full joy and contentment and fecurity is the utmoft, that any compofition of this kind can bear; and it is fure always to be the concluding one. If in the texture of the piece, there be interwoven any fcenes of fatisfaction, they afford only faint gleams of pleafure, which are thrown in by way of variety, and in order to plunge the actors into deeper diftrefs, by means of that contraft and difappointment. The whole art of the poet is employed, in rouzing and fupporting the compaffion and indignation, the anxiety and refentment of his audience.
They

They are pleafed in proportion as they are afflicted; and never are fo happy as when they
employ tears, fobs, and cries to give vent to
their forrow, and relieve their heart, fwoln with
the tendereft fympathy and compaffion.

THE few critics, who have had fome tincture of philofophy, have remarked this fingular
phænomenon, and have endeavoured to account
for it.

L'ABBE *Dubos*, in his reflections on poetry
and painting, afferts, that nothing is in general
fo difagreeable to the mind as the languid, lift-
lefs ftate of indolence, into which it falls upon
the removal of every paffion and occupation.
To get rid of this painful fituation, it feeks
every amufement and purfuit; bufinefs, gaming, fhows, executions; whatever will rouze
the paffions, and take its attention from itfelf.
No matter, what the paffion is: Let it be difagreeable, afflicting, melancholy, difordered;
it is ftill better, than that infipid languor, which
arifes from perfect tranquillity and repofe.

IT

IT is impoffible not to admit this account, as being, at leaft, in part fatisfactory. You may obferve, when there are feveral tables of gaming, that all the company run to thofe, where the deepeft play is, even tho' they find not there the fineft players. The view, or at leaft, imagination of high paffions, arifing from great lofs or gain, affects the fpectators by fympathy, gives them fome touches of the fame paffions, and ferves them for a momentary entertainment. It makes the time pafs the eafier with them, and is fome relief to that oppreffion, under which men commonly labour, when left entirely to their own thoughts and meditations.

WE find, that common lyars always magnify, in their narrations, all kinds of danger, pain, diftrefs, ficknefs, deaths, murders, and cruelties ; as well as joy, beauty, mirth, and magnificence. It is an abfurd fecret, which they have for pleafing their company, fixing their attention, and attaching them to fuch marvellous relations, by the paffions and emotions, which they excite.

THERE is, however, a difficulty of applying to the prefent fubject, in its full extent, this folution,

lution, however ingenious and satisfactory it
may appear. It is certain, that the same object
of distress which pleases in a tragedy, were it
really set before us, would give the most unfeigned uneasiness, tho' it be then the most effectual cure of languor and indolence. Mon-
sieur *Fontenelle* seems to have been sensible of
this difficulty; and accordingly attempts another
solution of the phænomenon; at least, makes
some addition to the theory abovementioned [a].

" PLEASURE and pain," says he, " which are
" two sentiments so different in themselves,
" differ not so much in their cause. From the
" instance of tickling, it appears, that the
" movement of pleasure pushed a little too far,
" becomes pain; and that the movement of pain,
" a little moderated, becomes pleasure. Hence
" it proceeds, that there is such a thing as a sor-
" row, soft and agreeable: It is a pain weakened
" and diminished. The heart likes naturally to
" be moved and affected. Melancholy objects
" suit it, and even disastrous and sorrowful,
" provided they are softened by some circum-
" stance. It is certain, that on the theatre the
" representation has almost the effect of reality;

[a] Reflexions sur la poetique. § 36.

" but

" but yet is has not altogether that effect.
" However we may be hurried away by the
" spectacle; whatever dominion the senses and
" imagination may usurp over the reason, there
" still lurks at the bottom a certain idea of
" falshood in the whole of what we see. This
" idea, tho' weak and disguised, suffices to di-
" minish the pain which we suffer from the
" misfortunes of those whom we love, and to
" reduce that affliction to such a pitch as con-
" verts it into a pleasure. We weep for the
" misfortune of a hero, to whom we are at-
" tached : In the same instant we comfort our-
" selves, by reflecting, that it is nothing but a
" fiction : And it is precisely, that mixture of
" sentiments, which composes an agreeable
" sorrow, and tears that delight us. But as
" that affliction, which is caused by exterior
" and sensible objects, is stronger than the con-
" solation, which arises from an internal re-
" flection, they are the effects and symptoms
" of sorrow, which ought to prevail in the
" composition."

THIS solution seems just and convincing;
but perhaps it wants still some new addition, in
order to make it answer fully the phænomenon,

2 which

which we here examine. All the paffions, excited by eloquence, are agreeable in the higheft
degree, as well as thofe which are moved by
painting and the theatre. The epilogues of *Cicero* are, on this account chiefly, the delight of
every reader of tafte ; and it is difficult to read
fome of them without the deepeft fympathy and
forrow. His merit as an orator, no doubt, depends much on his fuccefs in this particular.
When he had raifed tears in his judges and all
his audience, they were then the moft highly
delighted, and expreffed the greateft fatisfaction
with the pleader. The pathetic defcription of
the butchery made by *Verres* of the *Sicilian* cap-
tains is a mafter-piece of this kind : But I believe none will affirm, that the being prefent at
a melancholy fcene of that nature would afford
any entertainment. Neither is the forrow here
foftened by fiction : For the audience were convinced of the reality of every circumftance.
What is it then, which in this cafe raifes a pleafure from the bofom of uneafinefs, fo to fpeak ;
and a pleafure, which ftill retains all the features
and outward fymptoms of diftrefs and forrow ?

I Answer : This extraordinary effect proceeds from that very eloquence, with which the
melancholy

melancholy fcene is reprefented. The genius
required to paint objects in a lively manner, the
art employed in collecting all the pathetic circumftances, the judgment difplayed in difpofing
them; the exercife, I fay, of thefe noble talents, along with the force of expreffion, and
beauty of oratorial numbers, diffufe the higheft
fatisfaction on the audience, and excite the moft
delightful movements. By this means, the uneafinefs of the melancholy paffions is not only
overpowered and effaced by fomething ftronger
of an oppofite kind; but the whole movement
of thofe paffions is converted into pleafure, and
fwells the delight, which the eloquence raifes
in us. The fame force of oratory, employed on
an uninterefting fubject, would not pleafe half
fo much, or rather would appear altogether ridiculous; and the mind, being left in abfolute
calmnefs and indifference, would relifh none of
thofe beauties of imagination or expreffion,
which, if joined to paffion, give it fuch exquifite entertainment. The impulfe or vehemence,
arifing from forrow, compaffion, indignation,
receives a new direction from the fentiments of
beauty. The latter, being the predominant
emotions, feize the whole mind, and convert
the former into themfelves, or at leaft, tincture

4   them

them fo ftrongly as totally to alter their nature: And the foul, being, at the fame time, rouzed by paffion, and charmed by eloquence, feels on the whole a ftrong movement, which is altogether delightful.

THE fame principle takes place in tragedy; along with this addition, that tragedy is an imitation, and imitation is always of itfelf agreeable. This circumftance ferves ftill farther to fmooth the motions of paffion, and convert the whole feeling into one uniform and ftrong enjoyment. Objects of the greateft terror and diftrefs pleafe in painting, and pleafe more than the moft beautiful objects, that appear calm and indifferent [a]. The affection, rouzing the mind, excites a large ftock of fpirit and vehemence; which is all transformed into pleafure by the force of the prevailing movement. It is thus

[a] Painters make no fcruple of reprefenting diftrefs and forrow as well as any other paffion: But they feem not to dwell fo much on thefe melancholy affections as the poets, who, tho' they copy every emotion of the human breaft, yet pafs very quickly over the agreeable fentiments. A painter reprefents only one inftant; and if that be paffionate enough, it is fure to affect and delight the fpectator: But nothing can furnifh to the poet a variety of fcenes and incidents and fentiments, except diftrefs, terror, or anxiety. Compleat joy and fatisfaction is attended with fecurity, and leaves no farther room for action.

the

the fiction of tragedy foftens the paffion, by an infufion of a new feeling, not merely by weakening or diminifhing the forrow. You may by degrees weaken a real forrow, till it totally difappears; yet in none of its gradations will it ever give pleafure; except, perhaps, by accident, to a man funk under lethargic indolence, whom it rouzes from that languid ftate.

To confirm this theory, it will be fufficient to produce other inftances, where the fubordinate movement is converted into the predominant, and gives force to it, tho' of a different, and even fometimes tho' of a contrary nature.

Novelty naturally excites the mind and attracts our attention; and the movements, which it caufes, are always converted into any paffion, belonging to the object, and join their force to it. Whether an event excites joy or forrow, pride or fhame, anger or goodwill, it is fure to produce a ftronger affection, when new and unufual. And tho' novelty, of itfelf, be agreeable, it enforces the painful, as well as agreeable paffions.

K   HAD

HAD you any intention to move a person extremely by the narration of any event, the best method of encreasing its effect would be artfully to delay informing him of it, and first excite his curiosity and impatience before you let him into the secret. This is the artifice, practiced by *Iago* in the famous scene of *Shakespeare*; and every spectator is sensible, that *Othello's* jealousy acquires additional force from his preceding impatience, and that the subordinate passion is here readily transformed into the predominant.

DIFFICULTIES encrease passions of every kind; and by rouzing our attention, and exciting our active powers, they produce an emotion, which nourishes the prevailing affection.

PARENTS commonly love that child most, whose sickly infirm frame of body has occasioned them the greatest pains, trouble, and anxiety in rearing him. The agreeable sentiment of affection here acquires force from sentiments of uneasiness.

NOTHING

NOTHING endears fo much a friend as forrow for his death. The pleafure of his company has not fo powerful an influence.

JEALOUSY is a painful paffion, yet without fome fhare of it, the agreeable affection of love has difficulty to fubfift in its full force and violence. Abfence is alfo a great fource of complaint amongft lovers, and gives them the greateft uneafinefs : Yet nothing is more favorable to their mutual paffion than fhort intervals of that kind. And if long intervals be pernicious, it is only becaufe, thro' time, men are accuftomed to them, and they ceafe to give uneafinefs. Jealoufy and abfence in love compofe the *dolce piccante* of the *Italians*, which they fuppofe fo effential to all pleafure.

THERE is a fine obfervation of the elder *Pliny*, which illuftrates the principle here infifted on. *It is very remarkable,* fays he, *that the laft works of celebrated artifts, which they left imperfect, are always the moft prized, fuch as the* Iris *of* Ariftides, *the* Tyndarides *of* Nicomachus, *the* Medea *of* Timomachus, *and the* Venus *of* Apelles. *Thefe are valued even above their finifhed productions : The broken lineaments*

K 2 *of*

of the piece and the half formed idea of the painter are carefully studied; and our very grief for that curious hand, which had been stoped by death, is an additional encrease to our pleasure [a].

THESE inftances (and many more might be collected) are fufficient to afford us fome infight into the analogy of nature, and to fhow us, that the pleafure, which poets, orators, and muficians give us, by exciting grief, forrow, indignation, compaffion, is not fo extraordinary nor paradoxical, as it may at firft fight appear. The force of imagination, the energy of expreffion, the power of numbers, the charms of imitation; all thefe are naturally, of themfelves, delightful to the mind; and when the object prefented lays alfo hold of fome affection, the pleafure ftill rifes upon us, by the converfion of this fubordinate movement, into that which is predominant. The paffion, tho', perhaps, naturally, and when excited by the fimple appear-

[a] *Illud vero perquam rarum ac memoria dignum, etiam fuprema opera artificum, imperfectasque tabulas, ficut, Irin Ariftidis, Tyndaridas Nicomachi, Medeam Timomachi, & quam diximus Venerem Apellis, in majori admiratione effe quam perfecta. Quippe in iis lineamenta reliqua, ipfaeque cogitationes artificum fpectantur, atque in lenocinio commendationis dolor eft manus, cum id ageret, extinctae,* lib. xxxv. c. 11.

ance of a real object, it may be painful; yet is so smoothed, and softened, and mollified, when raised by the finer arts, that it affords the highest entertainment.

To confirm this reasoning, we may observe, that if the movements of the imagination be not predominant above those of the passion, a contrary effect follows; and the former, being now subordinate, is converted into the latter, and still farther encreases the pain and affliction of the sufferer.

Who could ever think of it as a good expedient for comforting an afflicted parent, to exaggerate, with all the force of oratory, the irreparable loss, which he has met with by the death of a favorite child? The more power of imagination and expression you here employ, the more you encrease his despair and affliction.

The shame, confusion, and terror of *Verres*, no doubt, rose in proportion to the noble eloquence and vehemence of *Cicero*: So also did his pain and uneasiness. These former passions were too strong for the pleasure arising from the beauties of elocution; and operated,

tho'

tho' from the fame principle, yet in a contrary manner, to the fympathy, compaffion, and indignation of the audience.

LORD *Clarendon*, when he approaches the cataftrophe of the royal party, fuppofes, that his narration muft then become infinitely difagreeable ; and he hurries over the King's death, without giving us one circumftance of it. He confiders it as too horrid a fcene to be contemplated with any fatisfaction, or even without the utmoft pain and averfion. He himfelf, as well as the readers of that age, were too deeply interefted in the events, and felt a pain from fubjects, which an hiftorian and a reader of another age would regard as the moft pathetic and moft interefting, and by confequence, the moft agreeable.

AN action, reprefented in tragedy, may be too bloody and atrocious. It may excite fuch movements of horror as will not foften into pleafure ; and the greateft energy of expreffion beftowed on defcriptions of that nature ferves only to augment our uneafinefs. Such is that action reprefented in the *ambitious Stepmother*, where a venerable old man, raifed to the height

of

of fury and defpair, rufhes againſt a pillar, and ſtriking his head upon it, beſmears it all over with mingled brains and gore. The *Engliſh* theatre abounds too much with ſuch images.

EVEN the common ſentiments of compaſſion require to be ſoftened by ſome agreeable affection, in order to give a thorough ſatisfaction to the audience. The mere ſuffering of plaintive virtue, under the triumphant tyranny and oppreſſion of vice, forms a diſagreeable ſpectacle, and is carefully avoided by all maſters of the theatre. In order to diſmiſs the audience with entire ſatisfaction and contentment, the virtue muſt either convert itſelf into a noble courageous deſpair, or, the vice receive its proper puniſhment.

MOST painters appear in this light to have been very unhappy in their ſubjects. As they wrought for churches and convents, they have chiefly repreſented ſuch horrible ſubjects as crucifixions and martyrdoms, where nothing appears but tortures, wounds, executions, and paſſive ſuffering, without any action or affection. When they turned their pencil from this ghaſtly mythology, they had recourſe commonly to

K 4 *Ovid,*

Ovid, whofe fictions, tho' paffionate and agreeable, are fcarce natural or probable enough for painting.

THE fame inverfion of that principle, which is here infifted on, difplays itfelf in common life, as in the effects of oratory and poetry. Raife fo the fubordinate paffion that it becomes the predominant, it fwallows up that affection, which it before nourifhed and encreafed. Too much jealoufy extinguifhes love: Too much difficulty renders us indifferent: Too much ficknefs and infirmity difgufts a felfifh and unkind parent.

WHAT fo difagreeable as the difmal, gloomy, difaftrous ftories, with which melancholy people entertain their companions? The uneafy paffion, being there raifed alone, unaccompanied with any fpirit, genius, or eloquence, conveys a pure uneafinefs, and is attended with nothing that can foften it into pleafure or fatisfaction.

DISSERTATION IV.

OF THE

STANDARD OF TASTE.

L

DISSERTATION IV.

Of the Standard of Taste.

THE great variety of Taftes, as well as of opinions, which prevail in the world, is too obvious not to have fallen under every one's obfervation. Men of the moft confined knowledge are able to remark a difference in the narrow circle of their acquaintance, even where the perfons have been educated under the fame government, and have early imbibed the fame prejudices. But thofe who can enlarge their view to contemplate diftant nations and remote ages, are ftill more furprifed at the great inconfiftence and contradiction. We are apt to call *barbarous* whatever departs widely from our own tafte and apprehenfion: But foon find the epithet of reproach retorted on us. And the higheft arrogance and felf conceit is at laft ftartled, on obferving an equal affurance on all fides, and fcruples, amidft fuch a conteft of fentiments, to pronounce pofitively in its own favour.

As this variety of tafte is obvious to the moft carelefs enquirer; fo will it be found, on exami-

nation,

nation, to be ſtill greater in reality than in appearance. The ſentiments of men often differ
with regard to beauty and deformity of all kinds,
even while their general diſcourſe is the ſame.
There are certain terms in every language, which
import blame, and others praiſe; and all men,
who uſe the ſame tongue, muſt agree in their
application of them. Every voice is united in
applauding elegance, propriety, ſimplicity, ſpirit
in writing; and in blaming fuſtian, affectation,
coldneſs, and a falſe brilliant: But when critics
come to particulars, this ſeeming unanimity va-
niſhes; and it is found, that they had affixed a
very different meaning to their expreſſions. In
all matters of opinion and ſcience, the caſe is oppoſite: The difference among men is there oftner
found to lie in generals than in particulars; and to
be leſs in reality than in appearance. An explication of the terms commonly ends the contro-
verſy; and the diſputants are ſurprized to find,
that they had been quarrelling, while at bottom
they agreed in their judgment.

Those who found morality on ſentiment,
more than on reaſon, are inclined to comprehend
ethics under the former obſervation, and to ſuppoſe, that in all queſtions, which regard conduct
and

and manners, the difference among men is really greater than at firſt ſight it appears. It is indeed obvious, that writers of all nations and all ages concur in applauding juſtice, humanity, magnanimity, prudence, veracity; and in blaming the oppoſite qualities. Even poets and other authors, whoſe compoſitions are chiefly calculated to pleaſe the imagination, are yet found, from *Homer* down to *Fenelon*, to inculcate the ſame moral precepts, and to beſtow their applauſe and blame on the ſame virtues and vices. This great unanimity is uſually aſcribed to the influence of plain reaſon; which, in all theſe caſes, maintains ſimilar ſentiments in all men, and prevents thoſe controverſies, to which the abſtract ſciences are ſo much expoſed. So far as the unanimity is real, the account may be admitted as ſatisfactory: But it muſt alſo be allowed, that ſome part of the ſeeming harmony in morals may be accounted for from the very nature of language. The word, *virtue,* with its equivalent in every tongue, implies praiſe; as that of *vice* does blame: And no one, without the moſt obvious and groſſeſt impropriety, could affix reproach to a term, which in general uſe is underſtood in a good ſenſe; or beſtow applauſe, where the idiom requires diſapprobation. *Homer's*

general

general precepts, where he delivers any fuch,
will never be controverted; but it is very obvious, that when he draws particular pictures of
manners, and reprefents heroifm in *Achilles* and
prudence in *Ulyffes*, he intermixes a much greater
degree of ferocity in the former, and of cunning
and fraud in the latter, than *Fenelon* would admit
of. The fage *Ulyffes* in the *Greek* poet feems to
delight in lies and fictions, and often employs
them without any neceffity or even advantage:
But his more fcrupulous fon in the *French* epic
writer expofes himfelf to the moft imminent
perils, rather than depart from the exacteft line
of truth and veracity.

THE admirers and followers of the *Alcoran*
infift very much on the excellent moral precepts,
which are interfperfed throughout that wild performance. But it is to be fuppofed, that the
Arabic words, which correfpond to the *Englifh*,
equity, juftice, temperance, meeknefs, charity,
were fuch as, from the conftant ufe of that
tongue, muft always be taken in a good fenfe;
and it would have argued the greateft ignorance,
not of morals, but of language, to have mentioned them with any epithets, befides thofe of
applaufe and approbation. But would we know,
whether

whether the pretended prophet had really attained a juſt ſentiment of morals? Let us attend to his narration; and we ſhall ſoon find, that he beſtows praiſe on ſuch inſtances of treachery, inhumanity, cruelty, revenge, bigotry, as are utterly incompatible with civilized ſociety. No ſteddy rule of right ſeems there to be attended to; and every action is blamed or praiſed, ſo far only as it is beneficial or hurtful to the true believers.

THE merit of delivering true general precepts in ethics is indeed very ſmall. Whoever recommends any moral virtues, really does no more than is implied in the terms themſelves. The people, who invented the word *modeſty*, and uſed it in a good ſenſe, inculcated more clearly and much more efficaciouſly, the precept, *be modeſt*, than any pretended legiſlator or prophet, who ſhould inſert ſuch a *maxim* in his writings. Of all expreſſions, thoſe, which, together with their other meaning, imply a degree either of blame or approbation, are the leaſt liable to be perverted or miſtaken.

It is very natural for us to ſeek a *Standard of Taſte*; a rule, by which the various ſentiments of men may be reconciled; or at leaſt, a de-

ciſion

cifion afforded, confirming one fentiment, and condemning another.

THERE is a fpecies of philofophy, which cuts off all hopes of fuccefs in fuch an attempt, and reprefents the impoffibility of ever attaining any ftandard of tafte. The difference, it is faid, is very wide between judgment and fentiment. All fentiment is right ; becaufe fentiment has a reference to nothing beyond itfelf, and is always real, wherever a man is confcious of it. But all determinations of the underftanding are not right ; becaufe they have a reference to fomething beyond themfelves, to wit, real matter of fact ; and are not always conformable to that ftandard. Among a thoufand different opinions which different men may entertain of the fame fubject, there is one, and but one, that is juft and true ; and the only difficulty is to fix and afcertain it. On the contrary, a thoufand different fentiments, excited by the fame object, are all right : Becaufe no fentiment reprefents what is really in the object. It only marks a certain conformity or relation betwixt the object and the organs or faculties of the mind ; and if that conformity did not really exift, the fentiment could never poffibly have a being. Beauty is no
quality

quality in things themfelves : It exifts merely in the mind which contemplates them ; and each mind perceives a different beauty. One perfon may even perceive deformity, where another is fenfible of beauty ; and every individual ought to acquiefce in his own fentiment, without pretending to regulate thofe of others. To feek the real beauty, or real deformity is as fruitlefs an enquiry, as to pretend to afcertain the real fweet or real bitter. According to the difpofition of the organs, the fame object may be both fweet and bitter ; and the proverb has juftly determined it to be fruitlefs to difpute concerning taftes. It is very natural, and even quite neceffary, to extend this axiom to mental, as well as bodily tafte ; and thus common fenfe, which is fo often at variance with philofophy, efpecially with the fceptical kind, is found, in one inftance at leaft, to agree in pronouncing the fame decifion.

But though this axiom, by paffing into a proverb, feems to have attained the fanction of common fenfe ; there is certainly a fpecies of common fenfe which oppofes it, or at leaft ferves to modify and reftrain it. Whoever would affert an equality of genius and elegance betwixt

L 5

Ogilby

Ogilby and *Milton*, or *Bunyan* and *Addison*, would be thought to defend no lefs an extravagance, than if he had maintained a molehill to be as high as *Teneriffe*, or a pond as extenfive as the ocean. Though there may be found perfons, who give the preference to the former authors; no one pays attention to fuch a tafte; and we pronounce without fcruple the fentiment of thefe pretended critics to be abfurd and ridiculous. The principle of the natural equality of taftes is then totally forgot; and while we admit of it on fome occafions, where the objects feem near an equality, it appears an extravagant paradox, or rather a palpable abfurdity, where objects fo difproportioned are compared together.

IT is evident, that none of the rules of compofition are fixed by reafonings *a priori*, or can be efteemed abftract conclufions of the underftanding, from comparing thofe habitudes and relations of ideas, which are eternal and immutable. Their foundation is 'the fame with that of all the practical fciences, experience; nor are they any thing but general obfervations, concerning what has been univerfally found to pleafe in all countries and in all ages. Many of the beauties of poetry and even of eloquence

I   are

are founded on falfhood and fiction, on hyper-
boles, metaphors, and an abufe or perverfion of
expreffions from their natural meaning. To
check the fallies of the imagination, and to reduce every expreffion to geometrical truth and
exactnefs, would be the moft contrary to the laws
of criticifm; becaufe it would produce a work,
which, by univerfal experience has been found
the moft infipid and difagreeable. But though
poetry can never fubmit to exact truth, it muft
be confined by rules of art, difcovered to the
author either by genius or obfervation. If fome
negligent or irregular writers have pleafed, they
have not pleafed by their tranfgreffions of rule
or order, but in fpite of thefe tranfgreffions:
They have poffeffed other beauties, which were
conformable to juft criticifm; and the force of
thefe beauties has been able to overpower cen-
fure, and give the mind a fatisfaction fuperior to
the difguft arifing from the blemifhes. *Ariofto*
pleafes; but not by his monftrous and improbable fictions, by his bizarre mixture of the ferious and comic ftyles, by the want of coherence
in his ftories, or by the continual interruptions
of his narration. He charms by the force and
clearnefs of his expreffion, by the readinefs and
variety of his inventions, and by his natural

L 6   pictures

pictures of the paffions, efpecially thofe of the gay and amorous kind: And however his faults may diminifh our fatisfaction, they are not able entirely to deftroy it. Did our pleafure really arife from thofe parts of his poem, which we denominate faults, this would be no objection to criticifm in general: It would only be an objection to thofe particular rules of criticifm, which would eftablifh fuch circumftances to be faults, and would reprefent them as univerfally blameable. If they are found to pleafe, they cannot be faults; let the pleafure, which they produce, be ever fo unexpected and unaccountable.

BUT though all the general rules of art are founded only on experience and on the obfervation of the common fentiments of human nature, we muft not imagine, that, on every occafion, the feelings of men will be conformable to thefe rules. Thofe finer emotions of the mind are of a very tender and delicate nature, and require the concurrence of many favourable circumftances to make them play with facility and exactnefs, according to their general and eftablifhed principles. The leaft exterior hindrance to fuch fmall fprings, or the leaft internal dif-

order,

order, difturbs their motion, and confounds the operation o the whole machine. When we would make an experiment of this nature, and would try the force of any beauty or deformity, we muft choofe with care a proper time and place, and bring the fancy to a fuitable fituation and difpofition. A perfect ferenity of mind, a recollection of thought, a due attention to the object; if any of thefe circumftances be wanting our experiment will be fallacious, and we fhall be unable to judge of the catholic and univerfal beauty. The relation, which nature has placed betwixt the form and the fentiment, will at leaft be more obfcure; and it will require greater accuracy to trace and difcern it. We fhall be able to afcertain its influence not fo much from the operation of each particular beauty, as from the durable admiration, which attends thofe works, that have furvived all the caprices of mode and fafhion, all the miftakes of ignorance and envy.

THE fame *Homer*, who pleafed at *Athens* and *Rome* two thoufand years ago, is ftill admired at *Paris* and at *London*. All the changes of climate, government, religion, and language have not been able to obfcure his glory. Authority

thority or prejudice may give a temporary vogue to a bad poet or orator; but his reputation will never be durable or general. When his compositions are examined by posterity or by foreigners, the enchantment is diffipated, and his faults appear in their true colours. On the contrary, a real genius, the longer his works endure, and the more wide they are spread, the more fincere is the admiration which he meets with. Envy and jealoufy have too much place in a narrow circle; and even familiar acquaintance with his person may diminifh the applaufe due to his performances: But when thefe obftructions are removed, the beauties, which are naturally fitted to excite agreeable fentiments immediately difplay their energy; and while the world endures, they maintain their authority over the minds of men.

IT appears then, that amidft all the variety and caprices of tafte, there are certain general principles of approbation or blame, whofe influence a careful eye may trace in all operations of the mind. Some particular forms or qualities, from the original ftructure of the internal fabric, are calculated to pleafe, and others to difpleafe; and if they fail of their effect in any particular
inftance,

instance, it is from some apparent defect or imperfection in the organ. A man in a fever would not insist on his palate as able to decide concerning flavours; nor would one, affected with the jaundice, pretend to give a verdict with regard to colours. In each creature, there is a found and a defective state; and the former alone can be supposed to afford us a true standard of taste and sentiment. If in the found state of the organs, there be an entire or a considerable uniformity of sentiment among men, we may thence derive an idea of the perfect and universal beauty; in like manner as the appearance of objects in day-light to the eye of a man in health is denominated their true and real colour, even while colour is allowed to be merely a phantasm of the senses.

Many and frequent are the defects in the internal organs, which prevent or weaken the influence of those general principles, on which depends our sentiment of beauty or deformity. Though some objects, by the structure of the mind, be naturally calculated to give pleasure, it is not to be expected, that in every individual the pleasure will be equally felt. Particular incidents and situations occur, which either throw
a false

a falfe light on the objects, or hinder the true
from conveying to the imagination the proper
fentiment and perception.

ONE obvious caufe, why many feel not the
proper fentiment of beauty, is the want of that
delicacy of imagination, which is requifite to
convey a fenfibility of thofe finer emotions.
This delicacy every one pretends to: Every one
talks of it; and would reduce every kind of tafte
or fentiment to its ftandard. But as our intention in this differtation is to mingle fome light of
the underftanding with the feelings of fentiment,
it will be proper to give a more accurate definition of delicacy, than has hitherto been attempted. And not to draw our philofophy
from too profound a fource, we fhall have recourfe to a noted ftory in *Don Quixote.*

'TIS with good reafon, fays *Sancho* to the
fquire with the great nofe, that I pretend to have
a judgment in wine: This is a quality heredi-
tary in our family. Two of my kinfmen were
once called to give their opinion of a hogfhead,
which was fuppofed to be excellent, being old
and of a good vintage. One of them taftes it;
confiders it, and after mature reflection pro-
nounces

nounces the wine to be good, were it not for a
fmall tafte of leather, which he perceived in it.
The other, after ufing the fame precautions,
gives alfo his verdict in favour of the wine; but
with the referve of a tafte of iron, which he
could eafily diftinguifh. You cannot imagine
how much they were both ridiculed for their
judgment. But who laughed in the end? On
emptying the hogfhead, there was found at
the bottom, an old key with a leathern thong
tied to it.

THE great refemblance between mental and
bodily tafte will eafily teach us to apply this ftory.
Though it be certain, that beauty and deformity,
no more than fweet and bitter, are not qualities
in objects, but belong entirely to the fentiment,
internal or external; it muft be allowed, that
there are certain qualities in objects, which are
fitted by nature to produce thofe particular feelings. Now as thefe qualities may be found in
a fmall degree or may be mixt and confounded
with each other, it often happens, that the tafte
is not affected with fuch minute qualities, or is
not able to diftinguifh all the particular flavours,
amidft the diforder, in which they are prefented.
Where the organs are fo fine, as to allow nothing
to.

to efcape them; and at the fame time fo exact
as to perceive every ingredient in the compofition : This we call delicacy of tafte, whether
we employ thcfe terms in the natural or meta-
phorical fenfe. Here then the general rules of
beauty are of ufe; being drawn from eftablifhed
models, and from the obfervation of what pleafes
or difpleafes, when prefented fingly and in a high
degree: And if the fame qualities, in a continued compofition and in a fmaller degree, affect
not the organs with a fenfible delight or uneafinefs, we exclude the perfon from all pretenfions
to this delicacy. To produce thefe general
rules or avowed patterns of compofition is like
finding the key with the leathern thong; which
juftified the verdict of *Sancho's* kinfmen, and
confounded thofe pretended judges, who had
condemned them. Though the hogfhead had
never been emptied, the tafte of the one w. s ftill
equally delicate, and that of the other equally
dull and languid : But it would have been more
difficult to have proved the fuperiority of the
former, to the conviction of every by-ftander.
In like manner, though the beauties of writing
had never been methodized, or reduced to general principles ; though no excellent models had
ever been acknowledged ; the different degrees

of

of tafte would ftill have fubfifted, and the judgment of one man been preferable to that of another; but it would not have been fo eafy to filence
the bad critic, who might always infift upon his
particular fentiment, and refufe to fubmit to his
antagonift. But when we fhow him an avowed
principle of art; when we illuftrate this principle
by examples, whofe operation, from his own
particular tafte, he acknowledges to be conformable to the principle; when we prove, that the
fame principle may be applied to the prefent
cafe, where he did not perceive nor feel its influence: He muft conclude, upon the whole, that
the fault lies in himfelf, and that he wants the
delicacy, which is requifite to make him fenfible
of every beauty and every blemifh, in any compofition or difcourfe.

'TIS acknowledged to be the perfection of
every fenfe or faculty, to perceive with exactnefs
its moft minute objects, and allow nothing to
efcape its notice and obfervation. The fmaller
the objects are, which become fenfible to the
eye, the finer is that organ, and the more elaborate its make and compofition. A good palate
is not tried by ftrong flavours; but by a mixture
of fmall ingredients, where we are ftill fenfible
of

of each part, notwithstanding its minuteness and its confusion with the rest. In like manner, a quick and acute perception of beauty and deformity must be the perfection of our mental taste, nor can a man be satisfied with himself, while he suspects, that any excellence or blemish in a discourse has passed him unobserved. In this case, the perfection of the man, and the perfection of the sense or feeling, are found to be united. A very delicate palate, on many occasions, may be a great inconvenience both to a man himself and to his friends; but a delicate taste of wit or beauty must always be a desirable quality; because it is the source of all the finest and most innocent enjoyments, of which human nature is susceptible. In this decision, the sentiments of all mankind are agreed. Wherever you can fix or ascertain a delicacy of taste, it is sure to be approved of; and the best way of fixing it is to appeal to those models and principles, which have been established by the uniform approbation and experience of nations and ages.

But though there be naturally a very wide difference in point of delicacy between one person and another, nothings tends further to encrease and improve this talent, than *practice* in a particular

ticular art, and the frequent furvey or contemplation of a particular fpecies of beauty. When objects of any kind are firft prefented to the eye or imagination, the fentiment, which attends them, is obfcure and confufed : and the mind is, in a great meafure, incapable of pronouncing concerning their merits or defects. The tafte cannot perceive the feveral excellencies of the performance ; much lefs diftinguifh the particular character of each excellency, and afcertain its quality and degree. If it pronounce the whole in general to be beautiful or deformed 'tis the utmoft which can be expected ; and even this judgment a perfon, fo unpractifed, will be apt to deliver with great hefitation and referve. But allow him to acquire experience in thofe objects, his feeling becomes more exact and nice : He not only perceives the beauties and defects of each part, but marks the diftinguifhing fpecies of each quality, and affigns it fuitable praife or blame. A clear and diftinct fentiment attends him through the whole furvey of the objects ; and he difcerns that very degree and kind of aaprobation or difpleafure, which each part is naturally fitted to produce. The mift diffipates, which feemed formerly to hang over the object : The organ acquires

greater

greater perfection in its operations; and can pronounce, without danger of miftake, concerning
the merits of each performance. In a word,
the fame addrefs and dexterity, which practice
gives to the execution of any work, is alfo acquired, by the fame means, in the judging of it.

So advantageous is practice to the difcernment
of beauty, that before we can pronounce judgment on any work of importance, it will even
be requifite, that that very individual performance be more than once perufed by us, and
be furveyed in different lights, with attention
and deliberation. There is a flutter or hurry
of thought, which attends the firft perufal of any
piece, and which confounds the genuin fentiment of beauty. The reference of the parts is
not difcerned: The true characters of ftyle are
little diftinguifhed: The feveral perfections and
defects feem wrapped up in a fpecies of confufion, and prefent themfelves indiftinctly to the
imagination. Not to mention, that there is a
fpecies of beauty, which, as it is florid and fu-
perficial, pleafes at firft; but being found incompatible with a juft expreffion either of reafon or
paffion, foon palls upon the tafte, and is then rejected with difdain, at leaft rated at a much lower
value.   It

IT is impoffible to continue in the practice of contemplating any order of beauty, without being frequently obliged to form *comparifons* between the feveral fpecies and degrees of excellency, and eftimating their proportion to each other. A man, who has had no opportunity of comparing the different kinds of beauty, is indeed totally un-qualified to pronounce an opinion with regard to any object prefented to him. By comparifon alone we fix the epithets of praife or blame, and learn how to affign the due degree of each. The coarfeft dawbing of a fign-poft contains a cer-tain luftre of colours and exactnefs of imitation, which are fo far beauties, and would affect the mind of a peafant or Indian with the higheft ad-miration. The moft vulgar ballads are not en-tirely deftitute of harmony or nature; and none but a perfon, familiarized to fuperior beauties, would pronounce their numbers harfh, or narra-tion uninterefting. A great inferiority of beauty gives pain to a perfon converfant in the higheft excellency of the kind, and is for that reafon pronounced a deformity: As the moft finifhed object, with which we are acquainted, is natu-rally fuppofed to have reached the pinnacle of perfection, and to be entitled to the higheft ap-plaufe.

plaufe. A man who has had opportunities of
feeing, and examining, and weighing the feveral
performances, admired in different ages and nations, can alone rate the merits of a work exhibited to his view, and affign its proper rank
among the productions of genius.

But to enable him the more fully to execute
this undertaking, he muft preferve his mind free
from all *prejudice*, and allow nothing to enter into
his confideration, but the very object, which is
fubmitted to his examination. We may obferve,
that every work of art, in order to produce its
due effect on the mind, muft be furveyed in a
certain point of view, and cannot be fully re-
lifhed by perfons, whofe fituation, real or imaginary, is not conformable to that required by the
performance. An orator addreffes himfelf to a
particular audience, and muft have a regard to
their particular genius, interefts, opinions, paffions, and prejudices ; otherwife he hopes in vain
to govern their refolutions, and inflame their
affections. Should they even have entertained
fome prepoffeffions againft him, however unreafonable, he muft not overlook this difadvantage ;
but before he enters upon the fubject, muft endeavour to conciliate their affection, and acquire
their

their good graces. A critic of a different age or nation, who fhould perufe this difcourfe, muft have all thefe circumftances in his eye, and muft place himfelf in the fame fituation as the audience, in order to form a true judgment of the oration. In like manner, when any work is addreffed to the public, though I fhould have a friendfhip or enmity with the author, I muft depart from this particular fituation; and confidering myfelf as a man in general, forget, if poffible, my individual being and my peculiar circumftances. A perfon, influenced by prejudice, complies not with this condition; but obftinately maintains his natural pofition, without entering into that required by the performance. If the work be addreffed to perfons of a different age or nation, he makes no allowance for their peculiar views and prejudices; but full of the manners of his own times, rafhly condemns what feemed admirable in the eyes of thofe for whom alone the difcourfe was calculated. If the work be executed for the public, he never fufficiently enlarges his comprehenfion, or forgets his interefts as a friend or enemy, as a rival or commentator. By this means, his fentiments are perverted; nor have the fame beauties and blemifhes the fame influence upon him, as if he had impofed a proper

M   violence

violence on his imagination, and had forgot himfelf for a moment. So far his tafte evidently
departs from the true ftandard ; and of confequence lofes all credit and authority.

It is well known, that, in all queftions, fubmitted to the underftanding, prejudice is moft
deftructive of found judgment, and perverts all
operations of the intellectual faculties : It is no
lefs contrary to good tafte ; nor has it lefs influence to corrupt our fentiments of beauty. It belongs to *good fenfe* to check its influence in both
cafes ; and in this refpect, as well as in many
others, reafon, if not an effential part of tafte,
is at leaft requifite to the operations of this latter
faculty. In all the nobler productions of genius,
there is a mutual relation and correfpondence of
parts ; nor can either the beauties or blemifhes
be perceived by him, whofe thought is not ca-
pacious enough to comprehend all thofe parts,
and compare them with each other, in order to
perceive the confiftence and uniformity of the
whole. Every work of art has alfo a certain end
or purpofe, for which it is calculated ; and is to
be deemed more or lefs perfect, as it is more or lefs
fitted to attain this end. The object of eloquence
is to perfuade, of hiftory to inftruct, of poetry to
pleafe

pleafe by means of the paffions and the imagination. Thefe ends we muft carry conftantly in our view, when we perufe any performance; and we muft be able to judge how far the means employed are adapted to their refpective purpofes. Befides, every kind of compofition, even the moft poetical, is nothing but a chain of propofitions and reafonings; not always indeed the jufteft and moft exact, but ftill plaufible and fpecious, however difguifed by the colouring of the imagination. The perfons, introduced in tragedy and epic poetry, muft be reprefented as reafoning and thinking, and concluding and acting, fuitable to their characters and circumftances; and without judgment, as well as tafte and invention, a poet can never hope to fucceed in fo delicate an undertaking. Not to mention, that the fame excellence of faculties which contributes to the improvement of reafon, the fame clearnefs of conception, the fame exactnefs of diftinction, the fame vivacity of apprehenfion, are effential to the operations of true tafte, and are its infallible concomitants. It feldom, or never happens, that a man of fenfe, who has experience in any art, cannot judge of its beauty; and it is no lefs rare to meet with a man, who has a juft tafte, without a found underftanding.

M 2

THUS,

THUS, though the principles of taſte be univerſal, and nearly, if not entirely the ſame in all
men ; yet few are qualified to give judgment on
any work of art, or eſtabliſh their own ſentiment
as the ſtandard of beauty. The organs of internal ſenſation are ſeldom ſo perfect as to allow
the general principles their full play, and produce a feeling correſpondent to thoſe principles.
They either labour under ſome defect, or are
vitiated by ſome diſorder; and by that means,
excite a ſentiment, which may be pronounced
erroneous. When the critic has no delicacy,
he judges without any diſtinction, and is only
affected by the groſſer and more palpable qualities
of the object : The finer touches paſs unnoticed
and diſregarded. Where he is not aided by
practice, his verdict is attended with confuſion
and heſitation. Where no compariſon has been
employed, the moſt frivolous beauties, ſuch as
rather merit the name of defects, are the objects
of his admiration. Where he lies under the influence of prejudice, all his natural ſentiments
are perverted. Where good ſenſe is wanting,
he is not qualified to diſcern the beauties of deſign and reaſoning, which are the higheſt and
moſt excellent. Under ſome or other of theſe

4   imper-

imperfections, the generality of men labour; and hence a true judge in the finer arts is observed, even during the most polished ages, to be so rare a character: Strong sense, united to delicate sentiment, improved by practice, perfected by comparison, and cleared of all prejudice, can alone entitle critics to this valuable character; and the joint verdict of such, wherever they are to be found, is the true standard of taste and beauty.

But where are such critics to be found? By what marks are they to be known? How distinguish them from pretenders? These questions are embarrassing; and seem to throw us back into the same uncertainty, from which, during the course of this dissertation, we have endeavoured to extricate ourselves.

But if we consider the matter aright, these are questions of fact, not of sentiment. Whether any particular person be endowed with good sense and a delicate imagination, free from prejudice, may often be the subject of dispute, and be liable to great discussion and enquiry: But that such a character is valuable and estimable will be agreed by all mankind. Where these

M 3   doubts

doubts occur, men can do no more than in other disputable queſtions, which are ſubmitted to the underſtanding: They muſt produce the beſt arguments, which their invention ſuggeſts to them; they muſt acknowledge a true and deciſive ſtandard to exiſt ſomewhere, to wit, real exiſtence and matter of fact; and they muſt have indulgence to ſuch as differ from them in their appeals to this ſtandard. It is ſufficient for our preſent purpoſe, if we have proved, that the taſte of all individuals is not upon an equal footing, and that ſome men in general, however difficult to be particularly pitched upon, will be acknowledged by univerſal ſentiment to have a preference above others.

But in reality the difficulty of finding, even in particulars, the ſtandard of taſte, is not ſo great as is repreſented. Though in ſpeculation, we may readily avow a certain criterion in ſcience and deny it in ſentiment, the matter is found in practice to be much more hard to aſcertain in the former caſe than in the latter. Theories of abſtract philoſophy, ſyſtems of profound theology have prevailed during one age: In a ſucceſſive period, theſe have been univerſally exploded: Their abſurdity has been detected: Other theo-

ries

ries and fyftems have fupplied their place, which again gave way to their fucceffors: And nothing has been experienced more liable to the revolutions of chance and fafhion than thefe pretended decifions of fcience. The cafe is not the fame with the beauties of eloquence and poetry. Juft expreffions of paffion and nature are fure, after a little time, to gain public vogue, which they maintain for ever. *Ariftotle* and *Plato*, and *Epicurus* and *Defcartes*, may fucceffively yield to each other: But *Terence* and *Virgil* maintain an univerfal, undifputed empire over the minds of men. The abftract philofophy of *Cicero* has loft its credit: The vehemence of his oratory is ftill the object of our admiration.

Though men of delicate tafte are rare, they are eafily to be diftinguifhed in fociety, by the foundnefs of their underftanding and the fuperiority of their faculties above the reft of mankind. The afcendant, which they acquire, gives a prevalence to that lively approbation, with which they receive any productions of genius, and renders it generally predominant. Many men, when left to themfelves, have but a faint and dubious perception of beauty, who yet are capable of relifhing any fine ftroke, which is pointed out to them. Every convert to the ad-

miration

miration of the true poet or orator is the cause of some new conversion. And though prejudices may prevail for a time, they never unite in celebrating any rival to the true genius, but yield at last to the force of nature and just sentiment. And thus though a civilized nation may easily be mistaken in the choice of their admired philosopher, they never have been found long to err in their affection for a favourite epic or tragic author.

But notwithstanding all our endeavours to fix a standard of taste, and reconcile the various apprehensions of men, there still remain two sources of variation, which, tho' they be not sufficient to confound all the boundaries of beauty and deformity, will often serve to vary the degrees of our approbation or blame. The one is the different humours of particular men; the other, the particular manners and opinions of our age and country. The general principles of taste are uniform in human nature: Where men vary in their judgments, some defect or perversion in the faculties may commonly be remarked; proceeding either from prejudice, from want of practice, or want of delicacy; and there is just reason for approving one taste and condemning another. But where there is such a diversity in the internal frame or external situation as is entirely

tirely blamelefs on both fides, and leaves no room to give one the preference above the other; in that cafe a certain diverfity of judgment is unavoidable, and we feek in vain for a ftandard, by which we can reconcile the contrary fentiments.

A young man, whofe paffions are warm, will be more fenfibly touched with amorous and tender images, than a man more advanced in years who takes pleafure in wife and philofophical prefections concerning the conduct of life and moderation of the paffions. At twenty, *Ovid* may be the favourite author; *Horace* at forty; and perhaps *Tacitus* at fifty. Vainly would we, in fuch cafes, endeavour to enter into the fentiments of others, and diveft ourfelves of thofe propenfities, which are natural to us. We chufe our favourite author as we do our friend, from a conformity of humours and difpofitions. Mirth or paffion, fentiment or reflection; which ever of thefe moft predominates in our temper, it gives us a peculiar fympathy with the writer, who refembles us.

ONE perfon is more pleafed with the fublime; another with the tender; a third with raillery. One has a ftrong fenfibility to blemifhes, and is extremely ftudious of correctnefs: Another has

M 5 a more

a more lively feeling of beauties, and pardons twenty abfurdities and defects for one elevated or pathetic ftroke. The ear of this man is entirely turned towards concifenefs and energy; that man is delighted with a copious, rich, and harmonious expreffion. Simplicity is affected by one; ornament by another. Comedy, tragedy, fatire, odes have each their partizans, who prefer that particular fpecies of writing to all others. It is plainly an error in a critic to confine his approbation to one fpecies or ftyle of writing and condemn all the reft. But it is almoft impoffible not to feel a predilection for that which fuits our particular turn and difpofition. Such preferences are innocent and unavoidable, and can never reafonably be the object of difpute, becaufe there is no ftandard, by which they can be decided.

For a like reafon, we are more pleafed with pictures of characters, which refemble fuch as are found in our own age or country, than with thofe which defcribe a different fet of cuftoms. 'Tis not without fome effort, that we reconcile ourfelves to the fimplicity of antient manners, and behold princeffes drawing water from a fpring, and kings and heroes dreffing their own victuals. We may allow in general, that the reprefentation of fuch manners is no fault in the author, nor deformity in the piece; but we are

not

not fo fenfibly touched with them. For this reafon, comedy is not transferred eafily from one age or nation to another. A *Frenchman* or *Eng-lifhman* is not pleafed with the *Andria* of *Terence*, or *Clitia* of *Machiavel*, where the fine lady, upon whom all the play turns, never once appears to the fpectators, but is always kept behind the fcenes, fuitable to the referved humour of the antient *Greeks* and modern *Italians*. A man of learning and reflection can make allowance for thefe peculiarities of manners; but a common audience can never diveft themfelves fo far of their ufual ideas and fentiments as to relifh pictures which no way refemble them.

AND here there occurs a reflection, which may, perhaps, be ufeful in examining the celebrated controverfy concerning antient and modern learning; where we often find the one fide excufing any feeming abfurdity in the antients from the manners of the age, and the others refufing to admit this excufe, or at leaft, admitting it only as an apology for the author, not for the performance. In my opinion, the proper bounds in this fubject have feldom been fixed between the contending parties. Where any innocent peculiarities of manners are reprefented, fuch as thofe abovementioned, they ought cer-

M 6   tainly

tainly to be admitted ; and a man who is fhocked
with them, gives an evident proof of falfe delicacy and refinement. The poets *monument more
durable than brafs*, muft fall to the ground like
common brick or clay, were men to make no
allowance for the continual revolutions of manners and cuftoms, and would admit nothing but
what was fuitable to the prevailing fafhion. Muft
we throw afide the pictures of our anceftors,
becaufe of their ruffs and fardingales ? But where
the ideas of morality and decency alter from one
age to another, and where vicious manners are
defcribed, without being marked with the proper
characters of blame and difapprobation; this
muft be allowed to disfigure the poem, and to be
a real deformity. I cannot, nor is it proper I
fhould, enter into fuch fentiments ; and however
I may excufe the poet, on account of the manners
of his age, I never can relifh the compofition.
The want of humanity and of decency, fo confpicuous in the characters drawn by feveral of
the antient poets, even fometimes by *Homer*
and the *Greek* tragedians, diminifhes confidera-
bly the merit of their noble performances, and
gives modern authors a great advantage over
them. We are not interefted in the fortunes
and fentiments of fuch rough heroes : We are
difpleafed to find the limits of vice and virtue fo

con-

confounded: And whatever indulgence we may give the writer on account of his prejudices, we cannot prevail on ourselves to enter into his sentiments, or bear an affection to characters, which we plainly discover to be blameable.

THE case is not the same with moral principles as with speculative opinions of any kind. These are in continual flux and revolution. The son embraces a different system from the father. Nay, there scarce is any man, who can boast of great constancy and uniformity in this particular. Whatever speculative errors may be found in the polite writings of any age or country, they detract but little from the value of those compositions. There needs but a certain turn of thought or imagination to make us enter into all the opinions, which then prevailed, and relish the sentiments or conclusions derived from them. But a very violent effort is requisite to change our judgment of manners, and excite sentiments of approbation or blame, love or hatred, different from those to which the mind from long custom has been familiarized. And where a man is confident of the rectitude of that moral standard, by which he judges, he is justly jealous of it, and will not pervert the sentiments of his heart for a moment, in complaisance to any writer whatever.

OF

OF all fpeculative errors, thofe which regard religion, are the moft excufable in compofitions of genius; nor is it ever permitted to judge of the civility or wifdom of any people, or even of fingle perfons, by the grofinefs or refinement of their theological principles. The fame good fenfe, that directs men in the ordinary occurrences of life, is not hearkened to in religious matters, which are fuppofed to be placed entirely above the cognizance of human reafon. Upon this account, all the abfurdities of the pagan fyftem of theology muft be overlooked by every critic, who would pretend to form a juft notion of antient poetry; and our pofterity, in their turn, muft have the fame indulgence to their forefathers. No religious principles can ever be imputed as a fault to any poet, while they remain merely principles, and take not fuch ftrong poffeffion of his heart, as to lay him under the imputation of *bigotry* or *fuperftition*. Where that happens, they confound the fentiments of morality and alter the natural boundaries of vice and virtue. They are therefore eternal blemifhes, according to the principle abovementioned; nor are the prejudices and falfe opinions of the age fufficient to juftify them.

'TIS

'Tis effential to the *Roman* catholic religion to infpire a violent hatred to every other worfhip, and reprefent all pagans, mahometans, and heretics as the objects of divine wrath and vengeance. Such fentiments, though they are in reality extremely blameable, are confidered as virtues by the zealots of that communion, and are reprefented in their tragedies and epic poems as a kind of divine heroifm. This bigotry has disfigured two very fine tragedies of the *French* theatre, *Polieucte* and *Athalia* ; where an intemperate zeal for particular modes of worfhip is fet off with all the pomp imaginable, and forms the predominant character of the heroes. " What " is this," fays the heroic *Joad* to *Jofabet*, finding her in difcourfe with *Mattan*, the prieft of *Baal*, " Does the daughter of *David* fpeak to " this traitor? Are you not afraid, left the earth " fhould open and pour forth flames to devour " you both? Or that thefe holy walls fhould fall " and crufh you together? What is his purpofe? " Why comes that enemy of God hither to poi- " fon the air, which we breath, with his horrid " prefence?" Such fentiments are received with great applaufe on the theatre of *Paris*; but at *London* the fpectators would be full as much pleafed to hear *Achilles* tell *Agamemnon*, that he

I   was

was a dog in his forehead and a deer in his heart, or *Jupiter* threaten *Juno* with a found drubbing, if she will not be quiet.

RELIGIOUS principles are also a blemish in any polite composition, when they rise up to superstition, and intrude themselves into every sentiment, however remote from any connection with religion. 'Tis no excuse for the poet, that the customs of his country had burthened life with so many religious ceremonies and observances, that no part of it was exempt from that yoak. It must be for ever ridiculous in *Petrarch* to compare his mistress, *Laura*, to *Jesus Christ*. Nor is it less ridiculous in that agreeable libertine, *Boccace*, very seriously to give thanks to God Almighty, and the ladies, for their assistance in defending him against his enemies.

F I N I S.

E R R A T A.

P. 7. L. 13. r. *set.* P. 9. L. 12. r. *be buried.* P. 42. L. 5. r. *conditions.* P. 70. L. 4. from the Bottom, read *foretel the issue.* P. 116. L. 16. read *corrupt.*

ESSAYS ON SUICIDE and
THE IMMORTALITY
OF THE SOUL

INTRODUCTION

David Hume had intended to include his two essays 'Of Suicide' and 'Of the Immortality of the Soul' in a volume of longer essays that he published in 1757; the volume that eventually emerged was called *Four Dissertations*, but it did not contain either of these essays, which were not published in English in his lifetime. He wrote to his printer, Andrew Millar, on 12 June 1755, that he had 'four short Dissertations' which he wanted to publish; they were 'The Natural History of Religion', another 'of the Passions; a third of Tragedy; a fourth, some Considerations previous to Geometry & Natural Philosophy'.[1] The last item was never actually printed, as Hume had been advised by Lord Stanhope 'that either there was some Defect in the Argument or in its perspicuity' (*Letters*, II, 253). Having decided not to print this essay, Hume then proposed to add the essays on suicide and the immortality of the soul, and Millar actually printed the work that would have been *Five Dissertations*.

Millar apparently printed several 'proof' copies of this volume; none has survived, but proof copies of the two relevant essays, with corrections in Hume's hand, are now in the National Library of Scotland. Hume eventually suppressed these two essays out of his 'abundant Prudence' (*Letters*, II, 253), and it is

---

[1] *The Letters of David Hume*, ed. J.Y.T Greig (Oxford: The Clarendon Press, 1932), I, 223. Hereafter cited in text as *Letters*, with relevant volume and page numbers.

probable that he had some trepidation about the furore the two essays would have created. For one thing, the irascible William Warburton had learned about the proposed publication and had obtained a copy of the suppressed volume which he found 'as abandoned of all virtuous principle, as of all philosophic force' and added that Hume was probably afraid of prosecution.[2] A prosecution was probably mooted, and given the hostility that Millar had met from his publication of the collected works of Henry St John, Viscount Bolingbroke, in 1754, he may have felt that publishing Hume's two inflammatory essays would have created more problems with civil and ecclesiastical authority than he could cope with. In any case, he and Hume seem mutually to have agreed to suppress the essays. William Rose, in his review of the two essays in *The Monthly Review* confirmed that 'a noble Lord, still living, threatened to prosecute Mr. Millar', and the frightened Millar persuaded Hume to cancel the essays and substitute some others.[3]

Because Millar had allowed various people to see and to retain copies of the trial printing of *Five Dissertations*, it was inevitable that, despite his and Hume's decision to suppress the two objectionable essays, the works would survive. James Beattie, in a

---

[2] From a letter written on 14 February 1756 to the Reverend Thomas Balguy and printed in Ernest Campbell Mossner, *The Life of David Hume* (Oxford: The Clarendon Press, 1980; 2nd ed.), p. 323. Mossner's discussion here and in his essay, 'Hume's *Four Dissertations*: An Essay in Biography and Bibliography', in *Modern Philology*, XLVIII (1950), 37-57, provides the best account of this troublesome printing history, and I have relied on Mossner's information for my account of *Four Dissertations*. References to Mossner's *Life* are cited in text hereafter.

[3] *The Monthly Review* (London: R. Griffiths, 1784), LXXX, 427; the review appears in the June issue.

letter of 17 December 1776, to Mrs. Elizabeth Montagu, noted that 'a few copies, however, got abroad; one of which is in the hands of a Gentleman in England'. By some means or another, the two essays came to the attention of a French publisher, who brought them out in a French translation in 1770, *Recueil Philosophique ou Mélange de Pièces sur la Religion & la Morale*, as 'Dissertation sur l'immortalité de l'âme' and 'Dissertation sur le suicide'. The volume was probably edited by Jacques André Naigenon and the translations were by Baron Paul-Henry Thiry d'Holbach' (Mossner, *Life*, p. 330). Shortly after Hume's death in 1776, an edition simply entitled *Two Essays* was published in London in 1777; neither author's name nor publisher's identity appeared on the title-page, and Hume's name was put only to the edition here reprinted.

Most readers in the eighteenth century would probably have regarded the essays as inflammatory, and Hume had barely touched on the topic in his other works. So far as I can tell, he used the word 'suicide' in his published works only in this essay. In the section called 'A Dialogue' at the end of his *Enquiry concerning the Principles of Morals*, he wrote that 'an Athenian man of merit' might conclude his life by a 'desperate act of self-murder' and later in the same 'Dialogue' asks, 'Have the gods forbid self-murder? An Athenian allows, that it ought to be forborn. Has the Deity permitted it? A Frenchman allows, that death is preferable to pain and infamy'.[4] Since one of the purposes of 'A Dialogue' is to illustrate different mores and morals in the behaviour

---

[4] David Hume, *Enquiries concerning Human Understanding and concerning Principles of Morals*, ed. L.A. Selby-Bigge, revised P.H. Nidditch (Oxford: Clarendon Press, 1975; 3rd ed.), pp. 329, 335.

of people living in other lands, Hume simply records an attitude that would perhaps be at odds with sentiment in Britain. Otherwise, it is not a subject that engages his attention in his philosophical writings to any great degree.

In view of Hume's endorsement of the moral efficacy of taking one's own life, it is perhaps worth quoting in detail his one recorded documentation of it. When he was acting as secretary to Lieutenant-General James St Clair and in France, he had direct experience of a man's suicide. Writing to his brother John Home of Ninewells, on 4 October 1746, he recorded the death of one Major Alexander Forbes. It is worth quoting the passage at length as it perhaps gives some context, or at least some personal dimension, to Hume's discussion of suicide, and the disbelief, loathing, and, often, sanctimoniousness that it elicited:

> He was, & was esteem'd a Man of the greatest Sense, Honour, Modesty, Mildness & Equality of Temper in the World. His Learning was very great for a man of any Profession, but a Prodigy for a Soldier. His Bravery had been try'd & was unquestion'd. He had exhausted himself with Fatigue & Hunger for two days; so that he was oblig'd to leave the Camp, & come to our Quarters, where I took the utmost Care of him, as there was a great Friendship betwixt us. He express'd vast Anxiety that he shou'd be oblig'd to leave his Duty, & Fear, least his Honour should suffer by it. I endeavourd to quiet his Mind as much as possible, & thought I had left him tolerably compos'd at Night; but returning to his Room early next Morning, I found him with small

Remains of Life, wallowing in his own Blood, with the Arteries of his Arm cut asunder. I immediately sent for a Surgeon, got a Bandage ty'd to his Arm, & recover'd him entirely to his Senses & Understanding. He liv'd above four & twenty hours after, & I had several Conversations with him. Never a man exprest a more steady Contempt of Life nor more determind philosophical Principles, suitable to his Exit. He beg'd of me to unloosen his Bandage & hasten his Death, as the last Act of Friendship I coud show him: But alas! we live not in Greek or Roman Times. He told me, that he knew, he coud not live a few Days: But if he did, as soon as he became his own Master, he wou'd take a more expeditious Method, which none of his Friends cou'd prevent. I dye, says he, from a Jealousy of Honour perhaps too delicate; and do you think, if it were possible for me to live, I woud now consent to it, to be a Gazing-Stock to the foolish World. I am too far advanc'd to return. And if Life was odious to me before, it must be doubly so at present. He became delirious a few Hours before he dy'd. He had wrote a short Letter to his Brother above ten hours before he cut his Arteries. This we found on the Table (*Letters*, I, 97 - 98).

What effect this experience had on Hume (he was then thirty-five years old) can only be conjectured, since Hume simply records the death and reveals only by implication his attitude and feelings. In later years, he did express dismay when his intimate friend, the Comtesse de Boufflers, threatened, as she had on several occasions, to commit suicide. Even here

Hume cannot seem to refer to the act; writing to her on 14 July 1764, he regrets that she is not happy: 'If there are any obstacles to your happiness, I should wish they were of a nature that could be removed; and that they admitted of some other remedy than the one you sometimes mention, on which I cannot think without terror' (*Letters* I, 452).

The views that Hume put forward in 'Of Suicide' were at odds with both ecclesiastical tradition and the law: Sir William Blackstone in his *Commentaries on the Laws of England* asserted that 'the law of England wisely and religiously considers, that no man hath a power to destroy life, but by commission from God' and held that anyone committing suicide, or attempting to do so, was 'guilty of a double offence; one spiritual, in invading the prerogative of the Almighty and rushing into his immediate presence uncalled for; the other temporal, against the king...'.[5] In Scotland, John Erskine took the attitude that suicide was 'as truly criminal as the murder of one's neighbour'. To take one's own life was to disobey God's law as well as man's and therefore it was 'a species of murder, [which] ought to be governed by the common rules of murder'.[6] So, Hume's willingness to suppress the essay during his lifetime was indeed prudent, as he could have been prosecuted for seeming to endorse not just the utility of suicide, but its morality, if not its legality. His own feelings seem ambivalent: on the one hand, he regretted that 'we live not in Greek or Roman Times', from which it

---

[5] Sir William Blackstone, *Commentaries on the Laws of England* (Oxford: The Clarendon Press, 1765-1769), IV, xiv, 189.

[6] John Erskine, *A Treatise of the Law of Scotland* (Edinburgh: John Bell, 1773), p. 717; IV, iv, 46.

is not unreasonable to infer that he would have agreed with Forbes that it would have been an act of friendship in helping him to hasten a life that was clearly going to end very soon; on the other hand, the possible suicide of the Comtesse de Boufflers filled him with 'terror'.

The concept of the immortality of the soul was perhaps not quite so incendiary as that of suicide, and Hume actually addressed the issue in the *Treatise of Human Nature*. There, he argued that people did not really believe in a 'future state' simply because the concept was impossible to relate to our experience or comprehension. Hume's qualification is, however, interesting: some had indeed imprinted upon their minds by repetition and cool reflection what the concept of a future state means, but otherwise 'there scarce are any, who believe the immortality of the soul with a true and establish'd judgment; such as is deriv'd from the testimony of travellers and historians'.[7] Hume returned to the topic in Section 11 of his *Enquiry concerning Human Understanding*, 'Of a Particular Providence and a Future State', the only section of the work to be written in dialogue form, undoubtedly as a means of attributing to a 'friend who loves sceptical paradoxes' some of the heterodox views advanced in the argument. But Hume's relentlessly empirical methodology and sceptical psychology reduce the belief in the immortality of the soul to a rather tawdry passion. Since Bishop Joseph Butler had put forward very powerful and very popular arguments about the immortality of the soul and a future life in his frequently-reprinted *Analogy of*

---

[7] David Hume, *A Treatise of Human Nature*, ed. L.A. Selby-Bigge, revised P. H. Nidditch (Oxford: The Clarendon Press, 1987; 2nd ed.), pp. 114-115; I, iii, ix.

Religion (1736), Hume's dismissal of the concept was unlikely to have met with much eagerness by believers.

Contemporary reviews were not very enthusiastic about the essays. The notice in *The Critical Review* for 1783 described them as consisting of some 'detached thoughts and arguments', calling the book a 'little manual of infidelity'. Although Hume's aim in the essays is clearly limited and his tone moderate and calm, the reviewer attributes to Hume an attempt to support 'mean and malignant' principles, which would have a tendency to destroy society, to undermine religion, to devalue human nature and its ambitions, to make the whole of creation gloomy and miserable, and, finally, 'to frustrate our sublimest views and expectations'. Even if Hume's arguments were convincing, which the reviewer finds unlikely since none of the wisest men in all ages have embraced, much less supported such views, what would be the effect but the 'wretched prospect of annihilation?' And if Hume is wrong, of course, the consequences might be inconceivable, which is a reversal of Hume's own argument. The reviewer makes only a passing comment on the notes, merely alluding to the assertion in the Preface that they are intended to expose Hume's sophistry.[8]

The reviewer in the *Critical Review* concentrated almost exclusively on Hume's essays, but William Rose, in the *Monthly Review*, had some comments for the editor as well; Rose does not call into question the 'uprightness and benevolence' of the editor's intentions but cannot 'applaud his judgment, or think it equal to his zeal'. Rose argues that in publishing

---

[8] *The Critical Review* (London: A. Hamilton, 1783), LVI, 475.

the essays only in order to refute them, the editor just
gives new life and currency to the 'poison' to which he
is trying to provide an 'antidote'. Hume's most ardent
admirers do not think the essays do his reputation any
good and they do not need to be elaborately
discredited by the editor, since they 'carry their own
confutation with them'. Rose's method of refutation,
however, is rather light-weight. Citing some of
Hume's arguments and comments, he asks what
would happen were a 'drunken libertine' to articulate
such 'nauseous stuff'? His fellow drunkards might
excuse him, but 'men of plain sense and decent
manners' would treat the views only with contempt.
The anonymous editor seems to do Hume the
courtesy of taking his views seriously and opposes
them seriously, but Rose asserts somewhat
condescendingly that combatting opinions or views
such as those advanced in Hume's essays 'requires no
great abilities', and grudgingly acknowledges that the
editor's notes 'contain some pertinent and judicious
observations'.[9]

The notice in the August, 1784 issue of the
Gentleman's Magazine confirms, or at least repeats in
substance, Rose's account of the suppression in the
1750s of the essays and takes very much Rose's line
about the wisdom of republishing noxious essays.
Those who vend poison cannot in any way justify
their efforts: those who 'swallow the poison' may not
accept the antidote, 'even were it stronger than that
here administered'. The reviewer then draws
attention to the next book reviewed in the journal,
Bishop George Horne's *Letters on Infidelity* (1784)
which contains 'a much better antidote than any here

[9] *The Monthly Review*, LXXX, 427-8.

prescribed'[10]. The 'poison' analogy occurred to other writers; even James Boswell in his journal entry for 25 January 1780 referred to Hume's *Dialogues concerning Natural Religion* as 'posthumous poison'.[11]

Bishop George Horne in his comment on various of Hume's writings in his *Letters on Infidelity* also kept the 'poison' analogy before his readers and attempts virtually a line-by-line refutation of the essay on suicide. Horne mentions Hume's opening tribute to philosophy as a remedy for superstition but asks if the 'remedy [may not] prove worse than the disease?' Throughout the three letters (4, 5, and 6) in which Horne comments on the essay, he maintains a judicious, analytic tone, and while many of his observations derive from Christian theology, others are as empirical as Hume's arguments. At one stage, indeed, he seems to agree that there may be circumstances in which suicide is justifiable. He refers to some 'Christian virgins' who chose to kill themselves rather than 'suffer the violation of their purity by their ruffian persecutors'. In so doing, they had obtained the 'suffrage of the Fathers', since theirs was a case that did not fit the general proscription against suicide. What is of particular interest is his assertion they 'we cannot readily blame those, who to preserve their honour, despised their life'. This is very much the argument that Hume's friend, Captain Forbes, had made to Hume. The virgins had committed one sin in order to avoid a greater one, though, as Horne adds

---

[10] *The Gentleman's Magazine* (London: D. Henry, 1784), LIV, 607.

[11] *Boswell, Laird of Auchinlech, 1778-1782*, ed. Joseph W. Reed and Frederick A. Pottle (New York: McGraw-Hill, 1977), p. 173.

parenthetically 'as their will would not have been concerned, they were perhaps mistaken'. They 'destroyed the temple' in order to prevent its profanation.[12] Horne's failure to pursue this argument, and to think of instances or contexts in which suicide would be preferable to some other 'sin' or immoral act, suggests that he may have seen possible merit in Hume's argument, but not in the way that Hume presented it.

Horne's intellectual honesty is in marked contrast to most of the attitudes taken towards Hume's essay, and he enlivens his discussion with witty, if irrelevant, scholia to Hume's text. For example, Hume compares diverting the Nile or the Danube to diverting a few ounces of blood (p. 12) and then implicitly wonders where the crime is. Horne agrees that it might not be a crime to divert the rivers but that the inhabitants of countries benefitting from the rivers might object: 'But I wish you had been so employed, instead of writing essays in defense of suicide' (*Letters on Infidelity*, p. 89). Hume doubtless would have enjoyed Horne's wit but might very well have responded by asking if those living in the countries through which the Nile and Danube flowed would have felt the same way. Hume's argument at this point is, one cannot help feeling, sophistical at best, and the analogy he suggests is misleading and does his argument more harm than good.

Although it was the essay on suicide that attracted most of the refutations and rebuttals, some responders did take notice of the other essay. The most obvious of these was the anonymous *Essay on the Immortality*

---

[12] George Horne, *Letters on Infidelity* (Oxford: The Clarendon Press, 1784), pp. 73, 123. Further references given in text.

of the Soul; Shewing The Fallacy and Malignity of a Sceptical one, lately published, together with such another on Suicide, and both ascribed, by the Editor to The Late David Hume, Esq. At its best, this performance is little more than assertion and hyperbole, but the author's justification invokes the poison analogy in extravagant language:

> The Poison is of such a refined, insinuating, and dangerous nature; and so easily, and generally procured, and administered; that every well-wisher to the Community, who has the least knack at this sort of Chymistry, ought to exert his skill in the composition of Antidotes of this kind, on such an inviting and urgent occasion; especially when we consider how much the present reigning taste for dissipation and profligacy favours the various and numerous Poisoners of the mind, in the administration of their alluring and fatal Nostrums.[13]

The evidence for such a taste for dissipation and profligacy is rather hard to find in the literature of the 1770s and 1780s. The author puts forward his rejection of Hume's argument against the immortality of the soul in a heavily repetitive style. Asserting a maxim that he attributes to 'natural philosophy', that nature does nothing in vain, he argues that human beings are distinguished by a love of happiness and that if we do not find happiness in this life, we must, as a matter of course, find it in a future life, since nature does nothing in vain. This argument he

---

[13] *Essay on the Immortality of the Soul; Shewing The Fallacy and Malignity of a Sceptical one, lately published, together with such another on Suicide, and both ascribed, by the Editor to The Late David Hume, Esq.* (London: Printed for the Author, 1784), pp. xii-xiii. Hereafter cited in text.

regards as having 'decisive coherency and energy' (p. 38).

In general, the reviews and responses to Hume's two suppressed essays reveal writers who do not seem either equipped or prepared to deal with either essay on its own merits, with the exception of the anonymous editor of the essays; and even the editor's notes often lack any semblance of argument. Most of the criticism seems to assert that Hume's views are simply repugnant to the vast majority of mankind, that no one could consider them seriously, or that they would subvert the foundations of society and religion. Equally, the tone of these rejoinders is often one of fear, fear of what would happen to society were the restraints imposed by our expectation of a future life to be discarded, fear of what would happen to religion and society if suicide became a plausible means of ending one's life. It is difficult to tell if Horne's somewhat jokey wish that Hume had spent his time diverting the course of two rivers rather than writing essays in favour of suicide and the mortality of the soul is genuine or not. It is an amusing riposte to one of the weakest sections of Hume's argument, and it may be that the weakness of the argument required nothing more than a jest to illustrate its feebleness.

While Hume would probably have enjoyed the mild controversy that the essays created, he might have been rather less amused by the inclusion of extracts from one of Jean-Jacques Rousseau's novels in the same volume as his two essays. Hume had befriended Rousseau in 1765, but, inevitably, found himself at odds with the deeply suspicious, if not paranoid Rousseau, and their quarrel became public.[14] The extracts are from Rousseau's *La Nouvelle Héloïse*, which was published early in 1761. It was translated almost immediately into English by William Kenrick as *Eloisa: Or, a Series of Original Letters* (London: R. Griffiths, 1761). This translation, like the original, was frequently reprinted. The anonymous editor of Hume's two essays reproduces, as the concluding pieces in the volume, letters 114 and 115 from *Eloisa* (II, 253 - 268, and 268 - 279), with only slight amendments to Kenrick's translation.

As it happens, Hume had read *La Nouvelle Héloïse* (for that matter, he had probably read all of Rousseau's published work before he met him). Hugh Blair had apparently asked Hume to find out from Rousseau whether the story was based on reality. Writing to Blair on 25 March 1766, Hume reported that he had indeed asked Rousseau and was told that the story 'had some general and distant Resemblance to Reality'. Even more interesting is Hume's assessment of the novel: 'I think this Work his Masterpiece.' Hume's enthusiasm for the work even led to him having one of the volumes on his table when Rousseau came to call, at least according to Rousseau (*Letters*, II, 28, 389n.). So, an inevitable irony in literary history emerges: Hume's two suppressed essays were linked after his death with extracts from the work he most admired from the pen of a man whom he came cordially to detest. While Hume might have been entertained by some of the hostility

---

[14] See Mossner's *Life of David Hume*, pp. 507-532 for the authoritative account of the dispute. Jerome Christensen in *Practicing Enlightenment: Hume and the Foundation of a Literary Career* (Madison, Wisconsin: The University of Wisconsin Press, 1987), pp. 243-273, has a different, if somewhat bizarre, interpretation of the dispute.

and humour in the responses to his two essays, he would not have liked being memorialized by the implicit refutation that the extracts from Rousseau's novel were supposed to effect.

John Valdimir Price
Honorary Fellow
University of Edinburgh
1992

E S S A Y S

ON

S U I C I D E,

AND

THE IMMORTALITY

OF THE

S O U L,

ASCRIBED TO THE LATE

D A V I D H U M E, Esq.

Never before publifhed.

With REMARKS, intended as an Antidote to the
Poifon contained in thefe Performances,

BY THE EDITOR.

TO WHICH IS ADDED,

TWO LETTERS ON SUICIDE,

FROM ROSSEAU'S ELOISA.

L O N D O N:

Printed for M. SMITH; and fold by the Bookfellers in Piccadilly,
Fleet-ftreet, and Paternofter-row.

1783.

(Price 3 s. 6 d. fewed.)

PREFACE.

THESE two Essays on *Suicide* and *the Immortality of the Soul*, though not published in any edition of his works, are generally attributed to the late ingenious Mr. Hume.

The well-known contempt of this eminent philosopher for the common convictions of mankind, raised an apprehension of the contents from the very title of these pieces. But the celebrity of the author's name, renders them, notwithstanding, in some degree objects of great curiosity.

Owing to this circumstance, a few copies have been clandestinely circulated, at a large price, for some time, but without any comment. The very mystery attending this mode of selling them, made them more an object of request than they would otherwise have been.

The

The prefent publication comes abroad under no fuch reftraint, and poffeffes very fuperior advantages.   The *Notes* annexed are intended to expofe the fophiftry contained in
the original Effays, and may fhew how little
we have to fear from the adverfaries of thefe
great truths, from the pitiful figure which e-
ven Mr. Hume makes in thus violently exhauft-
ing his laft ftrength in an abortive attempt to
traduce or difcredit them.

The two very mafterly Letters from the E-
loifa of Roffeau on the fubject of *Suicide*, have
been much celebrated, and we hope will be
confidered as materially increafing the value
of this curious collection.

The admirers of *Mr. Hume* will be pleafed
with feeing the remains of a favourite author
refcued in this manner from that oblivion to
which the prejudices of his countrymen had,
in all appearance, configned them; and even
the religious part of mankind have fome reafon
of triumph from the ftriking inftance here given of truth's fuperiority to error, even when
error has all the advantage of an elegant genius, and a great literary reputation to recommend it.

M.

ESSAY

E S S A Y   I.

On *S U I C I D E.*

ONE confiderable advantage that arifes
from Philofophy, confifts in the fovereign
antidote which it affords to fuperftition and
falfe religion.   All other remedies againft
that peftilent diftemper are vain, or at leaft
uncertain.   Plain good fenfe and the practice of the world, which alone ferve moft
purpofes of life, are here found ineffectu -
al : Hiftory as well as daily experience furnifh inftances of men endowed with the

ftrong-ſtrongeſt capacity for buſineſs and affairs, who have all their lives crouched under ſlavery to the groſſeſt ſuperſtition. Even gaiety and ſweetneſs of temper, which infuſe a balm into every other wound, afford no remedy to ſo virulent a poiſon ; as we may particularly obſerve of the fair ſex, who tho' commonly poſſeſt of theſe rich preſents of nature, feel many of their joys blaſted by this importunate intruder. But when ſound Philoſophy has once gained poſſeſſion of the mind, ſuperſtition is effectually excluded, and one may fairly affirm that her triumph over this enemy is more complete than over moſt of the vices and imperfections incident to human nature. Love or anger, ambition or avarice, have their root in the temper and affections, which the ſoundeſt reaſon is ſcarce ever able fully to correct, but ſuperſtition being founded on falſe opinion, muſt immediately vaniſh when true philoſophy has inſpired juſter ſentiments of ſuperior powers. The conteſt is here more equal between the diſtemper and the medicine,

cine, and nothing can hinder the latter from
proving effectual but its being falfe and fo-
phifticated.

It will here be fuperfluous to magnify
the merits of Philofophy by difplaying the
pernicious tendency of that vice of which it
cures the human mind. (1) The fuperftitious man fays Tully * is miferable in
every fcene, in every incident in life ; even
fleep itfelf, which banifhes all other cares
of unhappy mortals, affords to him matter of
new terror ; while he examines his dreams,
and finds in thofe vifions of the night prog-
noftications of future calamities. I may add
that tho' death alone can put a full period to
his mifery, he dares not fly to this refuge,
but ftill prolongs a miferable exiftence from
a vain fear left he offend his Maker, by u-
fing the power, with which that beneficent
being has endowed him. The prefents of
God and nature are ravifhed from us by this

* De Divin. lib. ii.

　　　　　　　cruel

cruel enemy, and notwithſtanding that one ſtep would remove us from the regions of pain and ſorrow, her menaces ſtill chain us down to a hated being which ſhe herſelf chiefly contributes to render miſerable.

'Tis obſerved by ſuch as have been re-duced by the calamities of life to the neceſ-ſity of employing this fatal remedy, that if the unſeaſonable care of their friends de-prive them of that ſpecies of Death which they propoſed to themſelves, they ſeldom venture upon any other, or can ſummon up ſo much reſolution a ſecond time as to exe-cute their purpoſe. So great is our horror of death, that when it preſents itſelf under any form, beſides that to which a man has endeavoured to reconcile his imagination, it acquires new terrors and overcomes his feeble courage : But when the menaces of ſuperſtition are joined to this natural timidity, no wonder it quite deprives men of all power over their lives, ſince even many pleaſures and enjoyments,

to

to which we are carried by a ſtrong propenſity, are torn from us by this inhuman tyrant. Let us here endeavour to reſtore men
to their native liberty, by examining all
the common arguments againſt Suicide, and
ſhewing that that action may be free from
every imputation of guilt or blame, according to the ſentiments of all the antient philoſophers. (2)

If Suicide be criminal, it muſt be a
tranſgreſſion of our duty either to God,
our neighbour, or ourſelves.—To prove
that ſuicide is no tranſgreſſion of our duty to
God, the following conſiderations may
perhaps ſuffice. In order to govern the
material world, the almighty Creator has
eſtabliſhed general and immutable laws, by
which all bodies, from the greateſt planet
to the ſmalleſt particle of matter, are
maintained in their proper ſphere and function. To govern the animal world, he
has endowed all living creatures with bodily and mental powers; with ſenſes, paſſions,

fions, appetites, memory, and judgment,
by which they are impelled or regulated
in that courfe of life to which they are deftined. Thefe two diftinct principles of the
material and animal world, continually
encroach upon each other, and mutually re-
tard or forward each others operation. The
powers of men and of all other animals are
reftrained and directed by the nature and
qualities of the furrounding bodies, and
the modifications and actions of thefe bodies are inceffantly altered by the operation
of all animals. Man is ftopt by rivers in
his paffage over the furface of the earth;
and rivers, when properly directed, lend
their force to the motion of machines,
which ferve to the ufe of man. But tho'
the provinces of the material and animal
powers are not kept entirely feperate, there
refults from thence no difcord or diforder in
the creation; on the contrary, from the
mixture, union, and contraft of all the various powers of inanimate bodies and living creatures, arifes that fympathy, harmony,

mony, and proportion, which affords the
fureſt argument of ſupreme wiſdom. The
providence of the Deity appears not immediately in any operation, but governs every
thing by thoſe general and immutable
laws, which have been eſtabliſhed from the
beginning of time. All events, in one
ſenſe, may be pronounced the action of the
Almighty, they all proceed from thoſe
powers with which he has endowed his
creatures. A houſe which falls by its
own weight, is not brought to ruin by his
providence, more than one deſtroyed by
the hands of men ; nor are the human faculties leſs his workmanſhip, than the laws
of motion and gravitation. When the
paſſions play, when the judgment dictates,
when the limbs obey ; this is all the operation of God, and upon theſe animate principles, as well as upon the inanimate, has he
eſtabliſhed the goverment of the univerſe.
Every event is alike important in the eyes of
that infinite being, who takes in at one
glance the moſt diſtant regions of ſpace, and
re-

remoteſt periods of time.   There is no e-
vent, however important to us, which he
has exempted from the general laws that
govern the univerſe, or which he has peculiarly reſerved for his own immediate action and operation. The revolution of ſtates
and empires depends upon the ſmalleſt caprice or paſſion of ſingle men ;   and the
lives of men are ſhortened or extended by
the ſmalleſt accident of air or diet, ſun-
ſhine or tempeſt.   Nature ſtill continues her progreſs and operation; and
if general laws be ever broke by particular volitions of the Deity, 'tis after a
manner which entirely eſcapes human obſervation.   As on the one hand, the elements and other inanimate parts of the creation carry on their action without regard
to the particular intereſt and ſituation of
men ; ſo men are entruſted to their own
judgment and diſcretion in the various
ſhocks of matter, and may employ every faculty with which they are endowed, in order to provide for their eaſe, happineſs, or
pre-

prefervation. What is the meaning then of that principle, that a man who tired of life, and hunted by pain and mifery, brave-ly overcomes all the natural terrors of death, and makes his efcape from this cru-el fcene : that fuch a man I fay, has incur-red the indignation of his Creator by en-croaching on the office of divine providence, and difturbing the order of the univerfe ? fhall we affert that the Almighty has refer-ved to himfelf in any peculiar manner the difpofal of the lives of men, and has not fubmitted that event, in common with others, to the general laws by which the univerfe is governed ? This is plainly falfe; the lives of men depend upon the fame laws as the lives of all other animals ; and thefe are fubjected to the general laws of matter and motion. The fall of a tower, or the infufion of a poifon, will deftroy a man equally with the meaneft creature ; an in-undation fweeps away every thing with-out diftinction that comes within the reach of its fury. Since therefore the lives of men

are for ever dependant on the general laws
of matter and motion, is a man's difposing
of his life criminal, becaufe in every cafe
it is criminal to encroach upon thefe laws,
or difturb their operation ? But this feems
abfurd ; all animals are entrufted to their
own prudence and fkill for their conduct in
the world, and have full authority as far as
their power extends, to alter all the operations of nature. Without the excercife of this
authority they could not fubfift a moment ;
every action, every motion of a man, inno-
vates on the order of fome parts of matter,
and diverts from their ordinary courfe the
general laws of motion. Putting together, therefore, thefe conclufions, we find
that human life depends upon the general
laws of matter and motion, and that it is
no encroachment on the office of providence to difturb or alter thefe general
laws : Has not every one, of confequence,
the free difpofal of his own life ? And may
he not lawfully employ that power with
which nature has endowed him ? In order

to

to deftroy the evidence of this conclufion,
we muft fhew a reafon why this particular
cafe is excepted; is it becaufe human life
is of fuch great importance, that 'tis a pre-
fumption for human prudence to difpofe of
it ? But the life of a man is of no greater
importance to the univerfe than that of an
oyfter. And were it of ever fo great importance, the order of human nature has
actually fubmitted it to human prudence,
and reduced us to a neceffity, in every incident, of determining concerning it.—
Were the difpofal of human life fo much
referved as the peculiar province of the
Almighty, that it were an encroachment on
his right, for men to difpofe of their own
lives ; it would be equally criminal to act
for the prefervation of life as for its deftruction. If I turn afide a ftone which is falling upon my head, I difturb the courfe of
nature, and I invade the peculiar province
of the Almighty, by lengthening out my
life beyond the period which by the general laws of matter and motion he had affigned it. (3)

C 2   A hair,

A hair, a fly, an insect is able to destroy
this mighty being whose life is of such importance. Is it an absurdity to suppose
that human prudence may lawfully dispose
of what depends on such insignificant
causes ? It would be no crime in me to divert the *Nile* or *Danube* from its course,
were I able to effect such purposes. Where
then is the crime of turning a few ounces
of blood from their natural channel ?—Do
you imagine that I repine at Providence
or curse my creation, because I go out of
life, and put a period to a being, which,
were it to continue, would render me miserable ? Far be such sentiments from me ; I
am only convinced of a matter of fact,
which you yourself acknowledge possible,
that human life may be unhappy, and that
my existence, if further prolonged, would
become ineligible ; but I thank Providence, both for the good which I have already enjoyed, and for the power with
which I am endowed of escaping the ill that
threatens

threatens me. * To you it belongs to repine
at providence, who foolifhly imagine that
you have no fuch power, and who muft ftill
prolong a hated life, tho' loaded with pain
and ficknefs, with fhame and poverty———
Do not you teach, that when any ill befals
me, tho' by the malice of my enemies, I
ought to be refigned to providence, and
that the actions of men are the operations
of the Almighty as much as the actions of
inanimate beings ? When I fall upon my
own fword, therefore, I receive my death
equally from the hands of the Deity as if
it had proceeded from a lion, a precipice,
or a fever. The fubmiffion which you require to providence, in every calamity that
befals me, excludes not human fkill and induftry, if poffible by their means I can a-
void or efcape the calamity : And why
may I not employ one remedy as well as
another ?—If my life be not my own, it
were criminal for me to put it in danger, as
well

* Agamus Dei gratias, quad nemo in vita teneri poteft.
SEN. Epift. 12.

well as to difpofe of it ; nor could one
man deferve the appellation of *hero*, whom
glory or friendfhip tranfports into the greateft dangers, and another merit the reproach
of *wretch* or *mifcreant* who puts a period to
his life, from the fame or like motives.—
—There is no being, which poffeffes any
power or faculty, that it receives not from
its Creator, nor is there any one, which by
ever fo irregular an action can encroach
upon the plan of his providence, or diforder the univerfe. Its operations are his
works equally with that chain of events
which it invades, and which ever principle
prevails, we may for that very reafon conclude it to be moft favoured by him. Be
it animate, or inanimate, rational, or irrational, 'tis all a cafe : its power is ftill derived from the fupreme Creator, and is a-
like comprehended in the order of his providence. When the horror of pain prevails over the love of life ; when a voluntary action anticipates the effects of blind
caufes, 'tis only in confequence of thofe
powers

powers and principles which he has implanted in his creatures. Divine providence is ſtill inviolate, and placed far beyond the reach of human injuries. 'Tis impious ſays the old Roman ſuperſtition * to divert rivers from their courſe, or invade the prerogatives of nature · 'Tis impious ſays the French ſuperſtition to inoculate for the ſmall-pox, or uſurp the buſineſs of providence by voluntarily producing diſtempers and maladies. 'Tis impious ſays the modern *European* ſuperſtition, to put a period to our own life, and thereby rebel againſt our Creator; and why not impious, ſay I, to build houſes, cultivate the ground, or ſail upon the ocean? In all theſe actions we employ our powers of mind and body, to produce ſome innovation in the courſe of nature; and in none of them do we any more. They are all of them therefore equally innocent, or equally criminal. *But you are placed by providence, like a centinal, in a particular ſtation,*

and

* TACIT. Ann. lib. i.

and when you desert it without being re-
called, you are equally guilty of rebellion
against your almighty sovereign, and have
incurred his displeasure.——I aſk, why
do you conclude that providence has
placed me in this ſtation? for my part
I find that I owe my birth to a long chain
of cauſes, of which many depended upon
voluntary actions of men. *But providence*
guided all theſe cauſes, and nothing hap-
pens in the univerſe, without its conſent and
co-operation. If ſo, then neither does
my death, however voluntary, happen
without its conſent ; and whenever
pain or ſorrow ſo far overcome my
patience, as to make me tired of life,
I may conclude that I am recalled from
my ſtation in the cleareſt and moſt expreſs
terms. 'Tis providence ſurely that has
placed me at this preſent in this chamber :
But may I not leave it when I think proper, without being liable to the imputaticn
of having deſerted my poſt or ſtation ?
When I ſhall be dead, the principles of
which

which I am compofed will ftill perform their part in the univerfe, and will be equally ufeful in the grand fabrick, as when they compofed this individual creature. The difference to the whole will be no greater than betwixt my being in a chamber and in the open air. The one change is of more importance to me than the other ; but not more fo to the univerfe.

—'Tis a kind of blafphemy to imagine that any created being can difturb the order of the world, or invade the bufinefs of Providence ! it fuppofes, that that being poffeffes powers and faculties, which it received not from its creator, and which are not fubordinate to his government and authority. A man may difturb fociety no doubt, and thereby incur the difplea-fure of the Almighty : But the government of the world is placed far beyond his reach and violence. And how does it appear that the Almighty is difpleafed with thofe actions that difturb fociety ? By the prin-

D   ciples

ciples which he has implanted in human nature, and which infpire us with a fentiment of remorfe if we ourfelves have been guilty of fuch actions, and with that of blame and difapprobation, if we ever obferve them in others :—Let us now examine, according to the method propofed, whether Suicide be of this kind of actions, and be a breach of our duty to our *neighbour* and to *fociety.*

A MAN who retires from life does no harm to fociety : He only ceafes to do good ; which, if it is an injury, is of the loweft kind.—All our obligations to do good to fociety feem to imply fomething reciprocal. I receive the benefits of fociety, and therefore ought to promote its interefts; but when I withdraw myfelf altogether from fociety, can I be bound any longer ? But allowing that our obligations to do good were perpetual, they have certainly fome bounds ; I am not obliged to do a fmall good to fociety at the expence of a great

great harm to myfelf ; why then fhould I prolong a miferable exiftence, becaufe of fome frivolous advantage which the public may perhaps receive from me ? If upon account of age and infirmities, I may lawfully refign any office, and employ my time altogether in fencing againft thefe calamities, and alleviating, as much as poffible, the miferies of my future life : why may I not cut fhort thefe miferies at once by an action which is no more prejudicial to fociety ?—But fuppofe that it is no longer in my power to promote the intereft of fociety, fuppofe that I am a burden to it, fuppofe that my life hinders fome perfon from being much more ufeful to fociety. In fuch cafes, my refignation of life muft not only be innocent, but laudable. And moft people who lie under any temptation to abandon exiftence, are in fome fuch fituation ; thofe who have health, or power, or authority, have commonly better reafon to be in humour with the world. (4)

D 2 A MAN

A MAN is engaged in a confpiracy for the public intereft ; is feized upon fufpicion ; is threatened with the rack ; and knows from his own weaknefs that the fecret will be extorted from him : Could fuch a one confult the public intereft better than by putting a quick period to a miferable life ? This was the cafe of the famous and brave *Strozi* of *Florence.*—— Again, fuppofe a malefactor is juftly condemned to a fhameful death, can any reafon be imagined, why he may not anticipate his punifhment, and fave himfelf all the anguifh of thinking on its dreadful approaches ? He invades the bufinefs of providence no more than the magiftrate did, who ordered his execution ; and his voluntary death is equally advantageous to fociety, by ridding it of a pernicious member.

THAT Suicide may often be confiftent with intereft and with our duty to ourfelves, no one can queftion, who allows that age,

fick-

ficknefs, or misfortune, may render life a burthen, and make it worfe even than annihilation. I believe that no man ever threw away life, while it was worth keeping. For fuch is our natural horror of death, that fmall motives will never be able to reconcile us to it ; and though perhaps the fituation of a man's health or fortune did not feem to require this remedy, we may at leaft be affured that any one who, without apparent reafon, has had recourfe to it, was curft with fuch an incurable depravity or gloominefs of temper as muft poifon all enjoyment, and render him equally miferable as if he had been loaded with the moft grievous misfortunes.—If fuicide be fuppofed a crime, 'tis only cowardice can impel us to it. If it be no crime, both prudence and courage fhould engage us to rid ourfelves at once of exiftence, when it becomes a burthen. 'Tis the only way that we can then be ufeful to fociety, by fetting an example, which if imitated, would preferve to every one his chance for happinefs in life, and

and would effectually free him from all danger of misery *

* It would be easy to prove that suicide is as lawful un-der the Christian dispensation as it was to the Heathens. There is not a single text of scripture which prohibits it. That great and infallible rule of faith and practice which must controul all philosophy and human reasoning, has left us in this particular to our natural liberty. Resignation to Providence is indeed recommended in scripture; but that implies only submission to ills that are unavoidable, not to such as may be remedied by prudence or courage. *Thou shalt not kill*, is evidently meant to exclude only the killing of others, over whose life we have no authority. That this pre-cept, like most of the scripture precepts, must be modified by reason and common sense, is plain from the practice of magi-strates, who punish criminals capitally, notwithstanding the letter of the law. But were this commandment ever so express against suicide, it would now have no authority, for all the law of *Moses* is abolished, except so far as it is established by the law of nature. And we have already endeavoured to prove that suicide is not prohibited by that law. In all cases Christians and Heathens are precisely upon the same foot-ing; *Cato* and *Brutus, Arrea* and *Portia* acted heroically; those who now imitate their example ought to receive the same praises from posterity. The power of committing suicide is regarded by *Pliny* as an advantage which men possess even above the Deity himself. "Deus non sibi po-test mortem conscifcere si velit quod homini dedit optimum in tantis vitæ pænis."   Lib. II. cap. 7. (5)

E S S A Y

E S S A Y   II.

ON THE

IMMORTALITY OF THE *SOUL.*

BY the mere light of reafon it feems difficult to prove the *Immortality* of the Soul; the arguments for it are commonly derived either from *metaphyfical* topics, or *moral* or *phyfical.* But in reality 'tis the Gofpel and the Gofpel alone, that has brought *life and immortality to light.*

I. METAPHYSICAL topics fuppofe that the foul is immaterial, and that 'tis im-

poffible

poſſible for thought to belong to a material ſubſtance. ——— (1) But juſt metaphyſics teach us that the notion of ſubſtance is wholly confuſed and imperfect, and that we have no other idea of any ſubſtance, than as an aggregate of particular qualities, inhering in an unknown ſomething. Matter, therefore, and ſpirit, are at bottom equally unknown, and we cannot determine what qualities inhere in the one or in the other. (2) They likewiſe teach us that nothing can be decided *a priori* concerning any cauſe or effect, and that experience being the only ſource of our judgments of this nature, we cannot know from any other principle, whether matter, by its ſtructure or arrangement, may not be the cauſe of thought. Abſtract reaſonings cannot decide any queſtion of fact or exiſtence.—But admitting a ſpiritual ſubſtance to be diſperſed throughout the univerſe, like the etherial fire of the *Stoics*, and to be the only inherent ſubject of thought, we have reaſon to conclude
from

from *analogy* that nature ufes it after the manner fhe does the other fubftance, · *matter*. She employs it as a kind of pafte or clay ; modifies it into a variety of forms and exiftences ; diffolves after a time each modification, and from its fubftance erects a new form. As the fame material fubftance may fucceffively compofe the bodies of all animals, the fame fpiritual fubftance may compofe their minds : Their confcioufnefs, or that fyftem of thought which they formed during life, may be continually diffolved by death. And nothing interefts them in the new modification. The moft pofitive affertors of the mortality of the foul, never denied the immortality of its fuftance. And that an immaterial fubftance, as well as a material, may lofe its memory or confcioufnefs, appears in part from experience, if the foul be immaterial.—Reafoning from the common courfe of nature, and without fuppofing any new interpofition of the fupreme caufe, which ought always to be excluded from philofo-

E   phy,

phy, what is incorruptible muſt alſo be in-
generable. The Soul therefore if immortal, exiſted before our birth ; and if the
former exiſtence no ways concerned us,
neither will the latter.—Animals undoubtedly feel, think, love, hate, will, and even
reaſon, tho' in a more imperfect manner
than men ; are their ſouls alſo immaterial
and immortal ? (3)

II. LET us now conſider the moral arguments, chiefly thoſe derived from the juſtice of God, which is ſuppoſed to be farther
intereſted in the farther puniſhment of the
vicious and reward of the virtuous.—But
theſe arguments are grounded on the ſuppoſition that God has attributes beyond
what he has exerted in this univerſe, with
which alone we are acquainted. Whence
do we infer the exiſtence of theſe attributes ?—'Tis very ſafe for us to affirm, that whatever we know the Deity to
have actually done, is beſt ; but 'tis very
dangerous to affirm, that he muſt always do
what

what to us feems beft.   In how many inftances would this reafoning fail us with
regard to the prefent world ?—But if any
purpofe of nature be clear, we may affirm,
that the whole fcope and intention of man's
creation, fo far as we can judge by natural
reafon, is limited to the prefent life. With
how weak a concern from the original inherent ftructure of the mind and paffions,
does he ever look farther ?   What comparifon either for fteadinefs or efficacy, betwixt fo floating an idea, and the moft doubtful perfuafion of any matter of fact that occurs in common life.   There arife indeed
in fome minds fome unaccountable terrors
with regard to futurity ; but thefe would
quickly vanifh were they not artificially
foftered by precept and education.   And
thofe who fofter them, what is their motive?
Only to gain a livelihood, and to acquire
power and riches in this world.   Their very zeal and induftry therefore is an argument againft them.

WHAT

WHAT cruelty, what iniquity, what injuſtice in nature, to confine all our concern,
as well as all our knowledge, to the preſent
life, if there be another ſcene ſtill waiting
us, of infinitely greater conſequence ?
Ought this barbarous deceit to be aſcribed
to a beneficent and wiſe being ?—Obſerve with what exact proportion the taſk
to be performed and the peforming powers are adjuſted throughout all nature. If
the reaſon of man gives him great ſuperio-
rity above other animals, his neceſſities
are proportionably multiplied upon him ;
his whole time, his whole capacity,
activity, courage, and paſſion, find ſufficient employment in fencing againſt the miſeries of his preſent condition, and frequently, nay almoſt always are too ſlender
for the buſineſs aſſigned them.—A pair of
ſhoes perhaps was never yet wrought to the
higheſt degree of perfection which that co-
modity is capable of attaining. Yet it is
neceſſary, at leaſt very uſeful, that there
ſhould be ſome politicians and moraliſts,
                                        even

even fome geometers, poets, and philofo ·
phers among mankind. The powers of
men are no more fuperior to their wants,
confidered merely in this life, than thofe of
foxes and hares are, compared to *their*
wants and to their period of exiftence.
The inference from parity of reafon is
therefore obvious.——

On the theory of the Soul's mortality, the
inferiority of women's capacity is eafily accounted for. Their domeftic life requires
no higher faculties, either of mind or body.
This circumftance vanifhes and becomes abfolutely infignificant, on the religious theory : the one fex has an equal tafk to per ·
form as the other ; their powers of reafon
and refolution ought alfo to have been e-
qual, and both of them infinitely greater
than at prefent. As every effect implies a
caufe, and that another, till we reach the
firft caufe of all, which is the Deity ; every
thing that happens is ordained by him, and
nothing can be the object of his punifhment or vengeance.——By what rule are pu-
nifhments

nifhments and rewards diftributed ? What is the divine ftandard of merit and demerit ? Shall we fuppofe that human fentiments have place in the Deity ? How bold that hypothefis. We have no conception of any other fentiments.—According to human fentiments, fenfe, courage, good manners, induftry, prudenee, genius, &c. are effential parts of perfonal merits. Shall we therefore erect an elyfium for poets and heroes like that of the antient mythology ? Why confine all rewards to one fpecies of virtue ? Punifhment, without any proper end or purpofe, is inconfiftent with *our* ideas of goodnefs and juftice, and no end can be ferved by it after the whole fcene is clofed. Punifhment, according to *our* conception, fhould bear fome proportion to the offence. Why then eternal punifhment for the temporary offences of fo frail a creature as man ? Can any one approve of *Alexder*'s rage, who intended to extirminate a whole nation becaufe they had feized his favorite horfe Bucephalus ? *

* Quint. Curtius lib. VI. cap. 5.

HEA-

HEAVEN and Hell ſuppoſe two diſtinct ſpecies of men, the good and the bad ; but the greateſt part of mankind float betwixt vice and virtue.—Were one to go round the world with an intention of giving a good ſupper to the righteous, and a ſound drubbing to the wicked, he would frequently be embarraſſed in his choice, and would find that the merits and the demerits of moſt men and women ſcarcely amount to the value of either.—To ſuppoſe meaſures of approbation and blame different from the human confounds every thing. Whence do we learn that there is ſuch a thing as moral diſtinctions, but from our own ſentiments ? —What man who has not met with perſonal provacation (or what good-natured man who has) could inflict on crimes, from the ſenſe of blame alone, even the common, legal, frivolous puniſhments ? And does any thing ſteel the breaſt of judges and juries againſt the ſentiments of humanity but reflection on neceſſity and public intereſt ?

By

By the Roman law thofe who had been guilty of parricide and confeffed their crime,
were put into a fack alone with an ape, a
dog, and a ferpent, and thrown into the river.　Death alone was the punifhment of
thofe whofe who denied their guilt, however fully proved.　A criminal was tried
before *Auguftus*, and condemned after a
full conviction, but the humane emperor,
when he put the laft interrogatory, gave it
fuch a turn as to lead the wretch into a de-
nial of his guilt. " You furely (faid the
" prince) did not kill your father."*　This
lenity fuits our natural ideas of *right* even
towards the greateft of all criminals,
and even though it prevents fo inconfiderable a fufference.　Nay even the moft bigotted prieft would naturally without reflection approve of it, provided the crime was
not herefy or infidelity ; for as thefe crimes
hurt himfelf in his *temporal* intereft and advantages, perhaps he may not be altogether fo
in-

* Suet. Auguf. cap. 3.

indulgent to them.   The chief fcource of
moral ideas is the reflection on the intereft
of human fociety.   Ought thefe interefts,
fo fhort, fo frivolous, to be guarded by pu-
nifhments eternal and infinite ?   The damnation of one man is an infinitely greater evil in the univerfe, than the fubver-
fion of a thoufand millions of kingdoms.
Nature has rendered human infancy peculiarly frail and mortal, as it were on purpofe
to refute the notion of a probationary ftate ;
the half of mankind die before they are
rational creatures.

III. The *Phyfical* arguments from the a-
nalogy of nature are ftrong for the mortality of the foul, and are really the only philofophical arguments which ought to be admitted with regard to this queftion, or indeed any queftion of fact.—Where any two
objects are fo clofely connected that all alterations which we have ever feen in the
one, are attended with proportionable alterations in the other ; we ought to conclude

F   by

by all rules of analogy, that, when there
are ftill greater alterations produced in the
former, and it is totally diffolved, there follows a total diffolution of the latter.--Sleep,
a very fmall effect on the body, is attended
with a temporary extinction, at leaft a great
confufion in the foul.—The weaknefs
of the body and that of the mind in infancy are exactly proportioned, their vigour in
manhood, their fympathetic diforder in
ficknefs; their common gradual decay in old
age. The ftep further feems unavoidable;
their common diffolution in death. The
laft fymptoms which the mind difcovers are
diforder, weaknefs, infenfibility, and ftupidity, the fore-runners of its annihilation.
The farther progrefs of the fame caufes encreafing, the fame effects totally extinguifh
it. Judging by the ufual analogy of nature, no form can continue when transferred to a condition of life very different
from the original one, in which it was placed. Trees perifh in the water, fifhes in
the air, animals in the earth. Even fo
fmall a difference as that of climate is often

ten fatal. What reason then to imagine, that an immense alteration, such as is made on the soul by the dissolution of its body and all its organs of thought and sensation, can be effected without the dissolution of the whole ? Every thing is in common betwixt soul and body. The organs of the one are all of them the organs of the other. The existence therefore of the one must be dependant on that of the other.—The souls of animals are allowed to be mortal ; and these bear so near a resemblance to the souls of men, that the analogy from one to the other forms a very strong argument. Their bodies are not more resembling ; yet no one rejects the argument drawn from comparative anatomy. The *Metempsychosis* is therefore the only system of this kind that philosophy can hearken to. (4)

NOTHING in this world is perpetual, every thing however seemingly firm is in continual flux and change, the world itself gives symptoms of frailty and dissolution. How contrary to analogy, therefore, to imagine

that

that one single form, feemingly the fraileſt of any, and ſubject to the greateſt diſorders, is immortal and indiſſolubie? (5) What daring theory is that! how lightly, not to fay how raſhly entertained! How to diſpoſe of the infinite number of poſthumous exiſtences ought alſo to embarraſs the religious theory. Every planet in every ſolar ſyſtem we are at liberty to imagine peopled with intelligent mortal beings, at leaſt we can fix on no other ſuppoſition. For theſe then a new univerſe muſt every generation be cr ated beyond the bounds of the preſent univerſe, or one muſt have been created at firſt fo prodigiouſly wide as to admit of this continual influx of beings. (6) Ought ſuch bold ſuppoſitions to be received by any philoſophy, and that merely on the pretext of a bare poſſibility? When it is aſked whether *Agamemnon, Therſites Hannibal, Varro,* and every ſtupid clown that ever exiſted in *Italy, Scythia, Bactria* or *Guinea,* are now alive ; can any man think, that a ſcrutiny of nature will furniſh arguments
ſtrong

ſtrong enough to anſwer ſo ſtrange a queſtion in the affirmative? The want of argument without revelation ſufficiently eſta-
bliſhes the negative.-·"*Quanto facilius* (ſays
Pliny *) " *certius que ſibi quemque credere*,
" *ac ſpecimen ſecuritatis antigene tali ſumere*
experimento." Our inſenſibility before the
compoſition of the body, ſeems to natural
reaſon a proof of a like ſtate after diſſolu-
tion.—Were our horrors of annihilation an
original paſſion, not the effect of our general love of happineſs, it would rather prove
the mortality of the ſoul. For as nature
does nothing in vain, ſhe would never give
us a horror againſt an impoſſible event.
She may give us a horror againſt an unavoidable event, provided our endeavours,
as in the preſent caſe, may often remove it
to ſome diſtance. Death is in the end unavoidable ; yet the human ſpecies could
not be preſerved had not nature inſpired us
with an averſion towards it. All doctrines
are to be ſuſpected which are favoured by

our

* Lib. 7. cap. 55,

our paffions, and the hopes and fears which gave rife to this doctrine are very obvious.

'Tis an infinite advantage in every controverfy to defend the negative. If the queftion be out of the common experienced courfe of nature, this circumftance is almoft if not altogether decifive. By what arguments or analogies can we prove any ftate of exiftence, which no one ever faw, and which no way refembles any that ever was feen? Who will repofe fuch truft in any pretended philofophy as to admit upon its teftimony the reality of fo marvellous a fcene? Some new fpecies of logic is requifite for that purpofe, and fome new faculties of the mind, that may enable us to comprehend that logic.

Nothing could fet in a fuller light the infinite obligations which mankind have to divine revelation, fince we find that no other medium could afcertain this great and important truth.

ANTI

ANTI SUICIDE.

(1) THIS elaborate eulogium on philofophy points obliquely at religion, which we chriftians confider as the only fovereign antidote to every difeafe incident to the mind of man. It is indeed hard to fay what reafon might do were it freed from all reftraints, efpecially if a fucceffion of philofophers were inceffantly improving on one another as they went on, avoiding and correcting the miftakes of thofe who preceded them in the fame purfuit, till at laft one complete and rational fyftem was effected. Great things might probably be accomplished in this manner. But no fuch plan in fact ever was or is likely to be finished. Neither prieftcraft, nor magifterial powers, however, cramped the progres of improving reafon, or baffled the genius of enquiring man. The principles of religion and virtue were freely canvaffed by the boldeft fpirits of antiquity. In truth, the fuperior advantage and neceffity of the chriftian religion feems manifeft from this particular circumftance,

ſtance, that it has taken away every poſſible reſtraint from natural religion, allowing it to exert itſelf to the utmoſt in finding out the fundamental truths of virtue, and in acquieſcing in them, in openly avowing and acknowledging them when revealed, in extending the views and expectations of men, in giving them more juſt and liberal ſentiments, and in publickly and uniformly diſclaiming any intention of eſtabliſhing a kingdom for its votaries or believers in this world.

THE doctrines of the goſpel are not intended to inſtruct us in the knowledge of every thing which may be really uſeful in the preſent life, far leſs of every thing, which, from curioſity alone, we may have a mighty deſire to know. Revelation conſiders mankind in their higheſt capacity, as the rational and accountable ſubjects of God, and as capable both of preſent and future happineſs or miſery, according to their behaviour. Its chief, if not its ſole deſign, is to give us thoſe views and impreſſions of our nature, of our ſtate, of the perfections, the counſels, the laws, and the government of God, which, under the influence of providence, are the immediate and infallible means of the purity, of the comfort, and of the moral order, rectitude, and excellence of our immortal ſouls. As corrupted and diſordered, we are incapable of true happineſs, till purified and reſtored to order. As guilty and
mortal

mortal creatures, we can have no true confolation without the hopes of pardon in a future and feperate ftate of exiftence. As furrounded with dangers, and obnoxious to e-
very difmal apprehenfion, we can poffefs no
folid, or permanent content, but in the fincere and well grounded convictions of that
gracious and righteous adminiftration fo mi-
nutely and explicity delineated in the fcrip-
tures. It is evident, therefore, that the principal excellence and utility of revealed truths
muft lie or confift in the influence they have
upon the fanctification and confolation of
our hearts. They tally exactly with the prefent circumftances of mankind, and are ad-
mirably adapted to cure every difeafe, every
diforder of the human mind, to beget, to cherifh, and confirm every pure, every virtuous, every pious difpofition.

MANKIND are certainly at prefent in a
ftate of the deepeft corruption and depravity, and at the fame time apt to continue
ftrangely infenfible of the mifery and danger to which, under the government of infinite wifdom, it neceffarily renders them.
Nothing can be conceived more fit to roufe
them from their lethargy, and to awaken
them to a juft fenfe of their condition, than
a meffenger from Heaven, clothed with divine authority, fetting before them the in-
G   trinfic

trinfic bafenefs, malignity, and wretched-
nefs of vice, together with the certain, the
dreadful, the eternal confequences of con-
tinuing in it.

COULD we enter upon a particular view
of all thofe maladies and diforders which infeft and deftroy the fouls of men, it were eafy to fhew, that a fteadfaft belief of religion
is, in truth, the moft natural and the beft antidote or remedy for each of them. It is obvious, at leaft, that the clear and full mani-
feftation, which the gofpel has given of the
character of God, and the laws of his moral
government, and of the terms of falvation
through faith in the religion of his fon, are
all finely calculated to root out the principles of fuperftition, and all falfe notions, deftructive to the virtue and happinefs of mankind, and to plant in their room whatever
has a natural and direct tendency to promote
our virtue, our perfection, our felicity.

M.

(2) CLEOMENES, king of Sparta, when
fuffering under misfortune, was advifed to
kill himfelf by Tharyceon. " Thinkeft
thou, wicked man, (faid he) to fhew thy fortitude by rufhing upon death, an expedient
always at hand, the daftardly refource of the
bafeft

bafeft minds? Better than we, by the fortune of arms, or overpowered by numbers, have left the field of battle to their enemies; but he who, to avoid pain, or calamity, or from a flavifh regard to the praife or cenfures of men, gives up the conteft, is overcome by his own cowardice. If we are to feek death, that death ought to be in action. It is bafe to live or die only for ourfelves. All we gain by fuicide is to get rid of prefent difficulty, without increafing our own reputation, or doing the leaft fervice to our country. In hopes, then, we may yet be of fome ufe to others, both methinks are bound to preferve life as long as we can. Whenever thefe hopes fhall have altogether abandoned us, death, if fought for, will readily be found.

(3) Of all the refined cobwebs, to which fophiftry has given birth, this feems at once the moft elaborate and the moft flimfy. It feems one of the firft and moft indifputable maxims in all found reafoning, that no ideas whatever fhould have a place in the premifes, which do not communicate a fenfible energy to the conclufion. But where is the connection between the beginning and end of this wire-drawn argument. What have the various beautiful facts, thus elegantly ftated, to do with a man's taking away his own

life ?   Though the greateſt philoſopher be of
no more conſequence to the general ſyſtem of
things than an oyſter, and though the life of
the one were, in every reſpect, as perfectly
inſignificant as that of the other, ſtill the
meaneſt of mankind is not without importance in his own eyes.   And where is he who
is guided uniformly, in all his actions, more
by a ſenſe of his relation to the univerſe at
large, than by the value he retains for himſelf, or the deference he has to his own opinion.

No deduction, however plauſible, can produce conviction in any rational mind, which
originates in a ſuppoſition groſsly abſurd. Is
it poſſible to conceive the author of nature
capable of authenticating a deed, which ultimately terminates in the total annihilation
of the ſyſtem ? By which of the creatures beneath us is the firſt law of their being thus da-
ringly violated ? And if ſuicide be eligible to
man, under any poſſible misfortune or diſ-
treſs, why not to them? Are not they alſo ſubject to the various miſeries which ariſe from
wayward accidents and hoſtile elements ?
Why, therefore, open a door for our eſcape
from thoſe evils of which others have their
ſhare, to whom, however, it muſt remain for
ever ſhut ?

In

IN truth, the exiſtence of all animals depends entirely on their inviolable attachment to ſelf-preſervation. Their attention to all poſſible means of ſelf-defence and ſuſtenance, is accordingly the obvious and common condition of all their natures. By this great and operative principle nature has chiefly conſulted her own ſafety. Our philoſopher's notions are ſo extremely hoſtile to her moſt eſſential inſtitutions, that ſhe could not poſſibly ſurvive a general conviction of them. And, in ſpite of all the ſophiſtry he is maſter of, the queſtion here will eternally recur, whether the wiſdom of nature, or the philoſophy of our author, deſerves the preference.

(4) THIS apology for the commiſſion, ariſing from man's inſignificance in the moral world, from the reciprocation of ſocial duty being diſſolved, or from the benefit reſulting from the voluntary diſmiſſion of being, is contrary to the foundeſt principles of juriſprudence, to the condition of human nature, and to the general eſtabliſhment of things.

THAT a man who retires from life *ad libitum*, does no harm to ſociety, is a propoſition peculiarly abſurd and erroneous. What is
law-

lawful for one, may be lawful for all, and no society can subsist in the conviction of a principle thus hostile to its being.

IT seems to be a maxim in human existence, that no creature has a right to decide peremptorily on the importance, utility, or necessity of his own being. There are an infinite variety of secret connections and associations in the vast system of things, which the eye of created wisdom cannot explore.

MAN is not, perhaps, so ignorant of anything, or any creature, as of himself. His own system, after all the art and inquisition of human ingenuity, is still to him the profoundest mystery in nature. His knowledge and faculties are adequate to the sphere of his duty. Beyond this, his researches are impertinent, and all his acquisitions useless. He has no adequate notions what the laws of the universe are with respect to any species of existence whatever. A cloud rests on the complicated movements of this great machine, which baffles all the penetration of mortals : and it will for ever remain impossible for man, from the most complete analysis of his present situation, to judge, with any degree of precision, of his own consequence, either as a citizen of the world at large, or as a member of any particular society.

FINAL

FINAL caufes form a fyftem of knowledge too wonderful for man. It is the perrogative of nature alone to decide upon them. In the fulnefs of time, her creative hand brought him into exiftence, and it belongs to her alone, in confequence of an arrangement equally wonderful and myfterious to difmifs him from his prefent mode of being. This is an authority with which fhe alone is invefted, and which, according to our apprehenfions, it is impoffible for her to delegate. Diffolution, as well as creation, is hers. and he who would attempt to infringe her fovereignty in this inftance, would ufurp a prerogative which does not belong to him, and become a traitor to the laws of his being. Nay, on this extravagant and licentious hypothefis, the right of affuming and relinquifhing exiftence is made reciprocal. For he who arrogates the liberty of deftroying himfelf, were he poffeffed of the power, might alfo be his own creator ; his imaginary infignificance to fociety being as inconclufive in the one cafe, as any chimerical advantage that may accidentally ftrike him can be in the other. It is a ftrange doctrine, which cannot be eftablifhed, but at the obvious expence of what feem the plaineft dictates of common fenfe.

INDEED, the abfurdities of this daring and paradoxical doctrine are endlefs and infinite.

When

When we come to pronounce on the condition of human infancy, and to feperate childhood, or non-age, from a ftate of maturity, we can fcarce trace one ufeful or falutary confequence it is calculated to produce in fociety. In this view children feem lefs adapted to ferve any fpecial or important end, than even beetles, gnats, or flies. Experience, however, has long, convinced the world of their prefent ineftimable value from their future deftination. And were a legiflator, from the plaufible pretext of their being a burden to the ftate, to exterminate the race of mankind in the infignificant ftage of infancy, his decree, like that of a certain monfter recorded in the gofpel, would fhock the fentiments of every nation under heaven, in whom there remained only the dregs of humanity.

It is not only impoffible for a man to decide, in any given period, of the progrefs of his exiftence, or what utility or confequence he may be to fociety; but without the faculty of prefcience, it is ftill more impracticable for him to divine what purpofes he may be intended to ferve in the many myfterious revolations of futurity. How far his mortal may be connected with his immortal life, muft reft with him who has the fole difpofal of it. But who told him that his load of mifery was too much to bear, that he was not able to fuf-
                                         tain

tain it ? or that his merciful father would not proportionate his sufferings to his abilities ? How does he know how short-lived the pressure of incumbent sorrow may prove ? It becomes not him to prescribe to his maker, or because his evils are enormous, to conclude they must be permanent. Rash man ! thy heart is in the hand of heaven, and he *who tempers the wind to the shorn lamb*, may either lighten the burthen that oppresses thee, or blunt the edge of that sensibility, from which it derives the greatest poignancy. What medicine is to the wounds of the body, that resignation is to those of the soul. Be not deficient in this virtue, and life will never prescribe a duty you cannot perform, or inflict a pang which you cannot bear. Resignation changes the grizzly aspect of affliction, turns sickness into health, and converts the gloomy forebdoings of despair into the grateful presentiments of hope. Besides, the most insignificant instruments are sometimes, in the hands of eternal providence, employed in bringing about the most general and beneficent revolutions. It is by making weakness thus subservient to power, evil to good, and pain to pleasure, that he who governs the world illustrates his sovereinty and omnipotence. Till, then, thou art able to comprehend the whole mysterious system of every possible existence, till thou art certain that thy life is totally insignificant, till thou art

con-

convinced it is not in the might of infinite power to render thee serviceable either to thyself or others, counteract not the benignity of providence by suicide, or, in this manner, by the blackest of all treasons, betray thy trust, and wage, at fearful odds, hostility against the very means and author of thy being.

One very obvious consequence arising from suicide, which none of its advocates appear to have foreseen, and which places it in a light exceedingly gross and shocking, is, that it supposes every man capable, not only of destroying himself, but of delegating the power of committing murder to another. That which he may do himself, he may commission any one to do for him. On this supposition, no law, human or divine, could impeach the shedding of innocent blood. And on what principle, of right or expediency, admit that which produces such a train of the most horrid and detestable consequences?

(5) The preceding note is, perhaps, the most audacious part in the whole of this very extraordinary performance. In our holy religion it is expressly declared that no murderer hath eternal life abiding in him; that murderers shall in no wise inherit the kingdom of God, and that it is the prerogative of heaven alone to kill and make alive. It is a fundamental

mental doctrine in the gospel, that, except ye repent, ye shall all likewise perish. And how are they to perform their duty, who, in the instant of dying, contract a guilt, which renders it indispensible. But this horrid supposition is repugnant to the whole genius of revelation, which inculates every virtue that can possibly administer to our present and future welfare. It inforces obedience and resignation to the righteous government of God. It inspires and produces those very dispositions which it recommends. All its doctrines, exhortations, and duties, are formed to elevate the mind, to raise the affections, to regulate the passions, and to purge the heart of whatever is hostile to happiness in this or another life. This impious slander on the christian faith is the obvious consequence of the grossest inattention to its nature and tendency. It is calculated chiefly to make us happy. And what happy man was ever yet chargeable with suicide ? In short, we may as well say, that, because the physician does not expressly prohibit certain diseases in his prescriptions, the very diseases are authenticated by the remedies devised, on purpose to counteract them.

H 2

IMMOR-

IMMORTALITY

OF THE

S   O   U   L.

(1) The ingenuity of Scepticifm has been long admired, but here the author boldly out-does all his former out-doings. Much has been faid againft the authenticity of religion, on the fuppofition that the evidence to which fhe appeals, is not either fufficiently general or intelligible to the bulk of mankind. But furely an argument is not conclufive in one cafe, and inconclufive in another. Admit this reafoning againft revelation to be valid, and you muft alfo admit it againft our author's hy-pothefis. There never at leaft was an ob-jection ftarted, that could, in the remoteft de-gree, affect the truths of the gofpel, more in-tricate, metaphyfical, and abftracted, than that by which our effayeft would deftroy the popu-lar doctrine of the foul's *immortality.* How many live and die in this falutary conviction, to whom thefe refined fpeculations muft for-ever remain as unintelligible as if they had

never

never been formed ! It is a fentiment fo con-
genial to the heart of man, that few of the fpecies would chufe to exift without it. ·Unable,
as they are, to account for its origin, they cordially and univerfally indulge it, as one of
their tendereft, beft, and laft feelings. It inhabits alike the rudeft and moft polifhed minds,
and never leaves any human breaft, which is
not either wholly engroffed by criminal pleafure, deadened by felfifh purfuits, or perverted by falfe reafoning. It governs with
all the ardor and influence of infpiration,
and never meets with any oppofition but from
the weak, the worthlefs, or the *will above
what is written.* All the world have uniformly confidered it as their laft refource in
every extremity, and for the moft part ftill regard and cherifh the belief of it, as an afylum
in which their beft interefts are ultimately fe-
cured or depofited, beyond the reach of all
temporary difafter or misfortune. Where,
therefore, is the probability of exterminating fo
popular and prevailing a notion, by a concate-
nation of ideas, which, perhaps, not one out of
a million in any country under Heaven is able
to trace or comprehend ?

(2) The natural perceptions of pleafure or
pain cannot be faid to act on the mind as one
part of matter does on another. The fubftance of the foul we do not know, but are
cer-

certain her ideas muft be immaterial. And thefe cannot poffibly act either by contact or impulfe. When one body impels another, the body moved is affected only by the impulfe. But the mind, whenever roufed by any pleafing or painful fenfation, in moft cafes looks round her, and deliberates whether a change of ftate is proper, or the prefent more eligible ; and moves or refts accorddingly. Her preceptions, therefore, contribute no further to action, than by exciting her active powers. On the contrary, matter is blindly and obftinately in that ftate in which it is, whether of motion or reft, till changed by fome other adequate caufe. Suppofe we reft the ftate of any body, fome external force is requifite to put it in motion ; and, in proportion as this force is greater or fmall, the motion muft be fwift or flow. Did not this body continue in its former ftate, no external force would be requifite to change it ; nor, when changed, would different degrees of force be neceffary to move it in different degrees of velocity. When motion is impreffed on any body, to bring it to reft, an *extra*force muft always be applied, in proportion to the intended effect. This refiftance is obferveable in bodies both when moved in particular directions, and to bear an exact proportion to the *vis impreffa*, and to the quantity of matter moved. Were it poffible to extract from matter the qualities of folidity and extenfion,

tenfion, the matter whence fuch qualities were extracted would no longer refift ; and confequently refiftance is the neceffary refult of them, which, therefore, in all directions muft be the fame. The degree of refiftance in any body being proportionate to the *vis impreffa,* it follows, when that body is confidered in any particular ftate, whether of motion or reft, the degrees of refiftance muft either indefinitely multiply, or decreafe, according to all poffible degrees of the moving force. But when the fame body is confidered abfolutely, or without fixing any particular ftate, the refiftance is immutable ; and all the degrees of it, which that body would exert upon the acceffion of any impreffed force, muft be conceived as actually in it. Nor can matter have any tendency contrary to that refiftance, otherwife it muft be equal or fuperior. If equal, the two contrary tendencies would deftroy each other. If fuperior, the refiftance would be deftroyed. Thus change would eternally fucceed to change without one intermediate inftant, fo that no time would be affigned when any body was in any particular ftate. Gravitation itfelf, the moft fimple and univerfal law, feems far from being a tendency natural to matter ; fince it is found to act internally, and not in proportion to the fuperfices of any body ; which it would not do, if it were only the mechanical action of matter upon matter.

From

From all this, it appears, that matter considered merely as such, is so far from having a principle of spontaneous motion, that it is stubbornly inactive, and must eternally remain in the same state in which it happens to be, except influenced by some other—that is, some immaterial power. Of such a power the human soul is evidently possessed ; for every one is conscious of an internal activity, and to dispute this would be to dispute us out of one of the most real and intimate perceptions we have.

Though a material automaton were allowed possible, how infinitely would it fall short of that force and celerity which every one feels in himself How sluggish are all the movements which fall under our observation. How slow and gradual their transitions from one part of space to another. But the mind, by one instantaneous effort, measures the distance from pole to pole, from heaven to earth, from one fixed star to another ; and not confined within the limits of the visible creation, shoots into immensity with a rapidity to which even that of lightning, or sunbeams, is no comparison. Who then shall assign a period, which, though depressed with so much dead weight, is ever active, and unconscious of fatigue or relaxation ? The mind is not only herself a principle of action, but probably actuates the body, without the

assist-

affiftance of any intermediate power, both from the gradual command which fhe acquires of its members by habit, and from a capacity of determining, in fome meafure, the quantity of pleafure or pain which any fenfible perception can give her. Suppofing the interpofing power a fpirit, the fame difficulty of fpirit acting upon matter ftill remains. And the volition of our own mind will as well account for the motion of the body, as the formal inteference of any other fptritual fubftance. And we may as well afk, why the mind is not confcious of that interpofition, as why fhe is ignorant of the means by which fhe communicates motion to the body.

(3) It is always bad reafoning to draw conclufions from the premifes not denied by your adverfary. Whoever, yet, of all the affertors of the foul's immortality, prefumed to make a monopoly of this great privilege to the human race? Who can tell what another ftate of exiftence may be, or whether every other fpecies of animals may not poffefs principles as immortal as the mind of man ? But that mode of reafoning, which militates againft all our convictions, folely on account of the unavoidable ignorance to which our fphere in the univerfe fubjects us, can never be fatisfactory. Reafon, it is true, cannot altogether folve every doubt which arifes concerning this important truth. But neither is there any other

I

ther truth, of any denomination whatever, a-
gainſt which ſophiſtry may not conjure up
a multitude of exceptions. We know no
mode of exiſtence but thoſe of matter and
ſpirit, neither of which have uniformly and
ſuccefsfully defied the extreme ſubtilty of ar-
gumentation. Still a very great majority of
mankind are ſtaunch believers in both. So well
conſtituted is the preſent difpofition of things,
that all the principles eſſential to human
life and happineſs continue, as it is likely they
ever will, to operate, in ſpite of every ſort of
clamour which ſophiſtry or ſcepticiſm has
raiſed or can raiſe againſt them.

(4) There is not a ſingle word in all this
elaborate and tedious deduction, which has
not been urged and refuted five hundred times.
Our ignorance of the divine perfections, as
is uſual with this writer, is here ſtated as an
unanſwerable exception to the concluſion uſually drawn from them. But he very artfully
overlooks, that this great ignorance will be
equally concluſive as applied to either ſide of
the argument. When we compare, however,
the character of God, as a wiſe ſuperinten-
dant, and generous benefactor, with the ſtate
in which things at preſent appear, where virtue is often depreſſed and afflicted, and vice apparently triumphs, it will be treated with
the infamy it merits, and virtue receive that
hap-

happinefs and honour, which, from its own intrinfic worth, it deferves, and, from its conformity to the nature of God, it has reafon to expect.

This fubject, perhaps, has been too much exaggerated, and fome pious men have weakly thought, the beft way to convince us that order and happinefs prevailed in a future ftate, was to perfuade us that there was none at all in this. External advantages have been taken for the only goods of human nature; and, becaufe, in this view, all things fpeak the appearance of mal-adminiftration, we have been taught to expect a government of rectitude and benevolence hereafter. Let us, on the contrary, candidly own that virtue is fovereignly and folely good, left, by depreciating her charms, we obliquely detract from the character of God himfelf. Let us confefs her undowered excellence fuperior to all the inconveniences that may attend her, even in the prefent fituation. But, without allowing fome difference between poverty and riches, ficknefs and health, pain and pleafure, &c. we fhall have no foundation to preference; and it will be in vain to talk of felecting where no one choice can be more agreeable or difagreeable to nature than another. Upon this difference, therefore, however it be called, let the prefent argument proceed.

I 2

If

If infinite goodnefs be the fpirit and cha-
racteriftic of this univerfal government, then
every advantage, however inconfiderable in
kind or degree, muft either be fuppofed immediately beftowed on virtue ; or, at leaft, that
fuch retributions will, at fome time, be made
her, as may not only render her votaries equal,
but fuperior to thofe of vice, in proportion
to their merit. But how different the cafe is
in human life, hiftory and obfervation may eafily convince us ; fo that one, whofe eyes are
not intent on the character of God, and the
nature of virtue, would often be tempted to
think this world a theatre merely intended
for mournful fpectacles and pomps of horror.
How many perfons do we fee perifh by the
mere wants of nature, who, had they been in different circumftances, would have thanked God
with tears of joy for the power of communica-
ting thofe advantages they now implore from
others in vain ? While, at the fame time,
they have, perhaps, the additional mifery of
feeing the moft endeared relations involved
in the fame deplorable fate ! How often do
we fee thofe ties which unite the foul and
body, worn out by the gradual advances of a
lingering difeafe, or burft at once by the fudden efforts of unutterable agony ? While the
unhappy fufferers, had they been continued
in life, might have diffufed happinefs, not
only through the narrow circle of their
friends

friends and neighbourhood, but as extensive-
ly as their country, and even the world at
large. How many names do we see buried in
obscurity, or soiled with detraction, which
ought to have shone the first in fame? How
many heroes have survived the liberties of
their country, or died in abortive attempts to
preserve them; and, by their fall, only left
a larger field for the lawless ravages of tyranny and oppression?

But were it possible, how long and insupera-
ble would be the task to enumerate all the
ingredients which compose the present cup
of bitterness? And is this the consummation
of things? Will supreme and essential goodness no way distinguish such as have invari-
ably pursued his honour, and the interest of his
government, from those who have industri-
ously violated the order he has appointed in
things? who have blotted the face of nature
with havock, murder, and desolation; and
shewn a constant intention to counteract all
the benevolent designs of providence? It is
confessed that the virtuous, happy in the pos-
session of virtue alone, make their exit from the
present scene with blessings to the Creator,
for having called them to existence, and given
them the glorious opportunity of enjoying
what is in itself supremely eligible. They
are conscious that this felicity can receive no
accession from any external lustre or advan

tage

tage whatever. Yet it feems highly neceffary
in the divine adminiftration, that thofe who
have been dazzled with the falfe glare of prof-
perous wickednefs, fhould at laft be unde-
ceived ;   that they fhould   at laft behold
virtue confpicuous, in all her native fplendor
and majefty as fhe fhines, the chief delight of
God, and ultimate happinefs of all intelligent
nature.

The language of religion, and our own
hearts, on this important argument, is equally
comfortable and decifive. It accumulates and
enforces whatever can infpire us with confidence in that God, who is not the God of the
dead, but of the living ; who reigns in the
invifible, as well as in the vifible world ; and
whofe attention to our welfare ceafes not with
our lives, but is commenfurate to the full extent of our being. Indeed the votaries of
the foul's mortality may as well be honeft for
once, and fpeak out what fo many fools think
in their hearts. For what is God to us, or
we to him, if our connection extends but to
the pitiful fpace allotted us in fuch a pitiful
world as this is ? To be fure, no abfurdity
will be rejected, which can fmother the feelings, or keep the vices of profligates in countenance ; but, if only made like worms and
reptiles beneath our feet, to live this moment,
and expire the next, to ftruggle in a wretched life with every internal and external calamity,

mity, that can affault our bodies, or infeft our minds ; to bear the mortifications of malignity, and the unmerited abhorrence of thofe who perhaps may owe us the greateft and tendereft efteem, and then, funk in everlafting oblivion, our fate would ftand on record, in the annals of the univerfe, an eternal exception to all that can be called good.

Suppofe a father poffeffed of the moft exquifite tendernefs for his fon, delighted with his fimilarity of form, his promifing conftitution, his ftrength, gracefulnefs, and agility, his undifguifed emotions of filial affection, with the various prefages of a fuperior genius and underftanding. Let us fuppofe this father pleafed with the employment of improving his faculties, and infpiring him with future hopes of happinefs and dignity : but that he may give him a quicker fenfibility to the misfortunes of others, and a more unfhaken fortitude to fuftain his own, he often prefers younger brethren, and even ftrangers, to thofe advantages which otherwife merit, and the force of nature would determine him to beftow on fo worthy an offspring. Let us go further, and imagine, if we can, that this father, without the leaft diminution of tendernefs, or any other apparent reafon, deftroys his fon in the bloom of life, and height of expectation : Who would not lament the fate of fuch a youth with inconfolable tears ?

Doomed

Doomed never more to behold the agreeable light of Heaven! never more to difplay his perfonal graces, nor exercife his manly powers, never more to feel his heart warm with benevolent regards, nor tafte the foul-tranfporting pleafure of obliging and being obliged! Blotted at once from exiftence, and the fair creation, he finks into filence and oblivion, with all his fublime hopes difappointed, all his immenfe defires ungratified, and all his intellectual faculties unimproved. Without mentioning the inftinctive horror which muft attend fuch an action, how abfurd to reafon, and how inconfiftent with the common feelings of humanity would it be to fuppofe a father capable of fuch a deed. Forbid it, God! forbid it, Nature! that we fhould impute to the munificent father of being and happinefs, what, even in the loweft of rational creatures, would be monftrous and deteftable!

(5) The truth is, that form which all mankind have deemed immortal, is fo far from being the fraileft, that it feems in fact the moft indiffoluble and permanent of any other we know. All the rational and inventtive powers of the mind happily confpire to proclaim her infinitely different in nature, and fuperior in dignity to every poffible modification of pure matter. Were mankind
joined

joined in fociety, was life polifhed and cultivated, were the fciences and arts, not only of
utility, but elegance, produced by matter ?
by a brute mafs ? A fubftance fo contrary
to all activity and intelligence, that it feems
the work of an omnipotent hand alone to
connect them. What judgment fhould we
form of that principle which informed and
enlightened a Galileo, a Copernicus, or a
Newton ? What infpiration taught them,
to place the fun in the center of this fyftem,
and affign the various orbs their revolutions
round him, reducing motions fo diverfe and
unequal, to uniform and fimple laws ? Was
it not fomething like that great eternal
mind, which firft gave exiftence to thofe lu-
minous orbs, and prefcribed each of them
their province ? Whence the infinite harmony and variety of found, the copious
flows of eloquence, the bolder graces and
more infpired elevations of poetry, but from
a mind, an immaterial being, the reflected
image of her all-perfect Creator, in whom eternally dwells all beauty and excellence. Were
man only endowed with a principle of ve-
getation, fixed to one peculiar fpot, and infenfible of all that paffed around him ; we
might, then, with fome colour, fuppofe that
energy, if it may be fo called, perifhable.
Were, he like animals poffeffed of mere vitability, and qualified only to move and feel,
ftill we might have fome reafon to fear that,

K   in

in some future period of duration, our Creator might resume his gift of existence. But can any one, who pretends to the least reflection, imagine that such a being as the human soul, adorned with such extensive intellectual powers, will ever cease to be the object of that love and care which eternally holds the universe in its embrace ? Did she obtain such a boundless understanding merely to taste the pleasure of exercising it? to catch a transient glance of its objects, and perish ? Formed, as she is, to operate on herself, and all things round her, must she cease from action, while yet the mighty task is scarce begun ? must she lose those faculties, by which she retains the past, comprehends the presents and presages the future? must she contemplate no more those bright impressions of divinity, which are discovered in the material world; nor those stronger, and more animated features of the same eternal beauty which shine in her own god-like form ? And must she be absorbed forever in the womb of unessential nothing ? Strange, that in the view, and even in the arms of infinite power and goodness, a dawn so fair and promising, should at one be clouded with all the horrors of eternal night ? Such a supposition would be contrary to the whole conduct and laws of nature.

The

The following Letters on SUICIDE are
extracted from ROSSEAU's ELOISA.

LETTER CXIV.

To Lord B————.

YES, my Lord, I confess it; the weight
of life is too heavy for my soul. I have
long endured it as a burden; I have lost every thing which could make it dear to me,
and nothing remains but irksomeness and
vexation. I am told, however, that I am
not at liberty to dispose of my life, without
the permission of that Being from whom I
received it. I am sensible likewise that you
have a right over it by more titles than one.
Your care has twice preserved it, and your
goodness is its constant security. I will ne-

ver

ver difpofe of it, till I am certain that I may
do it without a crime, and till I have not
the leaft hope of employing it for your fervice.

You told me that I fhould be of ufe to you;
why did you deceive me ? Since we have been
in London, fo far from thinking of employing me in your concerns, you have been kind
enough to make me your only concern. How
fuperfluous is your obliging folicitude ! My
lord, you know I abhor a crime, even worfe
than I deteft life ; I adore the fupreme Being
—I owe every thing to you ; I have an affection
for you ; you are the only perfon on earth
to whom I am attached. Friendfhip and duty may chain a wretch to this earth : fophiftry
and vain pretences will never detain him. En-
lighten my underftanding, fpeak to my heart ;
I am ready to hear you, but remember, that
defpair is not to be impofed upon.

You would have me apply to the teft of
reafon : I will ; let us reafon. You defire
me to deliberate in proportion to the importance

tance of the queftion in debate ; I agree to
it.   Let us inveftigate truth with temper and
moderation; let us difcufs this general propofition with the fame indifference we fhould
treat any other. Robeck wrote an apology
for fuicide before he put an end end to his
life. I will not, after his example, write a
book on the fubject, neither am I well
fatisfied with that which he has penned, but
I hope in this difcuffion at leaft to imitate
his moderation.

I have for a long time meditated on this
awful fubject.   You muft be fenfible that I
have, for you know my deftiny, and yet I am
alive. The more I reflect, the more I am convinced that the queftion may be reduced to this
fundamental propofition.   Every man has a
right by nature to purfue what he thinks good,
and avoid what he thinks evil, in all refpects
which are not injurious to others.   When
our life therefore becomes a mifery to ourfelves, and is of advantage to no one, we are
at liberty to put an end to our being. If there
is any fuch thing as a clear and felf-evident
                                        prin-

principle, certainly this is one, and if this be fubverted, there is fcarce an action in life which may not be made criminal.

Let us hear what the philofophers fay on this fubject. Firft, they confider life as fomething which is not our own, becaufe we hold it as a gift; but becaufe it has been given to us, is it for that reafon our own? Has not God given thefe fophifts two arms? nevertheless, when they are under apprehenfions of a mortification, they do not fcruple to amputate one, or both if there be occafion. By a parity of reafoning, we may convince thofe who believe in the immortality of the foul; for if I facrifice my arm to the prefervation of fomething more precious, which is my body, I have the fame right to facrifice my body to the prefervation of fomething more valuable, which is, the happinefs of my exiftence. If all the gifts which heaven has beftowed are naturally defigned for our good, they are certainly too apt to change their nature; and Providence has endowed us with reafon, that we may difcern the difference. If this rule
did

did not authorize us to chufe the one, and reject the other, to what ufe would it ferve a-
mong mankind ?

But they turn this weak objection into a
thoufand fhapes. They confider a man living upon earth as a foldier placed on duty.
God, fay they, has fixed you in this world, why
do you quit your ftation without his leave?
But you, who argue thus, has he not ftationed
you in the town where you was born, why
therefore do you quit it without his leave ? is
not mifery, of itfelf, a fufficient permiffion ?
whatever ftation Providence has affigned me,
whether it be in a regiment, or on the earth at
large, he intended me to ftay there while I
found my fituation agreeable, and to leave it
when it became intolerable. This is the voice of
nature, and the voice of God. I agree that we
muft wait for an order; but when I die a natural death, God does not order me to quit life,
he takes it from me ; it is by rendering life infupportable, that he orders me to quit it. In
the firft cafe, I refift with all my force ; in the
fecond, I have the merit of obedience.

Can

Can you conceive that there are some people so abſurd as to arraign ſuicide as a kind of rebellion againſt Providence, by an attempt to fly from his laws ? but we do not put an end to our being in order to withdraw ourſelves from his commands, but to execute them. What! does the power of God extend no farther than to my body ? is there a ſpot in the univerſe, is there any being in the univerſe, which is not ſubject to his power, and will that power have leſs immediate influence over me when my being is refined, and thereby becomes leſs compound, and of nearer reſemblance to the divine eſſence ? no, his juſtice and goodneſs are the foundation of my hopes; and if I thought that death would withdraw me from his power, I would give up my reſolution to die.

This is one of the quibbles of the Phædo, which, in other reſpects, abounds with ſublime truths. If your ſlave deſtroys himſelf, ſays Socrates to Cebes, would you not puniſh him, for having unjuſtly deprived you of your property;

perty; prithee, good Socrates, do we not belong to God after we are dead? The cafe you put is not applicable; you ought to argue thus: if you incumber your flave with a habit which confines him from difcharging his duty properly, will you punifh him for quitting it, in order to render you better fervice? the grand error lies in making life of too great importance; as if our exiftence depended upon it, and that death was a total annihilation. Our life is of no confequence in the fight of God; it is of no importance in the eyes of reafon, neither ought it to be of any in our fight; when we quit our body, we only lay afide an inconvenient habit. Is this circumftance fo painful, to be the occafion of fo much difturbance? my Lord, thefe declaimers are not in earneft. Their arguments are abfurd and cruel, for they aggravate the fuppofed crime, as if it put a period to exiftence, and they punifh it, as if that exiftence was eternal.

With refpect to Plato's Phædo, which has furnifhed them with the only fpecious argument that has ever been advanced, the queftion

L   is

is difcuffed there in a very light and defultory
manner. Socrates being condemned, by an unjuft judgment, to lofe his life in a few hours, had
no occafion to enter into an accurate enquiry
whether he was at liberty to difpofe of it himfelf. Suppofing him really to have been the
author of thofe difcourfes which Plato afcribes
to him, yet believe me, my lord, he would
have meditated with more attention on the fubject, had he been in circumftances which required him to reduce his fpeculations to practice ; and a ftrong proof that no valid objection can be drawn from that immortal work
againft the right of difpofing of our own lives,
is, that Cato read it twice through the very
night that he deftroyed himfelf.

The fame fophifters make it a queftion whether life can ever be an evil ? but when we
confider the multitude of errors, torments, and
vices, with which it abounds, one would rather be inclined to doubt whether it can ever
be a bleffing. Guilt inceffantly befieges the
moft virtuous of mankind. Every moment he
lives he is in danger of falling a prey to the
wicked, or of being wicked himfelf. To
ftruggle

ftruggle and to endure, is his lot in this world ;
that of the difhoneft man is to do evil,
and to fuffer. In every other particular
they differ, and only agree in fharing the miferies of life in common. If you required authorities and facts, I could recite you the oracles of old, the anfwers of the fages, and produce inftances where acts of virtue have been
recompenfed with death. But let us leave
thefe confiderations, my lord ; it is to you
whom I addrefs myfelf, and I afk you what is
the chief attention of a wife man in this life,
except, if I may be allowed the expreffion, to
collect himfelf inwardly, and endeavour, e-
ven while he lives, to be dead to every object of
fenfe ? The only way by which wifdom directs us to avoid the miferies of human nature,
is it not to detach ourfelves from all earthly
objects, from every thing that is grofs in our
compofition, to retire within ourfelves, and to
raife our thoughts to fublime contemplations ?
If therefore our misfortunes are derived from
our paffions and errors, with what eagernefs
fhould we wifh for a ftate which will deliver
us both from the one and the other ? What is

L 2 the

the fate of thofe fons of fenfuality, who indif-
creetly multiply their torments by their pleafures ? they in fact deftroy their exiftence by
extending their connections in this life ; they
increafe the weight of their crimes by their numerous attachments ; they relifh no enjoyments, but what are fucceeded by a thoufand
bitter wants ; the more lively their fenfibility, the more acute their fufferings ; the ftronger they are attached to life, the more wretched they become.

But admitting it, in general, a benefit to mankind to crawl upon the earth with gloomy fad-
nefs, I do not mean to intimate that the human
race ought with one common confent to deftroy themfelves, and make the world one immenfe grave. But there are miferable beings,
who are too much exalted to be governed by
vulgar opinion ; to them defpair and grievous
torments are the paffports of nature. It
would be as ridiculous to fuppofe that life can
be a bleffing to fuch men, as it was abfurd in
the fophifter Poffidonius to deny that is was an
evil,

evil, at the fame time that he endured all the torments of the gout. While life is agreeable to us, we earneftly wifh to prolong it, and nothing but a fenfe of extreme mifery can extinguifh the defire of exiftence ; for we naturally conceive a violent dread of death, and this dread conceals the miferies of human nature from our fight. We drag a painful and melancholy life, for a long time before we can refolve to quit it ; but when once life becomes fo infupportable as to overcome the horror of death, then exiftence is evidently a great evil, and we cannot difengage ourfelves from it too foon. Therefore, though we cannot exactly afcertain the point at which it ceafes to be a blefling, yet at leaft we are certain that it is an evil long before it appears to be fuch, and with every fenfible man the right of quitting life is, by a great deal, precedent to the temptation.

This is not all. After they have denied that life can be an evil, in order to bar our right of making away with ourfelves ; they confefs immediately afterwards that it is an evil,

evil, by reproaching us with want of courage to fupport it. According to them, it is cowardice to withdraw ourfelves from pain and trouble, and there are none but daftards who deftroy themfelves. O Rome, thou victrix of the world, what a race of cowards did thy empire produce! let Arria, Eponina, Lucretia, be of the number; they were women. But Brutus, Caffius, and thou great and divine Cato, who didft fhare with the gods the adoration of an aftonifhed world, thou whofe facred and auguft prefence animated the Romans with holy zeal, and made tyrants tremble, little did thy proud admirers imagine that paltry rhetoricians, immured in the dufty corner of a college, would ever attempt to prove that thou wert a coward, for having preferred death to a fhameful exiftence.

O the dignity and energy of your modern writers! how fublime, how intrepid are you with your pens? but tell me, thou great and valiant hero, who doft fo courageoufly decline the battle, in order to endure the pain of living fomewhat longer; when a fpark of fire lights

lights upon your hand, why do you with-draw it in such haste? how? are you such a coward that you dare not bear the scorching of fire? nothing, you say, can oblige you to endure the burning spark; and what obliges me to endure life? was the creation of a man of more difficulty to Providence, than that of a straw? and is not both one and the other equally the work of his hands?

Without doubt, it is an evidence of great fortitude to bear with firmness the misery which we cannot shun; none but a fool, how-ever, will voluntarily endure evils which he can avoid without a crime; and it is very often a great crime to suffer pain unnecessarily. He who has not resolution to deliver himself from a miserable being by a speedy death, is like one who would rather suffer a wound to mortify, than trust to a surgeon's knife for his cure. Come, thou worthy——cut off this leg, which endangers my life. I will see it done without shrinking, and will give that hero leave to call me coward, who suffers his leg to mortify, because he dares not undergo the same operation.

I ac-

I acknowledge that there are duties owing to others, the nature of which will not allow every man to difpofe of his life ; but, in return, how many are there which give him a right to difpofe of it ? let a magiftrate on whom the welfare of a nation depends, let a father of a family who is bound to procure fubfiftence for his children, let a debtor who might ruin his creditors, let thefe at all events difcharge their duty ; admitting a thoufand other civil and domeftic relations to oblige an honeft and unfortunate man to fupport the mifery of life, to avoid the greater evil of doing injuftice; is it, therefore, under circumftances totally different, incumbent on us to preferve a life oppreffed with a fwarm of miferies, when it can be of no fervice but to him who has not courage to die ? " Kill me, my child," fays the decrepid favage to his fon, who carries him on his fhoulders, and bends under his weight ; the " enemy is at hand ; go to battle with thy " brethren ; go and preferve thy children, " and do not fuffer thy helplefs father to fall
" alive

" alive into the hands of thofe whofe relations
" he has mangled." Though hunger, ficknefs, and poverty, thofe domeftic plagues,
more dreadful than favage enemies, may allow a wretched cripple to confume, in a fick
bed, the provifions of a family which can
fcarce fubfift itfelf, yet he who has no connections, whom heaven has reduced to the
neceffity of living alone, whofe wretched exiftence can produce no good, why fhould not
he, at leaft, have the right of quitting a ftation, where his complaints are troublefome, and
his fufferings of no benefit ?

Weigh thefe confiderations, my lord ; collect thefe arguments, and you will find that
they may be reduced to the moft fimple of nature's rights, of which no man of fenfe ever
yet entertained a doubt. In fact, why fhould
we be allowed to cure ourfelves of the gout,
and not to get rid of the mifery of life? do
not both evils proceed from the fame hand? to
what purpofe is it to fay, that death is painful?
are drugs agreeable to be taken ? no, nature
revolts againft both. Let them prove there-

M　　　　　　　　　　fore

fore that it is more juftifiable to cure a tranfi-
ent diforder by the application of remedies,
than to free ourfelves from an incurable evil
by putting an end to our life ; and let them
fhew how it can be lefs criminal to ufe the
bark for a fever, than to take opium for the
ftone. If we confider the object in view, it is
in both cafes to free ourfelves from painful
fenfations ; if we regard the means, both one
and the other are equally natural ; if we
confider the repugnance of our nature, it operates equally on both fides ; if we attend to
the will of providence, can we ftruggle againft
any evil of which it is not the author ? can
we deliver ourfelves from any torment which
the hand of God has not inflicted ? what are
the bounds which limit his power, and when
is refiftance lawful ? are we then to make no
alteration in the condition of things, becaufe
every thing is in the ftate he appointed ? muft
we do nothing in this life, for fear of infring-
ing his laws, or is it in our power to break
them if we would ? no, my lord, the occupation of man is more great and noble. God
did not give him life that he fhould fu-

pinely

pinely remain in a ftate of conftant inactivity.
But he gave him freedom to act, confcience to
will, and reafon to choofe what is good. He
has conftituted him fole judge of all his actions.
He has engraved this precept in his heart, Do
whatever you conceive to be for your own
good, provided you thereby do no injury to
others. If my fenfations tell me that death is
eligible, I refift his orders by an obftinate refolution to live; for, by making death defirable, he directs me to put an end to my being.

My lord, I appeal to your wifdom and can-
dour; what more infallible maxims can reafon deduce from religion, with refpect to fuicide? If Chriftians have adopted contrary tenets, they are neither drawn from the principles of religion, nor from the only fure guide,
the Scriptures, but borrowed from the Pagan
philofophers. Lactantius and Auguftine,
the firft who propagated this new doctrine,
of which Jefus Chrift and his apoftles take no
notice, ground their arguments entirely on
the reafoning of Phædo, which I have alrea-

M 2   dy

dy controverted ; ſo that the believers, who, in this reſpect, think they are ſupported by the authority of the Goſpel, are in fact only countenaced by the authority of Plato. In truth, where do we find, throughout the whole bible any law againſt ſuicide, or ſo much as a bare diſapprobation of it; and is it not very unaccountable, that among the inſtances produced of perſons who devoted themſelves to death, we do not 'find the leaſt word of improbation againſt examples of this kind ? nay, what is more, the inſtance of Samſon's voluntary death is authorized by a miracle, by which he revenges himſelf of his enemies. Would this miracle have been diſplayed to juſtify a crime ; and would this man, who loſt his ſtrength by ſuffering himſelf to be ſeduced by the allurements of a woman, have recovered it to commit an authoriſed crime, as if God himſelf would practice deceit on men ?

Thou ſhalt do no murder, ſays the decalogue ; what are we to infer from this ? if this commandment is to be taken literally, we

muſt

muft not deftroy malefactors, nor our enemies:
and Mofes, who put fo many people to death,
was a bad interpreter of his own precept.   If
there are any exceptions, certainly the firft
muft be in favour of fuicide, becaufe it is exempt from any degree of violence and injuftice, the two only circumftances which can
make homicide criminal; and becaufe nature,
moreover, has, in this refpect, thrown fufficient obftacles in the way.

But ftill they tell us, we muft patiently
endure the evils which God inflicts, and
make a merit of our fufferings.   This application however of the maxims of Chriftianity,
is very ill calculated to fatisfy our judgment.
Man is fubject to a thoufand troubles, his life
is a complication of evils, and he feems to
have been born only to fuffer.   Reafon directs him to fhun as many of thefe evils as he
can avoid ; and religion, which is never in
contradiction to reafon, approves of his endeavours.   But how inconfiderable is the account
of thefe evils, in comparifon with thofe he is
obliged to endure againft his will ?   It is with
refpect

respect to these, that a merciful God allows man to claim the merit of resistance ; he receives the tribute he has been pleased to impose, as a voluntary homage, and he places our resignation in this life to our profit in the next. True repentance is derived from nature ; if man endures whatever he is obliged to suffer, he does, in this respect, all that God requires of him ; and if any one is so inflated with pride, as to attempt more, he is a madman, who ought to be confined, or an impostor, who ought to be punished. Let us, therefore, without scruple, fly from all the evils we can avoid ; there will still be too many left for us to endure. Let us, without remorse, quit life itself when it becomes a torment to us, since it is in our own power to do it, and that in so doing we neither offend God nor man. If we would offer a sacrifice to the supreme Being, is it nothing to undergo death ? let us devote to God that which he demands by the voice of reason, and into his hands let us peaceably surrender our souls.

Such are the liberal precepts which good
sense

fenfe dictates to every man, and which religion authorifes *. Let us apply thefe precepts
to ourfelves. You have condefcended to dif-
clofe your mind to me; I am acquainted
with your uneafinefs; you do not endure lefs
than myfelf; and your troubles, like mine,
are incurable; and they are the more remedi-
lefs,

* A ftrange letter this for the difcuffion of fuch a fubject !
Do men argue fo coolly on a queftion of this nature, when
they examine it on their own accounts ? Is the letter a for-
gery, or does the author reafon only with an intent to be
refuted ? What makes our opinion in this particular
dubious, is the example of Robeck, which he cites, and
which feems to warrant his own. Robeck deliberated
fo gravely that he had patience to write a book, a large,
voluminous, weighty, and difpaffionate book; and when
he had concluded, according to his principles, that it was lawful to put an end to our being, he deftroyed himfelf with the
fame compofure that he wrote. Let us beware of the prejudices of the times, and of particular countries. When fuicide is out of fafhion we conclude that none but madmen
deftroy themfelves; and all the efforts of courage appear chimerical to daftardly minds; every one judges of others by himfelf. Neverthelefs, how many inftances are there, well attef-
tefted, of men, in every other refpect perfectly difcreet, who,
without remorfe, rage, or defpair, have quitted life for no o-
ther reafon than becaufe it was a burden to them, and have
died with more compofure than they lived ?

lefs, as the laws of honour are more immutable than thofe of fortune. You bear them, I
muft confefs, with fortitude. Virtue fupports
you; advance but one ftep farther, and fhe dif-
engages you.   You intreat me to fuffer; my
lord, I dare importune you to put an end to
your fufferings ; and I leave you to judge
which of us is moft dear to the other.

Why fhould we delay doing that which we
muft do at laft ? fhall we wait till old age and
decrepid bafenefs attach us to life, after they
have robbed it of its charms, and till we are
doomed to drag an infirm and decrepid body
with labour, and ignominy, and pain? We
are at an age when the foul has vigour to difengage itfelf with eafe from its fhackles, and
when a man knows how to die as he ought;
when farther advanced in years, he fuffers
himfelf to be torn from life, which he quits
with reluctance.   Let us take advantage of
this time, when the tedium of life makes
death defirable ; and let us tremble for fear
it fhould come in all its horrors, at the moment when we could wifh to avoid it.   I remember

member the time, when I prayed to heaven only for a fingle hour of life, and when I fhould have died in defpair if it had not been granted. Ah! what a pain it is to burft afunder the ties which attach our hearts to this world, and how advifable it is to quit life the moment the connection is broken! I am fenfible, my lord, that we are both worthy of a purer manfion; virtue points it out, and deftiny invites us to feek it. May the friendfhip which invites us preferve our union to the lateft hour! O what a pleafure for two fincere friends voluntary to end their days in each others arms, to intermingle their lateft breath, and at the fame inftant to give up the foul which they fhared in common! What pain, what regret can infect their laft moments? What do they quit by taking leave of the world? They go together; they quit nothing.

LETTER

LETTER CXV.

ANSWER.

THOU art diftracted, my friend, by a fatal paffion ; be more difcreet ; do not give counfel, whilft thou ftandeth fo much in need of advice. I have known greater e-vils than yours. I am armed with fortitude of mind; I am an Englifhman, and not afraid to die ; but I know how to live and fuffer as be-comes a man. I have feen death near at hand, and have viewed it with too much indifference to go in fearch of it.

It is true, I thought you might be of ufe to me ; my affection ftood in need of yours : your endeavours might have been ferviceable to me ; your underftanding might have en-lightened me in the moft important concern of my life ; if I do not avail myfelf of it, who are you to impute it to ? Where is it ? What

is

is become of it ? What are your capable of ?
Of what ufe can you be in your prefent condition ? What fervice can I expect from you?
A fenfelefs grief renders you ftupid and un-
concerned. Thou art no man ; thou art nothing ; and if I did not confider what thou
mighteft be, I cannot conceive any thing more
abject.

There is need of no other proof than your
letter itfelf. Formerly I could difcover in
you good fenfe and truth. Your fentiments
were juft, your reflections proper, and I liked
you not only from judgment but choice ; for
I confidered your influence as an additional
motive to excite me to the ftudy of wifdom.
But what do I perceive now in the arguments
of your letter, with which you appear to be
fo highly fatisfied ? A wretched and perpetual fophiftry, which in the erroneous deviations
of your reafon fhews the diforder of your mind,
and which I would not ftoop to refute, if I did
not commiferate your delirium.

To

To fubvert all your reafoning with one word, I would only afk you a fingle queftion. You who believe in the exiftence of a God, in the immortality of the foul, and in the free-will of man, you furely cannot fuppofe that an intelligent being is embodied, and ftation-ed on the earth by accident only, to exift, to fuffer, and to die. It is certainly moft pro-bable that the life of man is not without fome defign, fome end, fome moral object. I in-treat you to give me a direct anfwer to this point ; after which we will deliberately exa-mine your letter, and you will blufh to have written it.

But let us wave all general maxims, about which we often hold violent difputes, with-out adopting any of them in practice ; for in their applications we always find fome parti-cular circumftances which makes fuch an al-teration in the ftate of things, that every one thinks himfelf difpenfed from fubmitting to the rules which he prefcribes to others ; and it is well known, that every man who efta-blifhes

blifhes general principles deems them obliga-
tory on all the world, himfelf excepted. Once
more let us fpeak to you in particular.

You believe that you have a right to put
an end to your being. Your proof is of a very
fingular nature ; " becaufe I am difpofed to
" die, fay you, I have a right to deftroy my-
" felf." This is certainly a very convenient argument for villains of all kinds : they ought
to be very thankful to you for the arms with
which you have furnifhed them ; there can
be no crimes, which, according to your arguments, may not be juftified by the temptation
to perpetrate them ; and as foon as the im-
petuofity of paffion fhall prevail over the horror of guilt, their difpofition to do evil will
be confidered as a right to commit it.

Is it lawful for you therefore to quit
life ? I fhould be glad to know whether you
have yet begun to live ? what ! was you placed
here on earth to do nothing in this world ?
did not heaven when it gave you exiftence give
you fome tafk or employment ? If you have
ac-

accomplifhed your day's work before evening,
reft yourfelf for the remainder of the day;
you have a right to do it; but let us fee your
work. What anfwer are you prepared to
make the fupreme Judge, when he demands
an account of your time? Tell me, what
can you fay to him?—I have feduced a virtuous girl: I have forfaken a friend in diftrefs. Thou unhappy wretch! point out to
me that juft man who can boaft that he has
lived long enough; let me learn from him
in what manner I ought to have fpent my days
to be at liberty to quit life.

You enumerate the evils of human nature. You are not afhamed to exhauft com-
mon-place topics, which have been hackney-
ed over a hundred times; and you conclude
that life is an evil. But fearch, examine into
the order of things, and fee whether you can
find any good which is not intermingled with
evil. Does it therefore follow that there is no
good in the univerfe, and can you confound
what is in its own nature evil, with that
which is only an evil accidentally? You have

con-

confeffed yourfelf, that the tranfitory and paffive life of man is of no confequence, and only bears refpect to matter from which he will foon be difencumbered ; but his active and moral life, which ought to have moft in-fluence over his nature, confifts in the exercife of free-will. Life is an evil to a wicked man in profperity, and a bleffing to an honeft man in diftrefs : for it is not its cafual modificati-on, but its relation to fome final object which makes it either good or bad. After all, what are thefe cruel torments which force you to abandon life ? do you imagine, that under your affected impartiality in the enumeration of the evils of this life, I did not difcover that you was afhamed to fpeak of your own ? Truft me, and do not at once abandon every virtue. Preferve at leaft your wonted fincerity, and fpeak thus openly to you friend ; " I have loft " all hope of feducing a modeft woman, I am " oliged therefore to be a man of virtue ; I " had much rather die."

You are weary of living ; and you tell me, that life is an evil. Sooner or later you will

re-

receive confolation, and then you will fay life
is a bleſſing. You will ſpeak with more truth,
though not with better reaſon; for nothing
will have altered but yourſelf. Begin the alteration then from this day; and, ſince all the
evil you lament is in the diſpoſition of your
mind, correct your irregular appetites, and do
not ſet your houſe on fire to avoid the trouble of putting it in order.

I endure miſery, fay you: Is it in my power to avoid ſuffering? But this is changing
the ſtate of the queſtion: for the ſubject of
enquiry is, not whether you ſuffer, but whether your life is an evil? Let us proceed.
You are wretched, you naturally endeavour to extricate yourſelf from miſery.
Let us ſee whether, for that purpoſe, it is
neceſſary to die.

Let us for a moment examine the natural
tendency of the afflictions of the mind, as in
direct oppoſition to the evils of the body, the
two ſubſtances being of contrary nature. The
latter become worſe and more inveterate the
longer

longer they continue, and at length utterly
deftroy this mortal machine. The former, on
the contrary, being only external and tranfitory modifications of an immortal and uncom-
pounded effence, are infenfibly effaced, and
leave the mind in its original form, which is
not fufceptible of alteration. Grief, difquie-
tude, regret, and defpair, are evils of fhort duration, which never take root in the mind ;
and experience always falfifies that bitter reflection, which makes us imagine our mifery
will have no end. I will go farther ; I cannot imagine that the vices which contaminate
us, are more inherent in our nature than the
troubles we endure ; J not only believe that
they perifh with the body which gives them
birth, but I think, beyond all doubt, that a longer life would be fufficient to reform mankind,
and that many ages of youth would teach us
that nothing is preferable to virtue.

However this may be, as the greateft part
of our phyfical evils are inceffantly encreafing,
the acute pains of the body, when they are incurable, may juftify a man's deftroying him-
O   felf ;

felf; for all his faculties being diftracted with
pain, and the evil being without remedy, he
has no longer any ufe either of his will or of
his reafon ; he ceafes to be a man before he
is dead, and does nothing more in taking a-
way his life, than quit a body which incum-
bers him, and in which his foul is no longer
refident.

But it is otherwife with the afflictions of
the mind, which, let them be ever fo acute,
always carry their remedy with them. In fact,
what is it that makes any evil intolerable ?
Nothing but its duration. The operations of
furgery are generally much more painful than
the diforders they cure; but the pain occafioned by the latter is lafting, that of the operation is momentary, and therefore preferable.
What occafion is there therefore for any operation to remove troubles which die of courfe
by their duration, the only circumftance
which could render them infupportable ? Is
it reafonable to apply fuch defperate remedies to evils which expire of themfelves ? To
a man who values himfelf on his fortitude,
and

and who eftimates years at their real
value, of two ways by which he may
extricate himfelf from the fame troubles,
which will appear preferable, death or time?
Have patience, and you will be cured. What
would you defire more?

Oh! you will fay, it doubles my afflictions
to reflect that they will ceafe at laft! This
is the vain fophiftry of grief! an apoph-
thegm void of reafon, of propriety, and perhaps of fincerity. What an abfurd motive of defpair is the hope of terminating mifery *! Even allowing this fantaftical reflection, who would not chufe to encreafe the prefent pain for a moment, under the affurance
of putting an end to it, as we fcarify a
wound in order to heal it? and admitting any
charm in grief, to make us in love with fuf-

O 2   fering,

* No, my lord, we do not put an end to mifery by thefe
means, but rather fill the meafure of affliction, by burfting a-
funder the laft ties which attach us to felicity. When we
regret what was dear to us, grief itfelf ftill attaches us to the
object we lament, which is a ftate lefs deplorable than to be
attached to nothing.

fering, when we releafe ourfelves from it by
putting an end to our being, do we not at
that inftant incur all that we apprehend hereafter?

Reflect thoroughly, young man; what
are ten, twenty, thirty years, in competition
with immortality? Pain and pleafure pafs
like a fhadow; life flides away in an inftant;
it is nothing of itfelf; its value depends
on the ufe we make of it. The good that we
have done is all that remains; and it is that
alone which marks its importance.

Therefore do not fay any more that your
exiftence is an evil, fince it depends upon
yourfelf to make it a bleffing; and if it be an
evil to have lived, this is an additional reafon
for prolonging life. Do not pretend neither
to fay any more that you are at liberty to die;
for it is as much as to fay that you have power to alter your nature, that you have a right
to revolt againft the author of your being, and
to fruftrate the end of your exiftence. But
when you add, that your death does injury to
no

no one, do you recollect that you make this declaration to your friend?

Your death does injury to no one? I underſtand you! You think the loſs I ſhall ſuſtain by your death of no importance; you deem my affliction of no conſequence. I will urge to you no more the rights of friendſhip, which you deſpiſe; but are there not obligations ſtill more dear *, which ought to induce you to preſerve your life? If there be a perſon in the world who loved you to that degree as to be unwilling to ſurvive you, and whoſe happineſs depends on yours, do you think that you have no obligations to her? Will not the execution of your wicked deſign diſturb the peace of a mind, which has been with ſuch difficulty reſtored to its former innocence? Are not you afraid to add freſh torments to a heart of ſuch ſenſibility? Are not you apprehenſive leſt your death ſhould be attended

---

* Obligations more dear than thoſe of friendſhip! Is it a philoſopher who talks thus? But this affected ſophiſt was of an amorous diſpoſition.

tended with a lofs more fatal, which would deprive the world and virtue itfelf of its bright-eft ornament? And if fhe fhould furvive you, are not you afraid to roufe up remorfe in her bofom, which is more grievous to fupport than life itfelf? Thou ungrateful friend! thou indelicate lover! wilt thou always be taken up wholly with thyfelf? Wilt thou al-ways think on thy own troubles alone? Haft thou no regard for the happinefs of one who was, fo dear to thee? and cannot thou refolve to live for her who was willing to die with thee?

You talk of the duties of a magiftrate, and of a father of a family: and becaufe you are not under thofe circumftances, you think your-felf abfolutely free. And are you then under no obligations to fociety, to whom you are indebted for your prefervation, your talents, your underftanding? do you owe nothing to your native country, and to thofe unhappy people who may need your exiftence! O what an accurate calculation you make! a-mong the obligations you have enumerated,

you

you have only omitted thofe of a man and of
a citizen. Where is the virtuous patriot,
who refufed to enlift under a foreign prince,
becaufe his blood ought not to be fpilt but in
the fervice of his country; and who now, in a
fit of defpair, is ready to fhed it againft the exprefs prohibition of the laws ? The laws, the
laws, young man! did any wife man ever
defpife them ? Socrates, though innocent,
out of regard to them refufed to quit his prifon. You do not fcruple to violate them by
quitting life unjuftly; and you afk, what injury do I ?

You endeavour to juftify yourfelf by example. You prefume to mention the Romans : you talk of the Romans ! it becomes
you indeed to cite thofe illuftrious names.
Tell me, did Brutus die a lover in defpair, and
did Cato plunge the dagger in his breaft for
his miftrefs ? Thou weak and abject man !
what refemblance is there between Cato and
thee ? Shew me the common ftandard between that fublime foul and thine. Ah vain
wretch ! hold thy peace : I am afraid to profane

fane his name by a vindication of his conduct.
At that auguft and facred name every friend
to virtue fhold bow to the ground, and honour
the memory of the greateft hero in filence.

How ill you have felected your examples,
and how meanly you judge of the Romans, if
you imagine that they thought themfelves at
liberty to quit life fo foon as it became a burden to them. Recur to the excellent days of
that republic, and fee whether you will find a
fingle citizen of virtue, who thus freed himfelf from the difcharge of his duty even after
the moft cruel misfortunes. When Regulus
was on his return to Carthage, did he prevent
the torments which he knew were preparing
for him by deftroying himfelf? What would
not Pofthumus have given, when obliged to
pafs under the yoke at Caudium, had this refource been juftifiable? How much did e-
ven the fenate admire that effort of courage,
which enabled the conful Varro to furvive his
defeat? For what reafon did fo many generals voluntary furrender themfelves to their e-
nemies, they to whom ignominy was fo dreadful,

ful, and who were so little afraid of dying? It was because they considered their blood, their life, and their latest breath, as devoted to their country; and neither shame nor misfortune could dissuade them from this sacred duty. But when the laws were subverted, and the state became a prey to tyranny, the citizens resumed their natural liberty, and the right they had over their own lives. When Rome was no more, it was lawful for the Romans to give up their lives; they had discharged their duties on earth, they had no longer any country to defend, they were therefore at liberty to dispose of their lives, and to obtain that freedom for themselves which they could not recover for their country. After having spent their days in the service of expiring Rome, and in fighting for the defence of its laws, they died great and virtuous as they had lived, and their death was an additional tribute to the glory of the Roman name, since none of them beheld a sight above all others most dishonourable, that of a true citizen stooping to an usurper.

P

But

But thou, what art thou ? what haſt thou done? doſt thou think to excuſe thyſelf on account of thy obſcurity ? does thy weakneſs exempt thee from thy duty, and becauſe thou haſt neither rank nor diſtinction in thy country, art thou leſs ſubject to the laws ? It becomes you vaſtly to preſume to talk of dying, while you owe the ſervice of your life to your equals. Know, that a death, ſuch as you meditate, is ſhameful and ſurreptitious. It is a theft committed on mankind in general. Before you quit life, return the benefits you have received from every individual. But, ſay you, I have no attachments ; I am uſeleſs in the worʼd. O thou young philoſopher ! art thou ignorant that thou canſt not move a ſingle ſtep without finding ſome duty to fulfil ; and that every man is uſeful to ſociety, even by means of his exiſtence alone ?

Hear me, thou raſh young man ! thou art dear to me. I commiſerate thy errors. If the leaſt ſenſe of virtue ſtill remains in thy breaſt, attend, and let me teach thee to be reconciled

conciled to life. Whenever thou art tempted to quit it, fay to thyfelf————"Let me
" do at leaft one good action before I die."
Then go in fearch for one in a ftate of indi-
gence, whom thou mayeft relieve; for one under misfortunes, whom thou mayeft comfort;
for one under oppreffion, whom thou mayeft
defend. Introduce to me thofe unhappy
wretches whom my rank keeps at a diftance.
Do not be afraid of mifufing my purfe, or my
credit : make free with them ; diftribute my
fortune; make me rich. If this confideration reftrains you to-day, it will reftrain you
to-morrow ; if to morrow, it will reftrain you
all your life. If it has no power to reftrain
you, die ! you are below my care.

F I N I S.

E R R A T A.

Page 53, line 14, for *will*, read *wife*.
65, — 31, for *vitability*, read *vitality*.